D1587303

THE CHURCHES OF SURREY

Frontispiece   The brick west tower at St. Mary's, Thorpe.

THE
CHURCHES
OF
SURREY

by

Mervyn Blatch

PHILLIMORE

1997

Published for Surrey Local History Council by
PHILLIMORE & CO. LTD.,
Shopwyke Manor Barn,
Chichester, West Sussex

© Mervyn Blatch 1997

ISBN   1 86077 002 9

Printed and bound in Great Britain by
BUTLER AND TANNER LTD.
London and Frome

CONTENTS

*This book is dedicated
to my wife Eileen
who has given me indefatigable support
not only for this book
but throughout my married life.*

PREFACE

I have long felt that the churches of Surrey have not received the attention they deserve and this book is an attempt to correct the situation. Admittedly they may not figure in the first flight of English ecclesiastical architecture and must bow the head to those of Gloucestershire, Norfolk, Northamptonshire, Somerset, Suffolk and Yorkshire but, having lived in the county for more than 40 years, I have found that they have much to offer.

The descriptions of individual places of worship have been set out in alphabetical order, starting at Abinger and finishing at Wotton, the furnishings being described separately from the history. Not all churches are described in detail and I have had to be selective in my choice. I apologise to those churchgoers whose places of worship are not covered or only covered briefly but I have felt it necessary to keep the book within reasonable limits and in a form which makes the information readily accessible to those concerned. It will be obvious to the reader that I have leaned fairly heavily on the Buildings of England volume for Surrey. The author's succinct judgements have been of great help.

I have made no distinction between churches in the diocese of Southwark and the diocese of Guildford so far as the order in which they are described is concerned. Buildings quite close to one another may be in different dioceses, for instance Thames Ditton (Guildford) and Kingston (Southwark). Intending visitors are advised that opening times should be checked individually. It is my sincere wish that, once inside, visitors may find much to enjoy which they will have been glad to see.

I wish to thank the many incumbents who have been helpful and encouraging in providing information. Most of the photographs are my own. A list of acknowledgements is given below. One friend in particular had been of great help. Hamish Donaldson, despite his responsibilities as Chairman of the Guildford Diocesan Advisory Committee, has made special visits to churches to take photographs where I have lacked illustrations.

I cannot conclude this preface without expressing my gratitude to Kenneth Gravett but for whom this book would never have been written. His knowledge of the subject has been of immense value in supplementing the script and I very much appreciate the hours he has spent in helping me. Also deserving of my thanks is my wife, Eileen, who has been constantly at my side: I owe a great deal to her for her help and encouragement and, in recognition, I wish to dedicate this book to her.

ACKNOWLEDGEMENTS

The following have kindly provided illustrations for this book and are thanked for them:

Rev. John Ashe, Vicar of Godalming: 151
Hamish Donaldson: 30, 92, 102, 111, 199, 200, XXXIII
Kenneth Gravett: 44, 57, 160, 170
Ian Locke: 96
Rev. Graham Williams, Rector of Nutfield: tailpiece
London Borough of Sutton Heritage Services: 70
Minet Library: 58
Surrey Archaeological Society: 39, 59, 60, 61, 62, 64, 65, 66, 67, 119, 134, 178
Surrey Local History Council: 63
Trustees of the Cranston Library, Reigate: XXIV

In addition the following illustrations have been taken from published books:

C.T.Cracklow, *Views of all the Churches and Chapelries in the County of Surrey* (1826): 4
D. Lysons, *Environs of London*, Vol. I. (1796): XLIII
J.G. & L.A.B. Waller, *A Series of Monumental Brasses* (1864): 32

All of the rest of the illustrations were photographed by the author, including many taken especially for this work.

THE CHURCHES OF SURREY

Introduction

SIR JOHN BETJEMAN describes the story of Surrey Churches as 'mostly one of heavy restoration, of unpretentious fabrics or of new Victorian buildings'.[1] It is difficult, therefore, to disentangle the pre-Victorian picture from what we see today but we are fortunate in having the Cracklow drawings, also the Hassell and Petrie water-colours, to show us what Surrey churches looked like externally in the early part of the nineteenth century.[2] These confirm that they were indeed of modest proportions and bear out Betjeman's appellation of 'unpretentious fabrics'.

In medieval times there were two main factors which determined the state and appearance of churches in this country: the economic state of the area and the availability of building materials. In neither of these respects was Surrey well favoured although there was plenty of stone, even if not of the first quality, in the southern part of the county. As far back as Roman times, and even earlier, the poor soil and the impenetrable nature of the Weald with all its attendant dangers for travellers deterred settlers, and only in the river valleys did people reside. The sparseness of the population in Saxon times is borne out by the fact that Surrey had only 14 hundreds (a hundred, or rather a hundred and twenty, free English households banded together for mutual defence) compared with 61 in Sussex and 62 in Kent. A low population density continued until the end of the medieval period when a modest increase of wealth from new industries and the expansion of the London market began to change the picture. An interesting confirmation of the small number of people in the Weald is that many of the place-names refer to natural features (for example, *leigh*, a clearing: *fold*, pasture: *hurst*, a wood) rather than to persons.

With building materials there was more to offer although none to compare with the oolitic limestones which stretch up from Dorset through and across England to the Humber in a long crescent. The Surrey stones include the calcareous sandstone from the Upper Greensand formation called *Reigate* stone or often *firestone*, used in the old London Bridge, the Abbey and Palace of Westminster, Windsor Castle and St Mary Overie Priory at Southwark. Although suited for indoor work it has weathered badly in a smoky atmosphere. There is also *chalkstone* and a very hard and rather gritty sandstone called *carstone*. Together with *Bargate* stone, *Wealden* stone, *heathstone*, flint, brick, not to mention various *ironstone* and *puddingstone* rubbles, these materials produce a varied tapestry and give much local texture to Surrey churches. Some, like the churches at Chobham (*Colour Plate I*) and Shere, are a macedoine of many different materials; at Shere one finds Bargate stone, firestone, flints, Caen stone, re-used Roman tiles, clunch (*chalkstone*), Horsham slabs on part of the roof, Purbeck and Petworth marbles and brick. In general, however, local material was used: Wealden stone in the areas bordering on Sussex, flint on the North Downs and brick in the Thames valley. Surrey's most individual stones are the heathstone or sarsens found as isolated boulders in the sandy soil of the Bagshot Beds and elsewhere but in small quantities and difficult to work, and the durable but hard-to-course *Bargate* sandstone found around Guildford and Godalming – an attractive ferruginous material of warm brown and yellow tints particularly suited to the

1

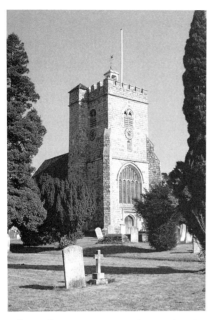

*1.   The west tower of Worplesdon
Church, built in heathstone.*

*2.   The Lych-gate at Betchworth
has graded Horsham slabs.*

Surrey scene and the county's best stone. Many church towers are built of heathstone (Ash, Chobham, Lingfield, top part of Old Woking, Pirbright, part of Puttenham and Seale), whilst at Worplesdon not only the tower but the nave, clerestory and aisles are all made of this hard, siliceous sandstone. Bargate stone is seen to advantage at Compton and Godalming (towers), Oxted (tower and porch), St Martha on the Hill at Chilworth and especially Wotton. Carstone is used at Bisley, Cobham and the base of Wonersh tower.

Horsham slates or slabs employed for roofing are – as the name implies – not a particularly Surrey material but they are a charming accompaniment to a number of the county's churches and can be found as far north as Chobham and Esher; unfortunately only part of these roofs are thus covered and the red tiles used to complete the protection often contrast unfavourably with the slates. The Horsham material is also seen on lych-gates. Betchworth is a good example where one can follow how the slates are laid in graduated fashion – large at the base and becoming smaller towards the ridge; other lych-gates roofed with this material include Chiddingfold and Shere. *Pudding-stone* – a conglomerate consisting of flint pebbles or lumps of sandstone held together by a natural cement of zinc oxide or some siliceous substance – was used *faute de mieux* in various churches (e.g. at Chobham and the chancel at Ripley); at St Nicholas, Pyrford, despite its imperfections, it has lasted with the help of much buttressing for over 800 years.

Apart from stone there is, as one would expect in such a well-wooded region, an abundance of timber used extensively and attractively in many spires, bellcotes and sometimes entire belfries; also for porches, roofs and furnishings. Until the nineteenth century, Frimley had a complete timber church and Bisley a timber-framed chancel. Shingles, formerly of cleft oak but now usually of Canadian cedar, are the commonest material for sheathing steeples and add to their charm. Brick did not come into use for Surrey churches until after the medieval period, but there are a number of seventeenth-century brick towers, whilst at Morden the entire fabric is of this material.

3.   *The north wall of the chancel at Ripley, showing*
coursed pudding-stone with ashlar quoins, string-course
and window jambs.

4.   *The former timber-framed church of 1606 at Frimley.*

Pre-Conquest

How did Christianity develop in Surrey? Before the county was evangelized there were Romano-Celtic temples at Farley Heath, near Albury towards the south-west, and Titsey to the east - which give some idea of the form of worship the early Roman settlers favoured. Surrey, however, became Christian about A.D. 393, although there is no early Christian church to be found in the county. Whatever may have existed was swept away by the Saxon invaders and it was not until St Augustine landed in Kent in 597 and the sub-king of Wessex had adopted Christianity in 635 that Surrey started to become Christian again. A milestone was the founding of Chertsey Abbey in 666 by the Benedictine St Erkenwald, later Bishop of London, who had been granted land by Frithwald, sub-king of the region under King Wulfhere of Mercia. About this time but probably a little later, Medehamstead (Peterborough) founded a daughter house at Woking. By 688, except for the deanery of Croydon which remained a *peculiar* (under the jurisdiction) of Canterbury and some other smaller exceptions (e.g. Chiddingfold), Surrey had become part of the diocese of Winchester. Chertsey, like Southwark, was a minster church (that is one which sent out missioners to evangelize and serve outlying areas) but in 871 it suffered the fate of many religious houses in the path of the advancing Danes and was sacked, Abbot Beocca and 90 of his monks being put to the sword. A new and confirmatory charter was granted by King Alfred in 889.

5.   *The west section of the upper part of the south wall of the nave at St Mary's, Stoke D'Abernon, showing the blocked Saxon door and the sundial.*

Domesday Book records 64 churches – together with some 160 manors – in Surrey but it may not have included all ecclesiastical buildings. Fetcham, Great Bookham and St Mary's, Guildford, believed to contain Saxon work, are not mentioned. Many of the churches were probably very primitive structures of wood and little has survived from the Anglo-Saxon period in Surrey – nothing to compare with Sompting or Worth in Sussex. All that remains are sections of walling and parts of towers in one or two churches, a capital at Betchworth, blocked openings at Stoke D'Abernon (one of which gave access to an upper storey for the lord), splayed windows at Thursley (containing Saxon woodwork) (*Colour Plate II*) and Witley, and, more substantially, the altered tower at St Mary's, Guildford. The good Bargate stone masonry of Compton tower may also have been pre-Conquest.

Twelfth Century

The Normans' opinion of Saxon work is shown by the fact that 61 of the Domesday churches were rebuilt soon after they took over – probably to underline that there was now strong and ordered government which would secure the country from the risk of another invasion. It is probably this sweeping away of the old and the wholesale rebuilding that led to the erection of the relatively unspoilt twelfth-century village churches of Farleigh, Pyrford and Wisley. Exceptionally, the new rulers left the Saxon abbot – Wulfwold – in charge at Chertsey (his abbacy lasted from 1058 to 1084), although a new abbey of imposing proportions was erected at the beginning of the twelfth century (*c.*1110). The county, however, remained poor and, apart from Chertsey and the other principal monastic foundations of Bermondsey, Merton, Southwark and Waverley, there were no substantial buildings of the scale of New Shoreham and Steyning in Sussex.

6.   *The twelfth-century church at Wisley retains its original size and proportions.*

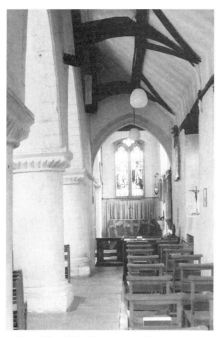

7.   *The Chobham south arcade,*
showing drum Norman piers
with scalloped capitals.

Nevertheless, many churches had to be enlarged after about 50 years; aisles were opened up and we can see Norman arcades at Chobham, Compton, Fetcham and Walton on Thames among many. Perhaps the most notable and the most complete arcades (although much restored) are those at Compton, especially when viewed in conjunction with the chancel arch and the unique double sanctuary. Chancels tended to be enlarged later. Norman examples are found at Addington (*Colour Plate VII*), Chaldon, Godalming, Little Bookham and Ripley; the last – although small – appears to have been designed for a rib-vault with corner shafts and elaborate capitals for the supporting piers; it also has an enriched string-course.

Doorways of the period occur in different parts of the county, the best being the west door at Old Woking, with roll mouldings and a door decorated with good ironwork of archaic form and the south door at Ewhurst, one of simple but elegant design. North doorways can be seen at Pyrford and Tandridge. The crop of towers is not outstanding. To name a few, there are Blechingley, Cobham (of carstone and flint),

8.   *The chancel at Ripley has shafts for vaulting and an ornate string-course.*

9.   *The west door at Old Woking.*

10.   *The south door at Ewhurst.*

11.   *The tower at Limpsfield.*

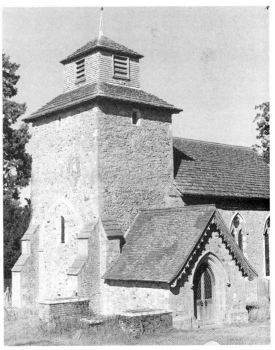

12.   *The west tower at Wotton.*

Godalming (of Bargate stone), Limpsfield (of ironstone and sandstone rubble), Mickleham, Oxted (short and rugged of Bargate stone), Shere and Wotton.

Among furnishings, there are plenty of fonts, mostly plain, of which Alfold has a large tub example, Thames Ditton one in the form of a block capital and Thursley one in the form of a tapered bowl (to which some give a Saxon date). Wall-paintings of the Norman period are minor but there is an interesting double mural at Pyrford – a rare example of such early wall-painting in Surrey (*Colour Plate V*).

13.   The font at Thames Ditton.   *14.   The font at Thursley.*

It would be presumptuous to rate any of the above as of national importance but there are two features of more than local significance: the double sanctuary at Compton and a rare lead font at Walton on the Hill. The sanctuary consists of a rib-vaulted lower chamber above which has been added an upper room at a later date: the reasons are not known but there may have been a need for a second chapel which, owing to the impossibility of extending laterally, could only be provided vertically. The wooden guardrail of Norman design in the upper chapel must be among the earliest church woodwork in the country. The lead font at Walton on the Hill dates from 1160, one of the few in this material to survive melting down for bullets in the Civil War, and a notable specimen. The decoration consists of a frieze at top and bottom enclosing eight (possibly twelve originally) delicately modelled figures in high relief, placed under round-headed arches. They wear haloes and hold books. The lead strip is in one piece. Although the number 12 suggests the Apostles, it is believed that the figures represent the four Latin Doctors of the Church (St. Ambrose, St Augustine, St Gregory, St Jerome) repeated.

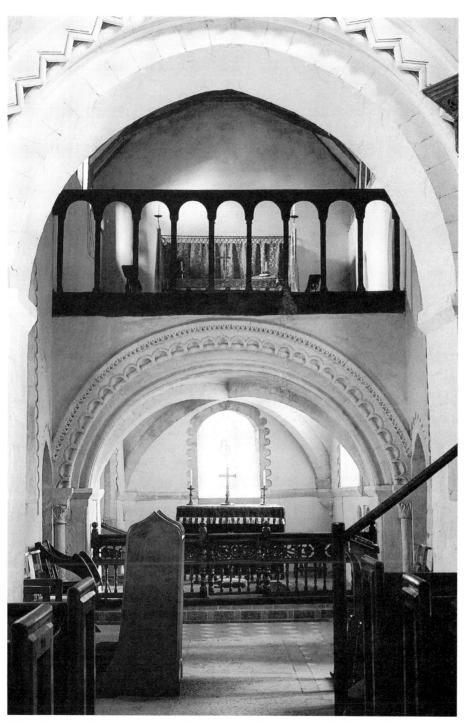

15.   *The double sanctuary at Compton, the lower chapel being vaulted and the upper one with a wooden screen, perhaps the oldest in England.*

16.   The Romanesque lead font at Walton on the Hill.

Thirteenth Century

The introduction of Gothic architecture into this country was followed during the thirteenth century by a period when monastic influence was very strong. Although there were relatively few monasteries in Surrey (only 17), the abbeys – more particularly Chertsey Abbey – owned many Surrey manors. The monastic institutions do not always seem to have

17.   The inscription at Great Bookham, recording the rebuilding of the chancel by Abbot Rutherwyk of Chertsey.

carried out their responsibilities properly and we read of Ash being taken away from Chertsey and given to the King 'by reason of voidance of the abbacy of Chertsey' who nevertheless appeared to have resumed ownership of the living later. The chancel of Effingham was repaired by order of William of Wykeham in 1388 because Merton Priory had neglected the church. Nor do the abbeys and priories seem to have exercised an influence upon ecclesiastical architecture proportionate to their wealth and power although, apart from St Mary Overie, Southwark, there is so little left of the Surrey monastic buildings that it is not possible to determine exactly how far the influence went. We do at least see tangible evidence at Egham and Great Bookham of the chancels being rebuilt by the great Chertsey abbot, Rutherwyk. At Burstow, even Canterbury appears to have failed in its duties for during a period in the fourteenth century the living passed to the Crown through 'voidance of the see'.

By the thirteenth century, the Mass had become – as the interesting Puttenham church guide states – 'more priestly and more mystical

18.   *The vaulted and apsidal chapel at St. Mary's, Guildford.*

19.   *The vaulted chancel at Stoke D'Abernon.*

20.   *The sedilia and piscina at Coulsdon.*

21.   *The chancel at Chipstead from the south.*

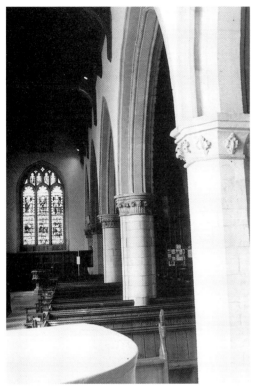

22.   *The south arcade at Reigate.*

23.   *Early stiff-leaf carving at Reigate.*

24.   *The east window at Ockham.*

and the fashion appeared in many churches of extending the chancel so that the priest, when celebrating, might be further removed from the people'.[3] This is seen at St Mary's, Guildford and Stoke D'Abernon, which have vaulted chancels whilst Coulsdon retains an attractive group of sedilia and piscina, the former with detached piers and richly moulded arches. The best example of a thirteenth-century chancel in the county is at Chipstead which has an array of narrow lancets on both north and south walls, the group of five on the north side being particularly fine; there are stone seats along parts of the walls. Additional aisles were also thrown out to provide more space; at Reigate the nave piers, although rebuilt by Scott, are of varying forms – octagonal, round and quatrefoil – with an early design of leaf-decorated capitals. Leatherhead has a good arcade with one carved capital.

25.   The tower at Thames Ditton.

26.   The west door at Merstham.

27.   Wanborough Church from the south.

The seven-light lancet east window at Ockham was clearly inserted later from a source not definitely known. Less rare is the two-light lancet window at East Clandon. Towers of this period occur at Chiddingfold, Chipstead (but date 1631 carved on it suggests that it was then renewed), Merstham, Thames Ditton and Wonersh (base): doorways at Ash and Merstham (both notable), and Wotton: fonts at Chelsham, Crowhurst, Gatton, Limpsfield and elsewhere. But perhaps the most striking feature is the tall lead-sheathed spire at Godalming – a rare phenomenon in the south-east (*Colour Plate VI*).

Two diminutive buildings, Okewood (in the heart of the Weald) and Wanborough (near Guildford) – a single-roomed chapel – afford examples of thirteenth-century hamlet churches, although the former has been spoilt by the addition of a north aisle in 1879. More substantial buildings are to be seen at Byfleet, Chipstead and Dunsfold, the last two being the leading Early English churches in the county. Chipstead has considerable nineteenth-century work but Dunsfold is a complete example of a village church of about 1270, when the Early English style was giving way to the Decorated. Being at the time under the Crown, it may have benefited from the skill of royal masons and is certainly a more accomplished work than a run-of-the-mill village church. William Morris called it 'the most beautiful country church in all England'.[4] The simple contemporary pews must be some of the oldest in the country. West Horsley has good small thirteenth-century medallions of stained glass in the east-end lancets (*Colour Plate VIII*) and, at the other end of the church, a notable St Christopher mural of impressive size dated about 1200 and only fully uncovered in 1972. Fragmentary paintings at Charlwood include the legend of St Margaret and the 'Three Living and Three Dead' in which three kings meet three skeletons who warn them that, as they now are, the kings will one day be. Two features of national interest remain to be mentioned – the D'Abernon brass and the Chaldon wall-painting. The well-known brass to Sir John D'Abernon, dating from *c.*1327 and although not the oldest

28. *Byfleet Church from the north east.*

29. *The west end of Dunsfold Church.*

30.   Early wooden pews in the nave at Dunsfold.

31.   The mural of St Christopher in the nave at West Horsley.

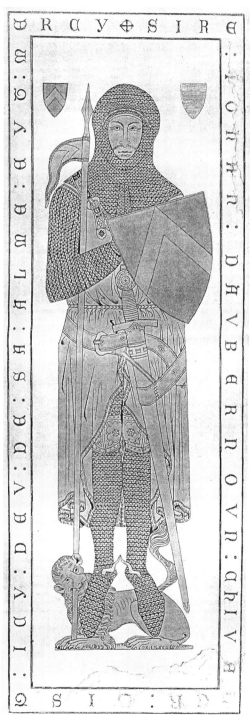

32.   The Brass of Sir John D'Abernon at Stoke D'Abernon (c.1327).

in the country as at one time thought, is a fine specimen of the brass engraver's craft. The wall-painting at Chaldon, although much restored, is a remarkable survival (*Colour Plate IV*). Covering the whole of the west wall, the theme is akin to the Ladder of Salvation and is of eastern origin, found also in Rumania. It depicts souls trying to scale a ladder towards the heavenly regions with fearsome demons picking many of them off, as they strive upwards, and thrusting them into boiling cauldrons.

Fourteenth Century

Much of Surrey in the Middle Ages was royal forest subject to the harsh forest laws, but where the land was held by monasteries the inhabitants were safe from harassment by the royal foresters, although liable to serf labour for the monks, a cause of violent resistance when labour became scarce after the Black Death of 1348/9. Before this disaster, however, monastic influence reached a peak in Surrey during the abbacy at Chertsey of Abbot Rutherwyk from 1307 to

33. The fourteenth-century extended chancel at Shere.

1346. He has been described by Eric Parker as 'an ardent and admirable landlord and a prelate of enduring energy and wisdom. No squire of modern days did more to improve his property. He laid out roads and had pathways raised from the level of flooded meadows; he set up mills and threw bridges over streams; he sowed oak plantations and taught forestry; he planned barns and granges for corn and dug stews and ponds for fish, and he was as enthusiastic a churchman as he was energetic as a farmer'.[5] He has also been described as an abbot of taste, a man of culture and an indefatigable builder. The rebuilding by him of the chancels at Egham and Great Bookham referred to earlier is recorded by inscribed stones. Chancels were extended at Ewell (old church), Godalming, Oxted, Sanderstead, Shere, Tatsfield and Walton on Thames, and the reverence accorded to the Virgin Mary led to a demand for more altars. Aisles were added and chapels formed (for example, Ham Chapel at Blechingley: Cudworth Chapel at Newdigate, built by the de la Poyles as a chantry or family chapel: St Margaret Chapel at Ockham). Window tracery, a particular feature

34. Geometric tracery at St. Peter's Church, Old Woking.

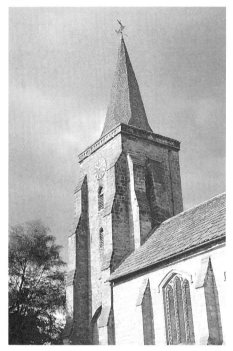

35 & 36   Two fourteenth-century west towers: Lingfield, with a broach spire, and Cranleigh, with a short cap and showing the put-log holes.

37.   The north nave arcade at Fetcham.   *38.   The font at Chipstead.*

of the Decorated style, is not noteworthy in Surrey; Kentish tracery (with downward-pointing cusps) is to be seen at Charlwood and Horley, curvilinear at Old Woking, Shere, Witley and Worplesdon (the last two identical), geometrical at Godalming, and intersecting at Dunsfold west window. (The other windows at Dunsfold are geometrical.) Other fourteenth-century windows are at Horne, Merton, Nutfield and Pyrford.

A splay-footed spire was added at Compton whilst the tower-framing at Horley and the lower part of the tower of Frensham date from this period; complete towers remain at Sanderstead and Lingfield (otherwise a predominantly Perpendicular church). Other features are roofs at Chertsey (chancel) and Tandridge, the south porch at Alfold and north doorway at Horley, the sedilia and piscina at Farnham, the piscina at Newdigate and the lych-gate at Limpsfield, and also fonts at Banstead, Chipstead and Ewhurst. Perhaps the most enjoyable single feature is the north arcade at Fetcham, described by Nairn as 'a great surprise, the arch shapes beautifully smooth and subtle, the appearance of having been designed for a church four times the size'.[6] The church where the Decorated style is most in evidence is Cranleigh where nave, aisles, chancel, clerestory and tower are all of this period although severely handled in 1864/6. The carstone tower is unusual in retaining its putlogs or scaffold holes which are normally filled in (these, however, are often seen in Italy, for example in the Torre del Mangia in Siena). There remain two items of more than local interest: a fourteenth-century nave window in the Victorian village church of Buckland, with the best medieval glass in Surrey, of dark blues and reds, depicting St Peter and St Paul under elaborate canopies (*Colour Plate X*) and a dignified female brass of the end of the century (about 1400) under a finely engraved ogee canopy at Horley.

Later Medieval Period

The Black Death of 1348/9 dealt a body-blow to the monasteries from which they never recovered and, for some time, there was little in the way of building. Secular influences increasingly exerted sway, but

39. Brass of an unknown lady at Horley.

unfortunately for Surrey these were not by wool merchants of the rising middle class coming forward with their wealth to beautify their local churches or to build chantry chapels for the repose of their souls, influences which have left such a rich heritage in other parts of the country. A certain amount of trade in cloth was carried out in Guildford and

40, 41 & 42.   Three timber steeples: a slender bell-turret and spire at Crowhurst; a spire and shingled bell-chamber, standing on four large rough posts inside, at Horley; and a timber west tower with a frame reaching to the ground, with a bottom stage of flint, at Great Bookham.

43. & 44.   The timber west porch at Bisley, with the entrance archway formed from a pair of solid timbers, and the lych-gate at Egham, the former porch and all that remains of the old church. This has an elegant framed archway with quatrefoils.

Godalming towards the end of the medieval period but this did not yield the wool-wealth that left such a beneficent mark in the churches of East Anglia, the West Country and the Humberside area of Yorkshire. In fact, there is no major Perpendicular ecclesiastical building in the county, the best being Lingfield, which is quite small and does not even have a clerestory. Surrey, however, can offer a large selection of timber-framed bellcotes and bell-turrets, some with spires (Alfold, Byfleet, Crowhurst, Horley and Thursley) and sometimes complete belfries rising from the ground in Essex style (Burstow, Great Bookham, Newdigate). At Horley and Tandridge the supporting timbers are inside the church. Horley is unusual in having the bell-chamber shingled, and Thursley, where the nave has been extended to the west, is set curiously on a timber cage over what is now the middle of the nave. Apart from shingling, weatherboarding and tiles are used for sheathing, although the smaller examples are mostly shingled. The local feature of belltower or bellcote with splay-footed spirelet, all shingled, was used by the Victorians at Buckland, Busbridge and Hascombe. It would be wrong, however, to assume that in Surrey wood was

45. *Merton chancel roof. Note also the tops of the arches of the wall arcades.*

more often employed than stone for steeples, for there are about 50 stone western towers of medieval date compared with about 30 bellcotes or towers in timber. Attractive porches can be seen at Bisley, Egham, Merton, Oxted, Pyrford, Reigate and Send, but roofs are generally plain. Merton, however, has a form of hammer-beam roof and Beddington one which is almost unrecognisable after nineteenth-century restoration.

The richly-carved screens which are such a feature of Devon and East Anglian churches will not be found in Surrey, except for a modest example at Charlwood. This has cresting above a line of angels and dragons holding initials and a vine trail below. At Chelsham half the former chantry-chapel parclose screen is now used as a chancel screen but cut down to half its height, whilst at Nutfield and (mutilated) Send much renovated ones remain. Gatton has a good screen from an unknown source.

Among private chapels, there are the Slyfield chapel at Great Bookham, a chantry chapel at Merstham, the Norbury chapel at Stoke D'Abernon and late examples at Holy Trinity, Guildford (Weston chapel) and St Mary's, Wimbledon (Cecil chapel). The two best towers are at Farnham and Worplesdon, the former with Victorian upper windows and crown, the latter enlivened with a cupola from the rectory stables. Others are at Ash and Chobham, both of heathstone (the former completed with a nineteenth-century shingled spire and the latter with a lead-sheathed spirelet), Kingston, Lambeth, Leatherhead, Old Woking (with a top of heathstone), Putney, Reigate and West Molesey. There is also the tower of *c.*1420 at Ewell with a stair-turret at the south-west corner; it is all that remains from the earlier church. A local speciality is the decoration of interior arches with crimped plaster as at Albury, Ash, Compton and Worplesdon.

46.   Screen at St Nicholas, Charlwood.

47.   'Crimped' plasterwork around a doorway at Worplesdon.

Of furnishings, the fonts are generally without decoration; they include octagonal examples with simple quatrefoil panels at Ashtead, Blechingley, Burstow, Epsom, Leatherhead and West Molesey. Crowhurst and Nutfield have pre-Reformation pulpits. Lingfield and Beddington have fine sets of misericords. St John the Baptist Church at Croydon has a fine fifteenth-century brass lectern (*Colour Plate XIV*). But no account of Surrey late medieval furnishings would be complete without mention of the collection of continental specimens at Gatton assembled by Lord Monson on a Grand Tour of Europe, including nave panelling of 1515 from Aarschot Cathedral and altar rails from Tongres, both in Belgium. There are no wall paintings worthy of mention but quite a lot of glass, the best being the fourteenth-century window at Buckland.

The medieval age cannot be left, however, without mentioning a rare example of a church built in the mid-sixteenth century. The old church of St George at Esher which Pevsner [7] describes as 'a delightful, most endearing little church' was constructed of chalk and flint in that

FOUR FIFTEENTH-CENTURY WEST TOWERS

48.   Farnham, St Andrew.

49.   Leatherhead, St Mary & St Nicholas.

50.   West Molesey, St Peter.

51.   Ewell, St Mary (Old Church).

52.   Octagonal font at Leatherhead.   *53.   West tower at Mortlake.*

54.   The west end of St George's Church, Esher, showing the Tudor stonework,
with the royal pew on the right and the added north aisle.

period. The tower of Mortlake, apart from the top storey and the lantern, is also of this time and was built on Henry VIII's order.

Post-Reformation

The Reformation was followed in Surrey, as in other parts of England, by a lull in church building and the main structural contributions were the brick towers of Barnes and Thorpe and the complete brick churches of Morden and Malden (except for its flintwork chancel). In furnishings, the chief items of interest are the numerous pulpits installed in accordance with an edict of 1603 that every church should be equipped with 'a comely and decent pulpit'. St Nicholas, Pyrford has a typical example of 1628, with sounding board and decorated with simple geometrical patterns; more elaborate ones occur at Stoke D'Abernon and West Molesey. At Chaldon there is a rare Cromwellian example dating from 1657 and at Mickleham a Belgian one dating from *c*.1600 (*Colour Plate XXVIII*). West galleries were installed at some churches (e.g. at Newdigate, Old Woking and Send) and altar rails were often provided no doubt to keep the sanctuary inviolate from dogs, etc., following the removal of screens.

55.   St. Lawrence, Morden (1636)   *56.   The pulpit at Pyrford.*

There is good seventeenth-century glass in the chapel of Abbot's Hospital, Guildford and at Morden. There is a wide range at Stoke D'Abernon, but it is mainly foreign (*Colour Plate XXV*). At Ashtead the east window (*Colour Plate XXVI*) contains glass from Herckenrode Abbey in the Netherlands, while at Great Bookham is more Flemish glass (*Colour Plate XXVII*) from the collection formerly at Costessy Hall (pronounced Cossey) in Norfolk.

57.   Plasterwork of 1592 in the Lumley Chapel ceiling at Cheam.

58.   The Hassell view of the west end of St Peter's, in (Old) Woking, showing the west gallery and the pulpit on the north side of the nave.

Brasses and Monuments

At Cheam, the chancel of the medieval church was converted into a chapel with a most attractive ceiling to house the Lumley monuments and it is pertinent here to say something about Surrey memorials. Mention has already been made of the Stoke D'Abernon and Horley brasses, to which should be added the fine early fifteenth-century set at Lingfield. There are small ones at Byfleet to a former rector (dating from about 1480) and at Shere to

59.   Brass of Walter Frilende (1376), at Ockham.

60.   Brass of John Bowthe, Bishop of Exeter (1478), at East Horsley.

SOME SURREY BRASSES

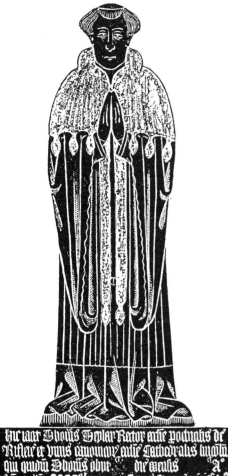

61.   *Thomas Taylar, priest (c.1480)*
at Byfleet.

62.   *John & Margaret Weston (1483)*
at Ockham.

63.   *The adoration of the shepherds (c.1500) at Cobham.*

65. *Palimpsest brass at Cobham. (Priest of c.1510 & man in armour of c.1550)*

64. *John & Susan Selwyn (1587) at Walton on Thames.*

66. *Peter & Richard Best (1587) at Merstham*

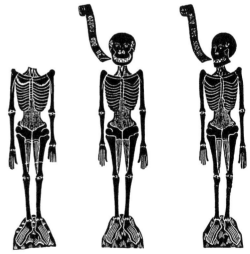

67. *A man & two wives as skeletons (15th. century) at Weybridge.*

John, Lord Audley (d.1491), but only the top half and inscription of the latter are original. Other examples occur at Ockham to Walter Frilende (d.1376) – the earliest priest's brass in Surrey – and John Weston (d.1483) and wife. At East Horsley there is an endearing kneeling figure of John Bowthe, Bishop of Exeter (d.1478), at Merstham and Stoke D'Abernon babes in chrisom robes and at Cobham a nativity scene. Others worthy of mention are that to Edward de la Hale, in armour, at Okewood, the skeletons at Weybridge and the palimpsest at Cobham.

68.   The monument at Lingfield to Reginald, first Lord Cobham of Sterborough (d.1361)

The best of the medieval stone monuments are those to members of the Cobham family at Lingfield, dating from 1361 and 1446, with engaging figures of angels and animals and – in one case – a Saracen's head under the feet. The Lumley monuments at Cheam date from the end of the sixteenth century and the beginning of the seventeenth and provide an interesting contrast in style with the plain tomb-chest of 1559 to Sir Thomas Cawarden at Blechingley. Immediately succeeding monuments are not outstanding and those at Holy Trinity, Guildford rather old-fashioned. A small memorial with kneeling figures to John Goodwine (d.1618) and his wife at Horne retains much of its original colouring (*Colour Plate XVII*). By the time of Charles I things had improved and at Egham there is a notable

69.   And the 'rascally-looking Saracen' at his feet.

70.   *Jane, Lady Lumley (1590) at Cheam.*

71.   *Archbishop George Abbot (1640) at Holy Trinity, Guildford.*

72.   *Sir John Denham (1638) at Egham.*

73.   *Broderick monument at Peper Harow.*

but macabre wall monument to Sir John Denham (d.1638), showing him with reconstituted body rising from the charnel house, with his unfortunate wife left behind; it is a work of great skill. There are two excellent busts at Peper Harow to Sir Thomas Broderick (d.1641) and his wife (d.1678), plus many good late seventeenth-century tablets, notably the one to Elisabeth Evelyn (d.1691) at St Martin's, Epsom with barley-sugar Corinthian columns and first-rate carving.

74.   The tablet to Elisabeth Evelyn at Epsom.

75.   Sir Robert & Lady Clayton at Blechingley.

The very large monument to Sir Robert Clayton (d.1707) at Blechingley is described by Nairn[9] as 'one of the most splendid early eighteenth-century monuments in the country': he is carved in a standing posture with his wife but the swagger is offset by the pathetic figure at the foot in embroidered clothes of their still-born child. It is stated that the monument was completed before Sir Robert's death so that he could admire it. By contrast at Ickenham in Middlesex, the same child is shown as a recumbent marble infant in swaddling clothes, pathetic in its loneliness. From an earlier church than the present one at St Paul's,

76.   The baby on the Clayton momument.

Clapham survives a memorial to Sir Robert Atkins (d.1689), his wife Rebecca (d.1711) and their three children, all of whom died before their parents. The craftsmanship is of a

77.   The Clayton baby at
Ickenham, Middlesex.

78.   Rebecca Atkins at
Clapham St Paul.

high order, particularly charming is the standing figure of Rebecca, the youngest child who
died in 1661 at the age of eight and who holds a skull in her hand.

Georgian Period

There was activity along the river Thames where the old churches had become dilapidated
and obsolete. St Mary's, Rotherhithe and St Mary's, Battersea were rebuilt, the latter to
accommodate what was said to be the 'second best carriage congregation in London'.[8] All
Saints, Wandsworth was largely rebuilt, a new place of worship was added at Kew,
Richmond nave was rebuilt, and Petersham received a large north transept. Away from the
inner surroundings of the metropolis, however, Holy Trinity, Guildford was the only large
Georgian church to have been erected in the county, the tower of the previous church
having collapsed. Other major structural work was the rebuilding in 1784 of the village
church of Pirbright and the south aisle at Carshalton.

   All Saints at Kingston upon Thames has an appealing brick top to the tower of 1708,
whilst Petersham has an eighteenth-century two-decker pulpit (*Colour Plate XX*) of pleasing
design, but the most rewarding church for eighteenth-century furnishings is St George's
Esher, which, in addition to a three-decker pulpit, has a well-carved reredos of 1722 and
the private Newcastle pew which was added in 1725 and has an impressive front towards
the church looking like a summer house. There is another pulpit (1720) with original stair
and sounding-board at Morden and a reredos at Carshalton, later gilded and painted by Sir
Ninian Comper (*Colour Plate XXII*).

QUEEN ANNE & GEORGIAN CHURCHES

79.   Kew, St Anne from the west.

80.   Holy Trinity, Guildford.

81.   The tower at Kingston upon Thames

82.   Pirbright, St Michael.

83.   The Newcastle pew at St George's, Esher from the nave of the church.

There are some notable monuments, Sir William Lewen (d.1721) at St Mary's, Ewell is exceptionally good; he is shown reclining and wearing a wig. Of almost the same date and semi-reclining is the effigy of Sir William Scawen (d.1722) at All Saints, Carshalton. An outstanding and very large monument by Joseph Rose the Elder in the north transept of St Mary's, Reigate commemorates Richard Ladbroke (d.1730). Rose was one of a number of little known English sculptors who sprung up at this time with fine work (cf. Crutcher at Blechingley who carved the Clayton monument). Ladbroke is shown in Roman dress; so, too are Colonel Arthur Moore (d.1735) at Great Bookham and Speaker Onslow (d.1778) at Holy Trinity, Guildford. Also at Great Bookham is a fine and uncommonly striking monument to Cornet Geary, who died in 1776 in an ambush at Flemington, New Jersey during the American War of Independence, with a delicately-carved relief of the scene of his death. Among smaller monuments there are two attractive busts in architectural frames at Ashtead to Lady Diana Feilding (d.1733), probably by Rysbrack, and at Sanderstead (unnamed). An urn and flambeau in an architectural frame commemorates Henry Ludlow (d. 1730) at Bramley.

Rysbrack, the great Flemish sculptor, is more substantially represented in Surrey by a monument at Ockham to Lord King, who started life as the son of a grocer, rising to become Lord Chancellor during the years 1725 to 1733 and dying in 1734. This large monument is housed in a chapel especially built for the purpose and is a fine composition. The faces are melancholy.

The other great sculptor of the eighteenth century, the Frenchman, Louis François Roubiliac, is represented in the county by a huge monument to Viscount Shannon at Walton on Thames. He was a great general and died a marshal in 1740. He leans proudly against a gun, with a large square tent behind. His daughter, beautifully carved, sits disconsolately at the side.

84. Sir William Scawen at Carshalton.

85. Speaker Onslow at Holy Trinity, Guildford.

86. Cornet Geary at Great Bookham.

87. Lady Diana Feilding at Ashtead.

88.   *Lord King at Ockham.*   89.   *Viscount Shannon at Walton on Thames.*

The Georgian era brings us to the period when Cracklow portrayed Surrey churches. Charles Thomas Cracklow was an architect and surveyor who set himself the task of making drawings of Surrey's 155 churches, including 10 chapels, as they appeared in the early 1820s, the complete set being first produced in 1826.[10] He only omitted Wanborough, then a farm building. The general impressions these drawings give, apart from the London places of worship and one or two outside like Mitcham, is one of quaint rusticity with many churches a patchwork of different styles and additions – 'atmospherick' perhaps sometimes but certainly not urbane. They have a delightful texture and the churchyards – not yet disfigured with alien marble, or, worse, polished granite – are uniformly attractive if often rather shaggy in appearance. One cannot discern the gentle decay into which many of them had slid, although only too obvious is the unsightly creeper which had wreathed itself round the towers of Great Bookham and West Horsley and must have been causing considerable deterioration. Ewhurst has a most remarkable steeple looking like an Essex belfry set centrally, whilst Farleigh has no bellcote at all and Oxted a little cupola above the tower. St Martha's Chapel, Chilworth was in a ruinous state. A large shire-type horse at the door of Limpsfield church seems to set the scene and the age perfectly.

Character of Surrey Churches and Churchyards

There is tremendous variety and one cannot pick out what might be called a Surrey style. As the Victoria County History points out,[11] there is a lack of individuality due to the absence of natural boundaries plus proximity to London and, as we have seen, the monastic institutions do not appear to have exercised an influence upon ecclesiastical architecture proportionate to their wealth and power. Moreover, the lack of important quarries meant that there were no local schools of masons, the absence of which meant a relative lack of local traditions and individual styles. The main influence appears to have come from Winchester whose bishop resided at Farnham and who had his London residence near St Mary Overie, Southwark, although Godalming had links with Salisbury. Surrey churches were added to and altered as circumstances demanded, but basically were designed for yeoman farmers rather than for large landlords, and for small populations without grandiose ideas. Occasionally as at Dunsfold, the workmanship is sophisticated but most is the handiwork of local masons working with a large variety of materials not of the first class and sparing in their use of decoration. They were suited to local needs and it would be unrealistic to expect major architectural buildings in a county which, up to the time of the Reformation, was so poor and little regarded except near the River Thames. Surrey medieval churches were, as elsewhere, a faithful reflection of the geological and economic conditions of the age.

The Railway Age

On 12th May 1838, less than a year after the accession of Queen Victoria to the throne, the London and Southampton Railway Company opened its line as far as Woking, linking 'windmill-studded' Vauxhall and Nine Elms to Woking Common where, as a print of the time shows, there was not a house to be seen and only a couple of stone-breakers at work in the foregound. This was the start of a revolution in transport to Surrey which was to change the character of the county, converting it from a sparsely populated area into one of the most densely inhabited parts of the country whose people looked ever more inward to London. Other lines to Surrey were soon to follow. Redhill was reached in 1841, Guildford in 1845, Epsom in 1847 and Richmond in 1848. In 1842, Redhill was linked to Ashford (Kent) and in 1849 to Reading.

Londoners, however, had discovered the charms of Surrey long before the railways came but the type of residence they had built for themselves was an adornment rather than the reverse, as we have only to see for ourselves along the riverside villages of Richmond, Kew and Ham, and even in the less fashionable Thames Ditton, Mortlake and Barnes. Further south, the natural Surrey parkland had been landscaped to good effect by discriminating owners, so that travellers approaching London from the south by stage coach could still enjoy the propect of fine villas, such as Grove Hill in Camberwell and Loughborough House in Brixton, lying amongst market-gardens spread out before the gentle rise of the tree-decked hills of Norwood. But the pleasant market-gardens on the Surrey side of London had already been doomed by the opening of Westminster Bridge in 1749 which cleared the way for coaches to Dover, Brighton and Portsmouth and provided the opportunity for developers to encroach on the villages of Camberwell, Peckham, Stockwell, Streatham and Clapham. A further blow was the enclosure of the common lands of Lambeth Manor in 1806 which opened the flood-gates to new construction. Although fiercely contested, it was of no avail and new streets were built in these areas until the villages gradually merged into one another; by 1868 they were solidly part of London and the view from Brixton towards Central London showed a completely built-up area. Previously, vegetables had been supplied to London from the market-gardens of Battersea and Lambeth, whilst fresh milk had come from numerous cow-keepers in Brixton, Camberwell, Peckham and beyond. Now the market-gardeners and cow-keepers had to go further afield.

90.   *Addlestone, St. Paul.*

The population of Surrey in the early years of the century rose from 105,857 (1801 census) to 182,337 (1841 census), an increase of 72% but still small in total. The need, therefore, for new places of worship was not as pressing as in the Metropolis where, in the same period, the population had doubled from one to two millions, largely due to the building of the docks, and over one-third of these lived in slum conditions. The social conscience was stirred to provide places of worship to combat the evils of living in such deprived conditions, and in 1818 the Church Building Act was passed – ostensibly as thanksgiving for victory at Waterloo – which set aside £ 1 million, increased in 1824 to £ 1 ½ millions, to cater for the spiritual needs of this huge increase of population. The Commissioners who administered the Act have been criticised for building on the cheap but they were honest churchmen concerned with using the money to provide maximum seating capacity and, in any case, church architecture was at a low ebb. Naturally, London received the bulk of the money but Commissioners' Churches were erected in Surrey at the following places:

	Date	Architect
Addlestone, St Paul	1836	James Savage
Croydon, St James	1827-9	Robert Wallace
Mitcham, St Peter & St Paul	1819-21	George Smith
Richmond, St John the Divine	1831-6	L. Vulliamy
Upper Norwood, All Saints	1827-9	James Savage

Epsom, St Martin's received a new facade of flint and stucco in 1824. None of these churches is of architectural moment. Addlestone and Richmond (St John the Divine), built of yellow stock and grey brick respectively, are not particularly inspiring and it is hard to equate the work of James Savage at Addlestone with his St Luke's, Chelsea, a notable landmark in the Gothic Revival, or his St James's, Thurland Road, Bermondsey, both churches of some distinction. St Peter & St Paul's, Mitcham, however, has attractive vaults and retains its medieval north-west tower, also a Rysbrack monument to Sir Ambrose (d.1713) and Lady Crowley (d.1727) in the form of profile portraits in a medallion. St John the Divine has pleasing balconies over the west gallery.

The most interesting place of worship to be built in Surrey during this period and a complete contrast to Commissioners' Gothic is St John the Baptist, Egham. Variously described as having 'simple and severe beauty' or as being 'very ugly', it was built by Henry Rhodes in 1817-20. Classical and rectangular in shape, the church has a shallow sanctuary and large ceiling, unsupported by any internal columns. Externally the west tower is surmounted by an oval cupola. Apart from the notable monument to Sir John Denham, the church is a period piece with many associations, the most famous of which is recorded around the gallery front by replicas of the coats of arms of the 25 barons chosen as sureties to defend Magna Carta.

At Frimley, J.T. Parkinson built St Peter's in 1825 which was a poor successor to the completely half-timbered church of 1606 and, at Ham, E. Lapidge designed St Andrew's, built in 1830-1. (The south aisle dates from 1860 and the chancel – the best part – from 1900-01, the latter designed by Bodley & Garner, using red brick as opposed to Lapidge's grey.) In addition, St Peter's, Chertsey received in 1806-08 a new nave with square piers in an unattractive Gothic style and Gatton, famous for its continental furnishings collected by Lord Monson, during the Grand Tour, was Gothicized in 1834. To round off this pre-Victorian period on a more cheerful note, St Nicholas, Peper Harow was given in 1826 a west tower of pleasant Gothic form.

91.   St. Peter's, Frimley. This church was built in 1825 with two rows of windows to light both above and below the galleries.

The Victorian Years

It is appropriate that we should enter the Victorian age at Peper Harow as this, and Albury (plus the east window at Farnham), are the only churches in Surrey where we encounter the work of Augustus Pugin, the great apostle of the Gothic Revival who had such a formative influence in the early years of the reign. Uncharacteristically, his work at Peper Harow, although Sir Thomas Jackson was involved later (1876-7), combines neo-Norman, Early English and Decorated features, possibly to give the impression of a slow-growth medieval building. Pugin's work was carried out in 1844, but before this the more typical Pugin is seen in the south transept of the old church in Albury Park, where in 1839 he redecorated it in a style quite different from the rough, plastered walls seen elsewhere in the church. The transept was later coloured in vivid tones and enlivened by rich stained glass, all of which comes as a surprise in these sedate surroundings. Commissioners' churches continued to be built (Croydon, St Peter's in 1849-51, Norbiton, St Peter's in 1841, both by Sir George Gilbert Scott, the latter in conjunction with his partner W.B. Moffatt, and Virginia Water in 1838-9 by W.F. Pocock). The early years of the reign, however, largely belong to Benjamin Ferrey, a somewhat pedestrian follower of Pugin. Between the years 1844 and 1857 he erected seven churches and one chapel (Coldharbour) in different parts of the county. The designs vary from the bizarre neo-Norman of Hale, Farnham (1844) with rose window and round south tower, to Kingswood on the other side of Surrey (1848-52), which is a replica of fourteenth-century Shottesbrooke in Berkshire and nicely set in wooded surroundings. Other Ferrey churches are Brockham (1846), cruciform in design and built of Reigate stone with limestone dressings, and Shalford (1846) of the warmer Bargate stone with attached north-west tower and copper-sheathed spire. The light tones of Brockham at the far side of the green make a charming composition with the adjacent houses. Christ Church, Esher of 1853 took the place, as parish church, of what to many today is the much more appealing St George's (in the centre of the town) which had become too small. Christ Church, although impressively set on the east side of the green, imposes more by its air of consequence and its stone broach-spire than by its architectural qualities. The remaining

92.   Pugin decoration in the south transept at Albury Old Church.

93.   Seale Church, Victorian Picturesque (1861-73).

new Ferrey churches are St Andrew's, Croydon and St Paul's, Dorking, both of 1857 and much added to later. Of churches already existing, he built the nave at Ripley in 1836, south arcade, south aisle and south chapel at Thames Ditton in 1864, as well as carrying out restoration work, much of it heavy-handed, at Chobham in 1866, Farnham (St. Andrew) in 1855 and Thursley (north aisle) in 1860. Much later, in 1884-95, he restored Burstow with a light hand.

The neo-Norman style encountered at Hale was also used by H.E. Kendall in the grey brick Holy Trinity of 1840 at Claygate which has two curious towers flanking the apse, octagonal towards the top and capped by spires; the style can be seen too in the 1842 red brick church at Albury by McIntosh Brooks which took the place of the old church in the Park, which was allowed to become a picturesque ruin. (Albury Old Church, as it is called, was finally made redundant in 1974 and vested in the Churches Conservation Trust who have restored it.) Other neo-Norman work, but outside the early Victorian period, is that carried out by Peacock in Mickleham in 1871 when, following on W.F. Robinson's work in 1823, he provided aisles of this style, a decorative east end with rose-window, plus a round tower on the south side. The Scott and Moffatt Commissioners' church at Norbiton, built in 1841 of yellow and white brick with north-west tower, was also of Norman design – one of Scott's earliest but not unworthy works. The best single piece, however, in this style is the central tower at Ewhurst by Robert Ebbals, who replaced the one that had fallen down in 1838. Other churches built in the opening years of the reign included an early example of John Loughborough Pearson's work – St James's, Weybridge. Pearson was to become one of the shining lights of the later Victorian period, but St James's, dating from 1848, was his first major work in Surrey and not one of his best. Nevertheless, the exterior is distinctive for its prominent and bold broach-spire and the interior for its harmonious proportions and skilful use of polychrome marble mosaic in the richly ornamented chancel, incorporating 22 types of marble. St Mary's Ewell was erected in 1847-8 by Henry Clutton.

St Peter's, Hambledon is a village church rebuilt in 1846 with a shingled bellcote forming a pleasant vignette with the adjoining houses. St Stephen's, Shottermill, Haslemere dates from 1838, but was enlarged in 1876 by J.W. Penfold who built the undistinguished parish church of Haslemere (St Bartholomew) in 1871. St Stephen's has a short tower and its virtues reside mainly in the Wealden stone used and in not straying too far from the traditional Surrey style. Holy Trinity, Lyne – well-sited and impressive from a distance – built in 1849 by Francis Brothers and the church at West Molesey, mainly constructed of yellow brick in 1843, but retaining its Perpendicular west tower of ragstone, are further examples of mid-nineteenth-century churches. In addition, substantial work was carried out at St John's, Merrow in 1843-5, and at St Mary's, Wimbledon by Scott and Moffatt in 1843. At Merrow, a north aisle was added later in 1881, and, at St Mary's, Wimbledon, Scott largely rebuilt the chancel in 1860; he had rebuilt the nave in 1843. Henry Woodyer set up office in Surrey in 1846. His first major work was the restoration in 1848 of St Martha on the Hill above Chilworth, which had become derelict, and which he almost entirely rebuilt in a manner well suited to the atmosphere of the lonely site. In addition, Byfleet received in 1841 a new south aisle and Godstone in 1845 a new north aisle.

1851-70

The years from 1851 to 1870 saw a gathering of momentum as more and more commuters took up their abode in the county and churches multiplied to cater for their needs. By 1861, the population of Redhill had out-stripped that of its smarter neighbour, Reigate. Surrey became a happy hunting-ground for architects. The leading figures were Henry Woodyer,

94.   St. Peter, Hascombe, from the south east, showing the south chapel.

who built and restored numerous churches in the county, and Sir George Gilbert Scott. Woodyer was a pupil of William Butterfield and the varied assortment of work that flowed from his drawing-board has left a strong visual impact on many a Surrey town and village. The restoration of St Martha on the Hill, Chilworth has already been mentioned; there followed the building by him of the town church of St Michael, York Town, Camberley (1849-51), nicely elevated in a typical Surrey coniferous setting but with an unimpressive interior. The prominent tower and spire of Bargate stone are additions of 1891.

Woodyer then turned to a quintet of village churches (Buckland, Burpham, Grafham, Hascombe and Wyke), Wyke being the earliest. Burpham is an unassuming but satisfying chapel of ease without aisles, of 1859; it has strange sedilia. Grafham, an apsed chapel of 1861-4, recalls an amusing deceit practised by the architect on the Bishop of Winchester by providing a wooden screen, despite objections from the latter on liturgical grounds, on the score that it was integral with and therefore necessary to the structure. The sentimental side of Woodyer is shown in a plaster corbel on the south wall of the chancel depicting a robin on its nest: it is believed that this is a memento of his daughter Hester who was called 'Chick' and the sad loss of his young wife, Frances, who died in childbirth ten months after their marriage. As it was near to his home, the architect had a special affection for the church which he paid for out of his own pocket (as did G.E. Street at Holmbury St Mary). Buckland, an admirable building of 1860 of Bargate stone, sticks well to traditional Surrey character and receives the accolade of 'This is Victorian village-church building at its best' from Ian Nairn. [12] The west end with bellcote is particularly successful. Inside, from the earlier church, the fourteenth-century figures of St Peter and St Paul under canopies in dark blues and reds is one of the finest examples of medieval stained glass in the county. Best of the five is Hascombe, 1864, an outstanding example of original Victorian work using local material (Bargate stone) and vernacular-style shingled bellcote with a separately roofed

Lady Chapel; the interior was subsequently in 1890 richly decorated in a highly individual Byzantine style with cusped and gilded apse-roof rafters and a painted reredos, incorporating the east window. The rood screen was lavishly coloured and the competent handling of the palette of colours makes the interior with its vivid stained glass one of the most exciting Victorian works in the county.

Following these rural pursuits, Woodyer designed and built his finest and largest church – St Martin's, Dorking – over the ten years 1868-77. The tall west tower and spire is an arresting sight from wherever one looks at it and nowhere better than in descending the road from Ranmore Common to the town. Internally, the excellent proportions, the acutely pointed arches and the richly shafted chancel arch all combine to create a satisfying vertical emphasis. Woodyer did other things in Surrey. They are of varying quality. He built St James's at Farnham in 1876 – a lack-lustre job; this was declared redundant in 1975 and has been converted into bed-sitting room accommodation for single people. He restored Compton sensitively. At Bramley, most of the church apart from the chancel is by Woodyer (1850 and 1876) and he rebuilt a large part of Capel in 1865, giving it an attractive Surrey-type shingled bell-turret and spire. Among his less worthy efforts must be counted the addition of the south transept at Byfleet in 1864 which broke up still further the proportions of the

95. *The west tower and spire of Woodyer's St. Martin's, Dorking.*

church, already compromised by the addition of a south aisle in 1841, and his all too comprehensive restoration at Chiddingfold.

If Woodyer was the most prolific architect in nineteenth-century Surrey, Sir George Gilbert Scott must be accounted one of the most productive in the whole country. A published list in 1878 named 730 buildings by him and it was not complete. His influence in the restoration of the major churches of the country was immense and, if one has reservations regarding some of his work, Scott himself claimed that he was strictly conservative in his restorations and that, but for them, many of our finest churches would have fallen down, so bad was their state of repair. He worked at a tremendous rate and his quality may sometimes have suffered from the poor workmanship of those serving under him. In many ways he is representative of Victorian architecture and one cannot go far without encountering his work. Scott founded a dynasty of architects and it is difficult sometimes to tell which member of the family is involved. In Surrey he started on a weak note with St John's, Woking, an aisleless chapel now almost unrecognisable under a modernisation scheme and earlier enlargements. In conjunction with Moffatt, he built St Peter's, Norbiton in 1843 and in the same year rebuilt the nave of St Mary's, Wimbledon; the latter's 196 ft. tower and spire was also his work. In 1847 he built Farncombe, adding to it later. He then designed in 1852 Holy Trinity, Westcott near Dorking and in 1856

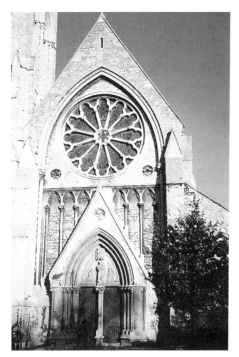

96. *The rose window at St Matthias, Richmond.*

97. *St. Bartholomew, Ranmore Common.*

St. John's, Shirley near Croydon, both in village style although St John's is quite a large building; the bell-turret with spike rests inside on two massive round piers. Holy Trinity, Westcott also has a bell-turret and is nicely perched above the village beside an open space, but somehow fails to convey a village atmosphere. These were followed by Scott's best work in Surrey – a trio of large churches, widely separated and showing fully his professional competence and sense of scale. The earliest of these (St. Matthias, Richmond) dating from 1858 is described by Nairn as 'the grandest church in Richmond'.[13] The north-west tower has a tall spire; internally the clerestory has lancet windows and there is strong vertical emphasis. A year later in 1859, Sir George went one better with his St Batholomew's at Ranmore Common, built for a wealthy patron, the son of Thomas Cubitt, the builder. It is faced entirely with cobbles (round flints) and the octagonal tower and spire combine to produce a *tour de force* of Victorian architecture in the county and a striking foil to the spire of Woodyer's St Martin's, Dorking in the valley below. Inside, everything betokens a rich man's church and is of the most lavish kind – multiple marble shafts to the piers under the crossing and furnishings to go with the church, especially the font. The third of the Scott major churches and his best is St Mary's, Shackleford built in 1865. Early English in style and built of Bargate stone, the central tower and spire, the large apse and the excellence of proportion give much distinction, and the central steeple acts as a fine focal point to the overall design; internally there is less to admire.

The remaining new place of worship – built in 1864 probably by an assistant – is Christ Church, Ottershaw, which thrusts its polychrome brick and stone apse towards the road from an elevated site. The tower and broach-spire date from 1885. Near Godalming at Busbridge is the work of another member of the Scott family (G.G. Junior most likely) – a central shingled-tower church of 1865-7.

Although not much can be said in favour of the exterior restoration of St Mary's, Reigate by Woodyer in 1845 and George Gilbert Scott, junior, in 1877-81, Scott carried out a notable restoration of the nave arcades inside. Dating from *c*.1200 and much influenced by the choir of Canterbury Cathedral which was rebuilt 1175-80, he rebuilt the arcades stone by stone and has left us a noble nave of five bays supported by four columns with carved capitals, terminating at each end in a respond. No two of the columns are exactly alike in form and ornamentation, while the columns on either side are out of alignment with those opposite. The width of the nave also varies from 18 feet at the west end to 20 feet at the east. The capitals show every type of foliage with a regular movement around the stone looking as if (to quote from Ian Nairn) 'growing radially out of the stone'.[14] Similar foliage is to be seen on the north-east capital of the nave arcade at Leatherhead and clearly of the same date and school.

Of other architects, Bodley built in 1867 a sensitive brick chapel of ease with shingled belfry at Valley End, Chobham. The brick is exposed

98. *Christ Church, Ottershaw.*

inside and there are large iron tie-rods. William Burges designed two churches in the eastern part of the county – a well-proportioned but otherwise undistinguished church at Outwood with a later stuccoed saddle-back tower (1876) and brick interior, and a far from ordinary place of worship – St Michael's, Lowfield Heath – beside Gatwick Airport. Dating from 1867, St Michael's is a charming building without aisles but with lean-to porch and elaborately carved rose window above. There is a south-west tower with pyramidal spire and the furnishings, notably the stained glass in the east window, are all in keeping. Edward Buckton Lamb erected two eccentric churches, one at Addiscombe near Croydon and the other at Englefield Green. St Mary Magdalene, Addiscombe (1868-70) is entered through a tower in the north-east corner (added in 1928-30) and the visitor is greeted with a design which concentrates upon a massive roof leading up to a central lantern. Less unorthodox is St Simon and St Jude's, Englefield Green; although of cruciform plan, the placing of a tower on the south transept and the longer arm of the nave being away from the road confuses the viewer; inside, alternate bands of ornamented brick, Bath limestone and Kentish rag produces a polychrome effect which evoked at the time a comment of the church being 'notoriously harlequinized'.[15] The tower of St Mary, Oatlands was not consecrated because the Vicar's Warden at the time feared that the removal of his hat when passing under the tower on his way from his nearby house to the station would expose him to the risk of catching frequent colds and, in deference to his wishes, the tower was only dedicated. Three small Ewan Christian (a relation of Fletcher Christian of the *Bounty*) buildings complete the picture for the 1851-70 period – St John, Churt of 1868 in local style and pleasantly sited, St Paul, Tongham of 1865, apsed with a high-pitched roof and unusual detached brick tower and All Saints, Tilford of 1867, a not unworthy church of Bargate stone. Churt and Tongham are, in effect, only chapels.

99.   St. Simon & St Jude's, Englefield Green, with the Fitzroy-Somerset Mausolea.

100.   St. Paul, Tongham, with detached bell tower.

There was the usual crop of new aisles added to older churches, going far to destroy their village character. But where were the larger congregations to be accommodated ? Churches enlarged in this way include Ash (1865 north aisle, now the nave), Beddington (outer north aisle 1850), Blechingley (north aisle 1856), Chobham (north aisle 1866), Ham (south aisle 1860) and Merton (south aisle 1856, north aisle 1866). Transepts were added or re-built at Ashtead (north 1862) and Chipstead (south rebuilt 1855). Seale was almost completely remodelled by J. Croft in 1861-73 making effective use externally of a contrast of clunch for the main fabric and green Bargate stone for the tower. At Beddington, further changes were made in 1869 when J. Clarke added the west vestries and probably provided at the same time the nave and chancel roofs together with the chancel arch; the chancel roof is enlivened with very large angels. All Saints, Kingston upon Thames was restored and given a Victorian look in 1862-6 and 1883, the latter by Pearson. Chessington's spire was restored in 1854 (Hesketh) and south aisle by Jackson in 1870, preserving its village character in a new housing estate. The period closes with the rebuilding of St John the Baptist, Croydon by Sir George Gilbert Scott in 1870 after a fire in 1867. This is the largest parish church in the county.

Late Victorian

Although commuters continued to flow into Surrey, the pace of church building slackened after 1870 but, if the churches were fewer in number, the quality was higher and reached a peak with two by John Loughborough Pearson in the Croydon area which may claim to be the finest of the Victorian era in the county. Further tracts of Surrey were made accessible by the opening of new rail routes – to Lingfield *via* Oxted in 1884 and an alternative route to Guildford via Cobham and East Horsley in the following year. Of towns that had been born out of the building of railways in Surrey, Redhill, as we have seen, had overtaken Reigate in population by 1861 whilst Surbiton (originally called New Kingston although three miles distant from Kingston's centre) grew to a town of 15,000 people by 1901. Woking's development, however, was stunted in that the London Necropolis Company purchased in 1852 about one quarter of the parish as the first and largest burial ground under an Act which provided for the interment of London citizens outside the capital for reasons of health. The Company was, therefore, at first more concerned with laying out the dead for burial by providing its splendidly landscaped necropolis at Brookwood than housing the living; it was only later that attention was paid to the spiritual needs of the latter and the first church in the centre of Woking (Christ Church) dates from 1889. Of other towns, Croydon more than trebled and Richmond doubled their populations between 1841 and 1861.

In 1888, the county of Surrey – one of the smallest in England – was mutilated by the formation of the county of London: 25,798 acres of the north east of Surrey were transferred to the metropolis. This not only deprived the county of its outlet to the sea, but also of many important centres intimately connected with its history, such as Rotherhithe, Southwark, Lambeth, Battersea and Putney. The loss of population was made up by the growth of towns still in the county, such as Redhill, Surbiton and Woking. Surrey suffered another loss of territory in 1965, when Richmond, Barnes, Kingston, Wimbledon, Merton, Morden, Mitcham, Sutton, Carshalton, Beddington and Croydon were incorporated into Greater London. But people who live in these towns have, for the most part, refused to relinquish their ties with Surrey and the main churches have been covered in this book. Those transferred in 1888 have not been included, but even these have not severed their links completely. The Surrey County Cricket Club has its headquarters at Kennington and commentators at the Boat Race still refer to the Surrey and Middlesex sides of the River Thames.

The two churches in the Croydon area mentioned earlier, St Michael's and St John the Evangelist, were built by Pearson in the 1880s when he was at the height of his powers. Neither church, however, has the crowning feature of a dominant steeple as Pearson provided for his masterpiece in north-west London, St Augustine's Kilburn. He was also involved with rebuilding the nave and chancel of St John, Redhill, covering the nave with transverse stone bows and a king-post roof. He also erected a church at Hersham (1887) of buff stone, which is interesting to compare with that built by him in Weybridge forty years earlier (1848). Both have steeples but neither is outstanding although Hersham is contemporary with Upper Norwood.

Turning to other architects, G. E. Street built St Mary's, Long Ditton in 1878-80 and St. Mary's, Holmbury St Mary in 1879, his last church which was not far from his home at Holmdale. Long Ditton is of buff stone with double bell-cote between nave and chancel. Holmbury St Mary was built by the architect at his own expense (like Woodyer at Grafham). It is a competent piece of work but it lacks warmth. Almost next door to Long Ditton, Sir Arthur Blomfield built a noteworthy church (St. Andrew) in 1871 at Surbiton of yellow and red brick. The west front has an apsed baptistry and the interior is distinctive for its very wide nave with narrow aisles. Blomfield also designed Christ Church, Epsom Common in 1876 of flint and stone with a north-west tower. At All Saints, Carshalton, most of what one sees from the pond is the work of Blomfield and his nephew (1893-1914). Dormansland (1883) was another building by him. Blomfield also provided the apse and transepts at St Peter & St Paul, Weston Street, Albury (1868). Sir Thomas G. Jackson, who at one time worked in Gilbert Scott's office, made various additions as well as carrying out discriminating restorations. The additions included the aisles at Ripley and Chessington (1869 and 1870), the aisle and bell-tower at East Clandon (1900) and the north aisle chapel at St John's, Caterham Valley (1881). His restoration work included the sensitive handling of the unspoilt village church of St Nicholas, Pyrford in 1869 and the south aisle at St Mary's, Chessington in 1870. Amongst other work, he was responsible for the new nave and chancel at St John's, (Old) Malden (1875), the rebuilding of the north tower with spire at St Peter and St Paul at West Clandon (1913) and the design of the glass, made by Powell's, in the seven-light east lancet window at All Saints, Ockham. St John's at Wimbledon (1875), however, was built entirely by Jackson: it is of red brick with no tower but with a curious bellcote between nave and chancel supported on a buttress.

With the disappearance of St Michael's, Weybridge (1874 demolished 1975), William Butterfield's sole remaining new ecclesiastical contribution to Surrey was the Guards' Chapel at Caterham. Late for him (1881), it is an interesting and less than usually aggressive example of his polychrome work – stock brick with patterns of black brick and chequered flint in the gable and tops of the aisles. The striking east end has large buttresses flanking the window. Butterfield restored Great Bookham in 1858 and 1885, and Stoke D'Abernon in 1853, his work at Stoke being superseded by later reconstruction. Other churches built in the last quarter of the century included: Bagshot, St Anne (1884) by Alec Cheer; East Molesey, St Mary (1864-70) by Talbot Bury, and St Paul (1854 – tower 1888) by Salter and Laforest; Guildford, St Nicolas (1870-5) by Ewan Christian to designs of S.S. Teulon, and St Saviour (1895) by H.S. Legg & Sons; Hook, near Chessington, St Paul (1881-3) by Carpenter and Ingelow; North Holmwood, St John (1875) by Rhode Hawkins; S. Croydon, St Augustine (1881-4) by J. Oldrid Scott; South Norwood, Holy Innocents (1894-5) by G.F. Bodley; South Wimbledon, All Saints (1891-3) by Micklethwaite and Somers; and Thornton Heath, St Alban (nave 1869, chancel 1894), Sir Ninian Comper's first church. W.F. Unsworth worked in the Woking area, producing Christ Church, Woking in 1887-93 and the more expensive but less successful All Saints, Woodham in 1893; he also reconstructed the chancel at Horsell and extended the nave and south aisle by one bay to cater for a marked increase in population towards the end of the century. A charming pair of small churches is now linked under one benefice: St Thomas's, Chilworth, originally built as the Gorhambury Institute in 1896, of red brick in English bond with battered buttresses at the corners and an appealing cupola, and St Martin's, Blackheath. St Martin's dates from 1893, and is Italianate outside with deep eaves and low walls, with inside an attractive barrel-vaulted chapel. Alterations consisted mainly of the addition of a north arcade at St Mary's, Addington in 1876 and north aisles at Bisley (1873) and Okewood (1879). In both cases the village character of the churches was destroyed although admittedly the north wall of Okewood was in a parlous state. East Sheen also received a north aisle in 1887. At Chobham, the additions consisted of a chancel and south transept. A curiosity is the riotously decorated and over-laden Watts Chapel of 1896 at Compton with Art Nouveau decoration inside and Celtic motifs outside; externally the Chapel is in the shape of a Greek cross (*Colour Plate XL*).

101. The font and font-cover at St. Nicolas, Guildford.

Victorian Furnishings

Victorian furnishings tend to be over-ornate, and the drawing of faces and figures in stained glass often weak and over-sentimental; this, coupled with the dense colours used and the amount of painting of detailed pictorial designs on thin, flat glass, casts a gloom over interiors; the effect neither revives the medieval atmosphere nor provides a suitable alternative; the uneven texture and the glowing colours which are such a delightful feature of medieval glass are not to be found. On the other hand, the furnishings cannot be dismissed out of hand and some which are enumerated below are works of good quality and an asset to the structure. Some of the Victorian glassmakers such as Hardman, Clayton & Bell, James Powell and William Morris working to designs by artists such as Willement,

Hedgeland, O'Connor, Wailes, Gibbs, William Morris, Burne-Jones, Kempe and Whall produced acceptable windows. One also must not overlook the fact that furnishings from an earlier church, particularly brasses and other monuments, are often given a place in the later building and some of these are of high quality. Reference has already been made to the standing monument to Sir William Lewen (d. 1721) in St Mary's, Ewell (1848). There are many others.

Fonts: The most notable Victorian fonts are at:-

Capel.	1865. Octagonal bowl with gilt incised ornament placed on a circular stem, the whole in polished brown marble.
Guildford, St Nicolas.	Soaring font canopy of gilded and painted wood completely enveloping the font.
Haslemere, St Bartholomew.	1870. Circular bowl on four columns and central pillar, the whole in polished black and red marble. Fawn-coloured base.
Hersham.	Of Caen stone, richly carved and supported on columns of red and green Devonshire marble.
Long Ditton.	Dedicated in 1891. Restrained and dignified oval-shaped, in green fluted design.
Okewood.	Fine restrained furnishing in black marble (*Colour Plate XXXIII*).
Ranmore Common.	Perhaps the most notable, this example, designed in thirteenth-century style, is of maroon and black marble. It is described by Pevsner as 'a dark, grand, moving piece'. [16]

Pulpits: Ranmore Common has a pulpit of variegated alabaster on fluted white marble columns (*Colour Plate XXXIV*). At Croydon, St Michael there is a Bodley pulpit with canopy, while at St Martin's, Dorking, there is one believed to have been brought from the Netherlands *c.*1837 and incorporating a panel depicting St Martin and the beggar (probably seventeenth century). The pulpit at Betchworth (*Colour Plate XXXII*) is described by Ian Nairn[17] as 'lush 1885 with five kinds of marble and inlaid mosaic panels of Faith, Hope and Love'.

Reredoses: Most Victorian reredoses are too ornate to afford much pleasure and, as with the glass, the faces are often too sentimentally drawn.

Stained glass: Among Victorian glass of note are the east windows of Titsey by Clayton & Bell (*Colour Plate XXXVI*). This firm's work is also to be seen at Hale (vivid medallions in the west window), Holmbury St Mary (east and west windows and in the north chapel from Street's designs), Limpsfield, Ranmore Common, Surbiton (Christ Church), and Worplesdon. Burne-Jones glass appears in the east and west windows of Busbridge (the west window being especially notable), one window of the north aisle at St Bartholomew's, Haslemere, two windows of the north aisle at Milford and the east window at Nutfield. They were all made by Morris & Co. Reference has already been made to the Hardman & Powell glass at Hascombe. Examples of Powell glass are to be seen at Chaldon, St Martin's, Dorking and North Holmwood. At St Mary's, Guildford, the west window of the north aisle is German work of *c.*1850 with Cambridge blue backgrounds to the heads.

Screens: Reference has been made above to the wooden screen which Woodyer inserted at Grafham against the Bishop of Winchester's wishes. There is an iron screen and rood at Busbridge by J. Starkie Gardner to the designs of Edwin Lutyens, one of the most notable of late nineteenth-century fittings.

Organs: With their love of large choirs it was natural that the Victorians favoured large organs which could only be fitted in with difficulty, masking windows and monuments. These are often an encumbrance and do not add to the visual pleasure of interiors. William Morris's organ (1869) at Beddington, however, is a most attractive instrument. The player's space is screened like a minstrel's gallery whilst the dado is painted with floral decoration and a tier of small figures (*Colour Plate XXX*).

Seating: Apart from poor stained glass, another depressing feature which the Victorians introduced was row upon row of pitch-pine pews, usually of commonplace design and often covered with yellow varnish, to accommodate the large surpliced choirs of men and boys and the congregation. Admittedly, box-pews, apart from their discomfort, were not suitable in a Gothic church, but the opportunity to provide a worthy substitute was not taken. The modern practice of replacing pews with chairs, provided the latter are well designed, is greatly to be encouraged. Not only are they visually more attractive but they provide flexibility for drama and other presentations as well as normal liturgical needs. It should be added that occasionally one comes across work of real craftsmen as at St Mary at Hill and St Michael's, Cornhill in the City of London although the former are box and not open pews.

102.   The rood & screen at Busbridge.

Victorian Churchyards

The visual harm inflicted on the interiors of our churches by the Victorians is unfortunately matched, if not exceeded, by what they did to the settings of the churches – namely the churchyards, where they imposed considerable visual harm. The background to this is well set out by Clifton-Taylor.[18] He points out that before the Reformation, there were few personal monuments. A simple churchyard cross served to commemorate all, irrespective of rank. There were a few table monuments and that was all. Later, in the Georgian period, it became fashionable to commemorate the departed with headstones and sometimes larger monuments. Made of local stone, skilfully carved and with beautifully-incised lettering, these – if in good condition – are an adornment to churchyards, nowhere seen to better advantage than at Painswick in Gloucestershire where a group of masons and carvers of exceptional skill were available. Churchyards with well kept and preferably not too many Georgian monuments can provide a beautiful setting to the parish church.

But, alas, the Victorians, in their pious desire to provide something they considered worthy, started soon after the middle of the century to import Italian marbles and to use granite (including pink stone), entirely alien to the setting and then to adorn them with simpering angels, open books, urns, broken columns, surrounding them with kerbs into which green chips were sometimes later spread. Even worse, the granite was often polished and black marble employed; jet-black stove-enamelled headstones were also erected. Disastrous as the effect was, succeeding generations made matters worse by importing mass-produced memorials so that they are as much to blame as the Victorians. Instead of the churchyard being a place in which to relax and wander pleasurably it has far too often become an area of ugliness and some of the monuments – admittedly often in the more remote parts of churchyards but by no means always – are in excessively poor taste. An added disfigurement is the employment of leaded lettering and inscriptions of unbelievable banality such as 'Cheerio, see you soon'. The matter is discussed at length by Alec Clifton-Taylor, [18] and some suggestions made but, if we are to provide a beautiful setting for our priceless heritage of parish churches, the most stringent rules are needed to prevent further desecration and a very tough attitude adopted with due regard to the feelings of relations, to correct what has been done. Dioceses have now published strict churchyard regulations which should arrest further deterioration. Fortunately, Surrey has many well kept churchyards; admirable examples are to be found at Effingham, Ewhurst, Frensham, Hascombe, Haslemere, Old Woking, Shalford and Wonersh; whilst, at Chobham, the number of monuments is reduced to just a handful enabling the public to enjoy a well kept grassy area coming right down to the main street.

Wood is sometimes used for memorials. The old grave-board (or bed-board as it is often called) is a long narrow board, supported on short posts at the head and foor of the grave. A good example can be seen at Abinger (*see fig. 107*).

Victorian Impact

How is one to assess the Victorian impact on Surrey's churches? The general tendency, judging from C.T. Cracklow's drawings, was for churches to slide into gentle if sometimes attractive decay and, if nothing had been done, many would probably have become ruinous. In addition to saving them from this, the Victorian architects had to cope with a tide of new residents who were not content to worship in homely village churches with box pews. When Cracklow assembled his drawings in the 1820s, he included 155 places of worship and these embraced those in London which were part of the county prior to 1888; by 1964, just before the 1965 changes in the county boundaries, the number of parishes in Surrey had increased to 263 and this excluded those churches now in Greater London. The population had risen from 157,000 in 1831 to 1,600,000 by 1964. Where were all these newcomers to worship and in what type of church? The type was unduly influenced by the ritual prescribed by the Oxford Movement, sponsored by the Camden Society, which insisted that the only proper place for divine service was a Gothic building, preferably in the Middle Pointed or Decorated style, ignoring the fact that one could not bring back to a totally different age the medieval spirit which inspired the form of the great Gothic churches. Box-pews must be ripped out, plaster and whitewash must be scraped away, thus destroying many wall-paintings still remaining under their Reformation coat of limewash and the church must be adorned with stained glass and colour.

The Victorians were, in effect, chasing a shadow without the substance. They have in consequence been severely criticised for their insensitive handling of medieval churches, licking them clean of texture and using machine-made bricks and tiles, nowhere more evident than in many horrid roofs with Victorian cresting: often they thought they could improve upon what they found by restoring an early form at the cost of removing a later one. As Ruskin put it – 'what copying can there be of surfaces that have been worn half an inch down?'. [19] To him, restoration 'meant the total destruction which a building can suffer'. Ian Nairn is not sparing in his punches and has used some pretty explosive adjectives which, for the sake of the churches concerned, I will not repeat here, but Nairn also gives praise where praise is due and there is no doubt that places of worship like St Michael's, Croydon; St John the Evangelist, Upper Norwood; St Bartholomew's, Ranmore Common; St Martin's, Dorking; St Mary's, Buckland and St Peter's, Hascombe are a welcome contribution to the ecclesiology of the county. And this omits some of Sir George Gilbert Scott's best work in Surrey (e.g. St Matthias, Richmond and St Mary, Shackleford) and the restoration of the arcade at St Mary's, Reigate by George Gilbert Scott, junior, and there are probably many others.

The addition of aisles and transepts was bound to result in village churches losing their character. But where a completely new building was needed much good work was done. There is no doubt that many of the architects were sincere, honest men anxious to do their best and some like Sir Thomas Jackson treated churches gently and with full regard to their character (as at St Nicholas, Pyrford). Others like Pearson, Woodyer and Scott were capable of excellent work, but Surrey is perhaps unfortunate in having so little of Bodley, or G.E. Street at his best.

The Twentieth Century

The first decade of the twentieth century produced one rarity – an appealing village church by Sir Edwin Lutyens, one of his few incursions into the realms of ecclesiastical architecture, St Martin's, Pixham, near Dorking, dating from 1903 (*Colour Plate XXXIX*). A tunnel-vaulted nave is allied to a domed sanctuary, the two parts being thus available by screening off, for different types of function. W. D. Caröe, who worked on churches in the

103.   West Byfleet, St John Baptist.

104.   Charterhouse School Chapel.

north-west of the county, used Lutyens motifs: the chimney of the vestry of the half-timbered St Paul's, Church Hill, Camberley (1902) and the west front of St Mary of Bethany, Woking (1907). Later, he built St John Baptist, West Byfleet (1910-12) which, although uneventful, has an interesting pyramidal, shingled, crossing spire and, inside, an attractive timber wagon roof over the nave. Anticipating events, Caröe & Passmore erected in 1912 an uninspired church at Oxshott (St. Andrew). Of other work, the following may be mentioned: Most of St Mary's, Barnes was rebuilt in 1904-06 by Charles Innes but the church went up in flames in 1978. St Saviour's, Brookwood, trim in shape, was erected in 1909, and St Mary's, Burgh Heath, with flint chequerwork exterior, was also built in the same year. All Saints, Grayswood (1900-02) by Axel Haig preserves the Surrey tradition in its style and bell-turret, and is nicely situated on the side of the green, but does not stand up well to closer inspection. Haslemere, St Christopher's between Haslemere and Shottermill was designed by Charles Spooner in 1902. The exterior with its low south tower and long nave roof without clerestory is not without interest. The use of Bargate stone which is galletted (use of stone chips in the mortar) also helps. Hindhead (1907-10) by J.D. Coleridge (nave completed 1930-1) is a large church but of no particular note. Norbury, built in 1908 by W.S. Weatherley, is a pleasing single-celled, yellow-and-red-brick place of worship with an attractive interior. All Saints, Petersham (1907-08), by John Kelly, is a large church of brick and red terracotta with a tall campanile on the side. Inside, use is made of a number of different marbles. Other activities in the Thames Valley were the addition of already mentioned chancels at Ham (Bodley & Garner – 1901) and at St John the Divine, Richmond (A. Grove – 1905), the former in red brick.

The 1914-18 War brought church building to a stop except for St John Baptist at Belmont, constructed in 1915, but, before the storm broke, new places of worship (in addition to the Caröe examples already mentioned at West Byfleet and Oxshott) were consecrated at St Thomas, Bourne in 1911 by H. Sidebotham, where the Lady Chapel is part of the 1862 church and the plain, whitewashed interior has a wagon roof with king posts, and St Barnabas, Mitcham in 1914, by H.P. Burke-Downing. Out of the ordinary run, St Barnabas is a hall church with very large arcades and is in the Bodley vein.

Ecclesiastical buildings did not pick up again until 1922-27 and then, very appropriately, with a war-memorial chapel at Charterhouse School. As the public schools probably suffered proportionately more in their mortality rate than any other section of the population, it was particularly fitting that a memorial chapel should be built in one of these schools. Designed by Sir Giles Gilbert Scott the chapel has an impressive interior with good proportions and a notable apse; tall lancets alternate with stone piers. The 1930s produced four churches, one on the very eve of the 1939-45 War at Weston Green, near Esher by Sir Edward Maufe, designer of Guildford Cathedral and also of the Coopers Hill R.A.F. Memorial above Runnymede. The church at Weston Green has a campanile in the north-east corner and tall windows. The whitewashed exterior encloses a noteworthy interior in which the arches die into the piers without capitals. The other three churches are Carshalton, the Good Shepherd, 1930 by Martin Travers and T.F.W. Grant, with a copper clerestory and an interior in Baroque style: Selsdon, a red, brick structure of 1935-36 by Newberry & Fowler, who have succeeded in producing an interesting church with narrow aisles having straight-headed, seven-light windows and an unassuming north-east tower; and Woldingham, built by Sir Herbert Baker in 1933 for Lord Craigmyle of the P. & O. Shipping Line. The church looks as though it had strayed from Norfolk with its flushwork words 'Praise Him/and Magnify Him/Forever' on the tower. There is more flushwork in the apse with words 'Glory to God in the Highest . . . ' set in agates. Although the style is not in the Surrey tradition of the past, perhaps the opulence is of the present.

Although after the 1939-45 War church attendances were falling, the shift of population further from London at the expense of the inner suburbs led to more churches being needed in the

105. West tower of St. Paul's, Woldingham.

outer commuter areas, but usually the sums available were modest and a typical example is the Church of the Good Shepherd at Pyrford, built between 1961 and 1964 at a cost of £ 54,000. The population of the village had risen from about a thousand before the war to over 5,000 by the time the church was built and the old Norman village church of St Nicholas, holding only about 110 people, was quite inadequate and, moreover, too far away from the residential centre. Other churches of this type (e.g. Burpham, and Wood Street), designed by David Nye were built in the 1960s in laminated wood. They are bright, cheerful, and well-suited to modern needs.

Guildford Cathedral

It is appropriate here to conclude by introducing Surrey's most famous twentieth-century building. The Diocese of Guildford, together with that of Portsmouth, was carved out of Winchester in 1927. For a time, Holy Trinity, Guildford was used as the mother church but was soon found to be too small. In 1932, 183 architects took part in an open competition for the design of a new cathedral and, in the following year, the summit of Stag Hill was provided as a free gift by the Onslow family. Sir Edward Maufe obtained the contract and work started before the 1939-45 War but came to a stop with the eastern parts still unfinished and the nave hardly begun. It was not until 1952 that progress could be made but, apart from minor features, the cathedral was ready for consecration in 1961. Although externally this episcopal building may appear ponderous in design, the architect has respected the limitations of the material (brick made from local clay) by not indulging in ornamentation and by good massing. The mighty 156-ft high tower, capped by a 15-ft

106.   *Guildford Cathedral nave.*

copper-gilded Angel weighing nearly a ton, gives a feeling of strength and dominates the scene from its spendid hill-top site. Inside, the brick is rendered with plaster, and limestone is used for the dressings, creating an air of light and space with narrow aisles, which provide interesting vistas. The brass stag set into the stone floor of the open crossing marks the highest point of Stag Hill and the beautiful symbolic carpet designed by Sir Edward Maufe, the architect, makes a fine setting for this focal point of the church. Other furnishings include a charmingly modelled Madonna and Child in Lignum Vitae in the Lady Chapel and a 45-ft high Dorsal curtain of a pleasing golden colour behind the main altar. Although conservative in style, the interior of this Mother Church of the Diocese of Guildford must be considered uplifting and the clarity of the design very satisfying.

Envoi

Surrey is no longer a poor county and the affluence that has come to this part of England, and the comparatively large proportion of churchgoers, is now operating to the benefit of the county's ecclesiastical heritage. There is now probably more loving care bestowed on Surrey churches than at any time since the Middle Ages, care that is a great deal more sensitive to the medieval mason and craftsman than that shown by our Victorian forebears. The fabrics may be modest, the Victorian restoration may be heavy-handed but one cannot go far without finding something of interest or beauty and sometimes something outstanding. Perhaps as good an example as any of long history, medieval changes and Victorian insensitivity is to be found at St Mary's church at Stoke D'Abernon where, with the aid of the scholarly account by C.A. Ralegh Radford,[20] one can trace its history right back to the eighth or even seventh century and see how a slow-growth medieval place of worship – in this case closely linked and almost embraced by the manor – developed. Despite a particularly thorough-going Victorian restoration, it can offer one of the oldest brasses in the country, some of the best stained glass in the county (English, French, German and Dutch, dating from the end of the fifteenth and the beginning of the sixteenth century, and Flemish from *c*.1610), an elaborate Jacobean pulpit, the Vincent effigies, a notable thirteenth-century oak chest and a noble vaulted chancel. This surely is a rich heritage.

A return to simpler values and greater respect for the character of our ecclesiastical architecture has halted much of the harm and the system of Faculty Jurisdiction enables dioceses through their Advisory Committees to keep a close watch on changes. No doubt the Victorians believed that what they were doing was to the glory of God but liturgical needs are not static and we have to ensure that we do not yield to what may be temporary new forms of worship, forgetting the verdict which posterity may give of what we do. We are responsible for preserving our great heritage whilst keeping the Church alive and responsive to its congregations' needs.

THE INDIVIDUAL CHURCHES

ABINGER, St James

This is a church going back a long way, an earlier church being mentioned in Domesday, with basically a Norman nave, early thirteenth-century chancel and fifteenth-century belfry but the victim of a double disaster this century. In 1944, a flying bomb reduced the church, except for the north chapel, to a heap of rubble and, after rebuilding, the bellcote was struck by lightning during a thunderstorm in 1964, causing a fire which led to considerable damage. Restorations were sensitively carried out by Frederick Etchells preserving the original design but lengthening the church by 10 feet. The building is situated on high ground and the parish is the longest in the county.

The exterior shows a pleasing building in Surrey vernacular style, constructed of yellow Wealden sandstone, with a shingled bell-turret. Despite rebuilding in its original style (Norman nave, Early English chancel and north chapel), the interior has a clinical and rather plain appearance with the windows of the aisleless nave high up on the walls. The stained glass of the east window, however, affords a striking contrast and the north chapel is satisfying.

107.   Abinger Church from the south.

Furnishings

The stained glass of the east window is by Lawrence Lee and was made in 1967 (*Colour Plate XLII*). Nairn gives it warm praise – 'Much the best modern glass in the county, portraying the Living Cross in vivid abstract colouring'.[21] There are three fifteenth-century alabaster reliefs in the south porch, near the altar and beside the font. The one in the porch is of the Crucifixion and the relief by the font depicts the beheading of John the Baptist. The carved chest in the north chapel dates from *c*.1525 and was originally in a church in Normandy.

ADDINGTON, St Mary the Blessed Virgin

An ancient foundation, St Mary's has a Norman chancel of *c*.1080 with three widely stepped and recessed windows of *c*.1140 at the east end plus a smaller one in the apex (*Colour Plate VII*). The nave consists of a south arcade, of three bays with two piers (one round and one octagonal), dating from *c*.1210, a narrow aisle and a north arcade of 1876. The church, after falling into disrepair, was largely rebuilt in 1773 and the Norman north tower refaced in brick shortly after. In 1843, the walls and tower were refaced in knapped flint and the tower capped with a concave pyramid roof. In 1876, the tower was heightened and the pyramid roof replaced with the present roof to produce the more dignified tower and, in 1897, the chancel was renovated and painted during the memorial redecoration to Archbishop Benson.

Alderman Barlow Trecothic, former Lord Mayor of London, bought the local manor and estate in 1768 and it was he who initiated the church restoration in 1773 and built in the same year Addington Palace. In 1808, the Palace was acquired by the Trustees of the Archbishop of Canterbury as a country residence in the place of Croydon Palace and was used for this purpose until 1896. It is now the Royal School of Church Music. One of the Archbishops, William Howley, who crowned Queen Victoria, initiated the refacing work in St Mary's in 1843 before the north aisle was added. During the Middle Ages, St Mary's was served from St Mary Overie, Southwark (now the Cathedral). The refacing of the exterior has stripped St Mary's of its medieval aspect but the tower lends an air of consequence to this historic church, so closely linked in the nineteenth century with the Primacy of the Church of England.

The chancel interior is one of the most remarkable in Surrey for, apart from the Norman character and style of it, there are a number of most interesting memorials. Norman chancels are rare in the county because, with the growth of monastic influence in the thirteenth century, larger areas were required for the daily offices and they were consequently rebuilt. In addition to the windows already referred to earlier, there are two other Norman ones on the north and south sides (the south blocked) and a low side-window, which retains its old iron bars added in c.1350; its head is a trefoiled ogee arch in the Decorated style and is in the same embrasure as the small blocked Norman window above. The east-end, twelfth-century triplet of windows is the only example remaining in Surrey.

Furnishings

The 1897 paintings on the chancel walls include St Damian and St Cosmas on the north and south sides whilst, on the east wall, there is St Katherine with her wheel on the right and St Mary, the patron saint of the church, on the left; the four statues in the recesses at the base of the windows are of Archbishops Cranmer, Theodore, Benson and Laud. The contemporary statue of St Mary on a pedestal at the east end of the south aisle was brought back from Oberammergau. The bishop's chair in the centre of the chancel dates from 1897. Stained glass of 1891 and 1898 in the south aisle and in the apex of the east end of the chancel is by C.E. Kempe. The west window commemorates Crawford Tait, son of Archbishop Campbell Tait, probably the greatest of the Addington Archbishops; the latter is commemorated by a window at the west end of the north aisle showing him between St Augustine and Archbishop Stephen Langton, who led the barons against King John. There is also a window in the south wall of the chancel to Catherine Tait, wife of the Archbishop.

Most of the notable memorials and brasses are to members of the Leigh and Trecothic families who, apart from a break of some thirty years in the eighteenth century and two years after the Trecothic era, lived in the Manor from 1447 to 1536 as tenants and as owners until 1808, when the trustees of the Archbishops acquired it. The Leighs are on the north side of the chancel and the Trecothics on the south. There is also on the Leigh side beneath a memorial to Elizabeth Lovell and her daughter Lady Sarah Leigh, the wife of Sir Francis Leigh (both d.1691), an altar tomb which once housed the Leigh brass (see below); this was removed to make way for a recumbent effigy of Archbishop Howley but the effigy has been

*108.   The Addington 'Pickle Jar'
– Barlow Trecothick's Monument.*

transferred to Canterbury. This altar tomb was converted from the former Easter Sepulchre. The most impressive monument is that on the north-west side of the chancel to Sir Oliph Leigh (1560-1612) and his wife (*Colour Plate XVIII*), of alabaster and black Sussex marble, containing life-size stiffly reclining effigies of them. Above are kneeling figures of their parents (Nicholas and his wife) and grandparents (John and his wife), flanked and separated by obelisks. The Trecothic memorials include a monument to Grizzel Trecothick (d.1761) first wife of Barlow Trecothick (d.1775), the first members of the family to spell their name that way, and whose monument is in the form of a large marble urn irreverently referred to as the 'Addington Pickle Jar'. Erected by his second wife, it was moved from the east wall.

The brasses include the one to John Leigh (d.1509), his wife and five children, now on the floor in the north-west corner of the chancel, but previously part of the altar tomb which became the monument to Archbishop Howley, and, on the other side, one to Thomas Hattecliff (d.1540) wearing full plate armour and with his coat of arms above. An attractive and much more recent brass commemorates Archbishop Longley (d.1868) showing Christ giving His commission to St Peter.

In the churchyard there is a jumble of assorted headstones, including in the south-west corner a cross some 20 feet high which is a memorial to five of the archbishops who were buried here, but the sixth archbishop associated with Addington – Archbishop Benson (d.1896) – was buried in Canterbury Cathedral.

ADDISCOMBE, St Mary Magdalene

E. Buckton Lamb, one of the most eccentric of mid-Victorian architects, has erected in this eastern area of Croydon a building, which Pevsner describes as 'one of the wildest of all Gothic Revival churches' – more roof than wall. Built between 1868 and 1870, the church of St Mary Magdalene was not consecrated until 1878 and the north-east tower not completed until 1930. Entrance is through the tower placed next to the apse and leads into a centrally-planned 'nightmarish' (Pevsner)[22] interior with the most extravagant roof resting on marble columns which stand on brackets. Numerous beams spread over the aisles create an enormous roof which leads up to a small timber lantern over the centre of the crossing. The effect is to give an impression of great space but the walls appear purely subsidiary, not integrating with the main structure. This is a church worth visiting for its eccentricity and as evidence that Victorian architects were not slavish imitators of the medieval.

ADDLESTONE, St Paul

The church of St Paul, Addlestone, with a west tower, was built in 1836-38 by James Savage (better known for his St Luke's, Chelsea) as a daughter church to St Peter's, Chertsey. The material is stock brick (Yellow Suffolks) with stone dressings and slate roof and the style Early English with lancet windows. The chancel was added in 1855 and extended in 1903/04. St Paul's became a separate parish in 1857 consequent upon the growth of population following the arrival of the railway in 1848. There were major reconstructions in 1883 and 1903/04. The south-east porch was removed in 1979.

A plain Jane but set in a spacious churchyard and harmonious in style, this church has an hexagonal east end. Whilst being of minor architectural merit, St Paul's does not deserve the harsh strictures of Ian Nairn.[23] The interior is broad in proportion to length and, whilst St George's Chapel to the north and the Lady Chapel enhance its interest, the rood and screen are unduly obtrusive and the white nave piers make the chancel feel remote. There are no arcades and the roof is poor. The rood screen was erected as a memorial to those killed in the 1914-18 War. St George's Chapel was fitted out and dedicated in 1947 in space formerly occupied by the organ; the grill in the upper part of the archway leading into the Chapel commemorates those who fell in the 1939-45 War.

Furnishings
The font is of 1874, on a plinth all in marble, with an oak cover with brass fittings. The pulpit is panelled in oak and supported on five green marble columns. It has an oak rail with wrought-iron supports. The Royal arms of Queen Victoria are in stone on the west gallery. There is much stained glass of varying quality. The best of it is found in the two westernmost windows on the north side, with striking, brightly coloured representations of St George and St Swithin, St Martin and St Lawrence (holding his gridiron).

There is a tablet on the north wall to Major-General Sir George Wood (d.1824) and his brother Vice-Admiral Sir James Athol Wood (d. 1829) and also Frances Vic Wood, Sir George's wife (d.1860). Lt. Col. de Visme, who served under Wellington in the Peninsular War and died in Jersey in 1860 aged 75 is commemorated by a plaque on the south wall of the nave; he was instrumental in saving the local Crouch Oak by fencing it to keep away village maidens to whom its bark was reputed to be a love charm when steeped in water.

The churchyard is well kept with headstones lined up. Fanny Kemble's mother is buried here.

ALBURY, St Peter and St Paul

The old church

109.   Albury Old Church from the south before the restoration of the chancel.

The old church, which now stands on its own in the grounds of Albury Park mansion, goes back to pre-Conquest times and is mentioned in Domesday. Traces of Saxon work appear in the base of the tower, which also retains a small Saxon window in its north wall and in the typical herring-bone masonry also in the north wall. The main part of the tower is Norman, built in the mid-twelfth century at the same time as a chancel. The latter, however, was replaced in the thirteenth century by a larger chancel which in the nineteenth century was allowed to fall into ruin and since 1875 until recently has stood roofless. The south aisle was rebuilt about 1300 to replace a narrower aisle whilst the south transept is a little earlier (*c.*1290), although redecorated in 1839. A north transept was added in the seventeenth century but this has disappeared and there was at one time a spire but, by 1820, this was replaced by the present unusual Turkish-looking, bulbous shingled cupola.

The isolation of the church is due to the high-handed action of Admiral Captain Finch who purchased the Albury estate from his brother in 1780. He did not like the village being so close to his mansion and, by a process of enclosing the village green, annexing part of the churchyard and generally harassing the villagers, he forced them to move a mile west to a hamlet at Weston Street.

In November 1974 the old church was vested in the Redundant Churches Fund (now Churches Conservation Trust) who have since cared for and restored it. The altar, pews, bells, plate and the thirteenth-century font of Sussex marble had already been transferred to the new church when it was built in 1842.

The isolation of the church helps to create a picturesque composition, completely surrounded as it is by the grounds of Albury Park. The late fifteenth-century north porch is well preserved with richly moulded timbers and delicate bargeboarding. The north door retains its original fourteenth-century hinges and lock together with a contemporary key of fine craftsmanship.

Although only the church and the village inn were left when Henry Drummond purchased the estate in 1819, he was interested in the church to the extent of having his family mortuary chapel placed in the south transept. This accounts for the lavish interior decoration, carried out under the direction of Augustus Pugin. The lively stained glass is by William Wailes and the wall decoration by T. Earley; Henry Drummond's altar-tomb is placed against the south wall. There is a faint wall-painting of St Christopher in the south aisle. The monuments are not of particular note but they include a slab with Lombardic lettering of *c*.1330 to Wm. de Weston and a brass to John Weston (d.1440) on the south aisle floor, showing him in full armour.

William Oughtred (rector from 1610 to 1660) was a distinguished mathematician; in 1631, he produced *Clavis Mathematicae* (subtitled 'The key of the Mathematicks new forged and filed'), which became the standard mathematical textbook embodying practically everything that was then known of algebra and arithmetic: he is credited also with being the originator of the 'X' sign for multiplication. One of the pupils who came to Oughtred was Christopher Wren.

Samuel Horsley (rector from 1774 to 1779) was an outstanding eighteenth-century cleric, who became Bishop of St David's, Wales, in 1788, of Rochester in 1793 and of St Asaph, Wales, in 1802.

The new church

Drummond provided another building for the churchgoers who had moved to Weston Street. Dating from 1842, it was designed by McIntosh Brooks. Built in brick in imitation of a church in Normandy, Drummond had expected stone and was disappointed to find this material on his return from his travels. Italianate, it has no aisles to the nave. There is a north-west tower. The apse and transepts were the work of Sir Arthur Blomfield following the same style and dating from 1868. The north transept was re-ordered as a Memorial Chapel by Sir Edward Maufe (architect of Guildford Cathedral) after the Second World War.

ALBURY, The Catholic Apostolic Church

Henry Drummond was a supporter of Edward Irving, the founder of the Catholic Apostolic Church. Irving's belief was that the Second Advent was at hand and he gathered round him people of like mind. Groups and congregations came into being to pray for the outpouring of the Holy Spirit, especially in preparation for the Second Advent, including prophecy and the ministries of apostles, prophets, evangelists and pastors. Albury became their spiritual centre and Drummond provided for the sect a new church commonly referred to as the 'Apostles' Chapel'. It was designed in 1840 in Commissioners' Gothic style by William McIntosh Brooks, who also designed the new church in Weston Street, with a large and impressive west tower and an octagonal chapter house on the north side. Although still maintained, it is no longer used regularly.

110.   The Catholic Apostolic Church, Albury – the chapter house.

111.   The timbers supporting the belfry at the west end of the nave at Alfold.

ALFOLD, St Nicholas

112.   The font at Alfold.

This church goes back to A.D. 1100 and one can envisage the original nave and chancel by viewing the interior from the west end. The south aisle was added about 1280 but later removed and it was not until a restoration in 1842 that the early arches were re-discovered and the aisle rebuilt upon the former foundations; the arches die into the round piers without capitals. The north arcade and chancel arch are early fourteenth century.

Not typically Surrey (Alfold is on the Sussex border), St Nicholas displays the Sussex characteristic of an immense catslide roof sweeping down to a few feet above the ground over both nave and aisles; it is partly covered with Horsham slates. There is a small, shingled bell-turret with spire. The south porch is a good example of fourteenth-century woodwork. The church makes a picturesque scene with the nearby cottages.

The rebuilding of the south aisle, the use of Bargate stone and the furnishings provide an agreeable interior matching one's expectations from viewing the exterior. A striking fifteenth-century framework supports the bell-turret.

Furnishings
One of the oldest (probably eleventh-century) and best preserved in Surrey, the font is of massive tub shape having a bowl decorated with blind arches each with a Maltese cross and encircling cable moulding symbolising the all-embracing Sacrament of Baptism. The top of the Communion Table is of polished Sussex marble and is said to have been discovered, during the 1842 restoration, under the north aisle where further examples of this material are to be seen. The seventeenth-century Jacobean pulpit retains its sounding-board. The north door has fine wrought-iron work. Nearby is a chest bearing the names of the two churchwardens of 1687. The church records contain an entry that Mary Woods was buried in wool on 7th April 1683; this was obligatory between the years 1678 and 1815 in order to encourage the woollen trade.

ASH, St Peter

A church at Ash was mentioned in Domesday. Subsequently the benefice was granted to Chertsey Abbey but, owing to failure by the monks to carry out their responsibilities 'by reason of voidance of the Abbey of Chertsey', the advowson passed to the Crown. It appears, however, that it was later returned to the monastery until the Dissolution when the Crown re-possessed it for a short time until Edward VI passed it to Winchester College (still the patrons). The pre-Conquest church, probably of wood, was succeeded by a flint building of which the south aisle and Lady Chapel remain. In 1865/6 St Peter's was insensitively enlarged with a north aisle – now the nave – to the design of H. Woodyer.

The tower, constructed of hard siliceous heath or sarsen stone, is fifteenth-century in date and together with the shingled nineteenth-century spire which took the place of the slender spire shown in Cracklow's drawing of the 1820's, is the most striking external feature. The timber and brick sixteenth-century porch leads to the south door of *c*.1170 which, although round-headed, is Gothic and one of the best Early Gothic survivals in Surrey.

The 1865/6 restoration has left an indifferent interior, although there is a very small Norman window reset in the north aisle near the pulpit and a thirteenth-century lancet on the south side of the chancel, the glass of which depicts the Parable of the Sower. The chancel arch rests on moulded capitals; on the top of the north pier is carved a toad and on the south a toadstool. The plaster surround of the inside of the tower arch is crimped.

113.   St. Peter's, Ash – the west tower.

114.   The wooden font at Ash.

115.   The Transitional Norman south doorway at Ash.

Furnishings

The font is one of two made of wood in Surrey (the other is at Chobham); a circular central post and eight octagonal columns support an octagonal bowl cut from one piece of wood. A well-preserved Royal Arms of George III is to be seen under the tower.

Among the several memorials, some of which have been moved, the one of most interest is the tablet to John Harris (rector from 1718 to 1760) on the east wall of the chancel beneath which he is buried; it is adorned with skulls and bones.

ASHTEAD, St Giles

St. Giles goes back to pre-Norman times and appears to have been rebuilt more than once. A stone church was built by Lawrence of Rouen *c*.1225 and evidence of Norman work is to be seen in the Roman tiles incorporated in the nave – probably from a nearby Roman villa. The first known rector, instituted in the thirteenth century, was Robert de Montfort; he was moved to Somerset after quarrelling with his bishop. A reconstruction of 1520 embodied Norman work and the massive squat tower with rising stair-turret dates from this period (*c*.1540). Much, however, of what is visible today is the work of thorough-going renewals mainly initiated and paid for by the Rev. William Legge, rector from 1826 to 1871. In 1830, a south door in the chancel was blocked up and the present south door in the nave inserted; the porch was presumably added at the same time. Later, the cedar-wood ceiling took the place of a low, plaster one and a panelled, wagon-roof ceiling was installed in the chancel; the north transept was built and the organ installed in it; the reredos and altar-rails were provided and the vestry was added in 1891. Little medieval work remains.

Dominated by the tower, the church is set in a triangular earthwork, apart from the village and near Ashtead Park. An attractive Victorian addition is the Horsham slate roof. This material is also used on the lych-gate.

Although Ian Nairn[24] describes the roofs as 'very frilly', they are the most striking features of the interior. The cedar-wood nave roof with scissor braces on the sides and quatrefoils in the spandrels has central king-posts. The frieze which runs round the nave in a clockwise direction has been carved with the words of the 'Te Deum' starting just above the font. The chancel roof – of quite different design – is panelled with poppy-heads on the underside. The Communion 'Ter Sanctus' is carved on the frieze. The nineteenth-century north transept is unusually deep.

Furnishings

There is a fifteenth-century octagonal font with quatrefoil and shield decorations, and an interesting cover. The oak pulpit dates from 1891. By far the most interesting furnishing is the sixteenth-century stained glass in the east window (*Colour Plate XXVI*) illustrating the Crucifixion which came from the Flemish Cistercian Abbey of Herckenrode, near Maastricht in the Netherlands (suppressed in 1801). St George and the dragon appear in the bottom left-hand corner. The colours – primarily gold and blue – are muted and Nairn [25] refers to the 'elaborate Mannerist architectural backgrounds' which he considers the best details. There is much more of this glass in the Lady Chapel of Lichfield Cathedral. The artist may have been Lambert Lombard (born in Liège in 1506). The west window in the tower ringing chamber is claimed also to be Flemish.

St. Giles has a number of good monuments, including one by Grinling Gibbons (but not at his best) and another in Rysbrack style. Brasses of 1590/1 can be seen on the floor of the nave and a brass to Dorothea Quennel (wife of a seventeenth-century rector) placed on a wall. There are several tablets of the early eighteenth century of which the best is the one to

Sarah Bond (d.1712); Sarah Bond was sister-in-law to the owner of the land on which London's Bond Street was established. The Grinling Gibbons monument, carved in 1693, commemorates Henry Newdigate who died much earlier in 1629; the carving is quite rough. The Rysbrack-style monument – of excellent workmanship – is to Lady Diana Feilding (d.1733) in the form of a bust in a circular, black-marble surround enclosed in a fine Palladian frame; it is on the north wall of the nave towards the west end (*see fig. 87*).

Beside a swing gate leading into the grounds of the old Manor House (now the City of London Freemen's School) and in the south-east corner of the churchyard is a most interesting monument in the form of a table tomb to Peter Hamelot, a Huguenot refugee who became Rector, and his wife and mother. We read that 'when the Papish fury destroyed the Protestants in France he left his patrimony and came into England. He was chosen Pastor of this Church 25th March 1699 and died the 14th day of April 1742, aged 81 years'.

Samuel Pepys, after his visit to St Giles', in 1663 wrote as follows:- 'So to Ashted Church, where we had a dull Doctor, one Downe, worse than I think even Parson King was, of whom we made so much scorn, and after sermon home, and staid while our dinner a couple of large chickens were dressed, and a good mess of cream'. Pepys mentioned Ashtead several times as he had a 'cozen' who lived there.

ASHTEAD, St George, Lower Ashtead

A simple brick church by Sir Arthur Blomfield's firm, but built after his death. Dating from 1906 but not completed until 1962, it took the place of a corrugated iron building, known as the 'Iron Church', built in 1881. The interior is satisfying, able to seat 500 people, with the arcade arches tending to die into the piers without capitals.

BANSTEAD, All Saints

All Saints is included in Domesday Book and the pre-Conquest church may have been built by Chertsey Abbey who had been granted the lands of Banstead. In Henry I's reign, however, the Lord of the Manor presented the living to the Augustinian Priory of St Mary Overie, Southwark with which it rested until the Dissolution. The present building, consisting of nave, chancel, aisles terminating in north and south chapels and west tower, was built, except for the aisles and vestry, basically between 1190 and 1220. The north doorway dates from the fifteenth century. The first recorded vicar is 'Ranulph before 1282'; a gap in the list between 1348/9 and 1367 was doubtless caused by the ravages of the Black Death. Since the Reformation there have been many restorations including the repair of the chancel in 1631, 'the

116.   Banstead Church from the west.

beautifying of the Parish Church' in 1761, the rebuilding of the south chapel (now called the Lambert Chapel) by the Lambert family in 1837 and a thorough going-over by G.E. Street in 1861 when the three-lancet east window was replaced by a fifteenth-century-type window and the chancel floor raised; this unfortunately covered the old stone paving and the Early English bases of the chancel arcade piers. Later in 1867, the Lambert family rebuilt the south aisle.

117.   The double piscina in the chancel at All Saints' Church, Banstead.

Banstead has grown from a village of 882 people in 1811 to a population today which numbers over 44,000 and new parishes have been created at St Mark's, Tattenham Corner and St Paul's, Nork Park. All Saints has much to offer and is well worth a visit. And, although now it is centrally situated in the busy High Street, it is said that, at the beginning of this century, no buildings at all would have been visible from the north door.

The flint and stone exterior has been completely renewed and shorn of its medieval texture with dormer windows inserted in the roof, but the sturdy tower – its walls are exceptionally thick – with a broadly-splayed tall spire pointing sharply upwards is a striking feature.

The effects of the restoration are far less apparent in the interior and there is much to see and enjoy. The two-bay nave arcade dates from the earliest building period (end twelfth century) with crocketed capitals and spurs on the bases of the octagonal piers. The bays are widely spaced and the arches are out of alignment with one another. The chancel chapels are of two bays; the octagonal pier on the south side has a plain capital but that on the north is most unusual in that the sides are alternately hollowed and sunk with four leaf crockets on the capital leaving fillets at the angles. The north chapel retains its narrow lancets and original roof, and the acutely pointed arch from the north aisle is of Caen stone.

Furnishings

The octagonal fourteenth-century font is also made of Caen stone and each of the eight sides is decorated with a different tracery design; the pedestal and base are modern. None of the stained glass is old but the west window was designed by Dante Gabriel Rossetti and William Morris and was made by Morris & Company. On the east wall of the Lambert Chapel is a copy, painted by Miss M.W. Taylor, a local artist, and presented to the church about 1950, of Millais's *Christ in the Home of His Parents.*

There are several monuments of interest. In the south aisle is a notable memorial to Sir Daniel Lambert who was Lord Mayor of London in 1741; it is tall and narrow with an achievement on top and an inscription in the concave central part. Also in the south aisle is a hanging monument without figure but with a nicely decorated predella to Nicholas Lambert (d.1815). Other monuments include a well-executed Rococo cartouche to Mrs. Elizabeth Tilly (d.1748) on the south wall of the Lambert Chapel and a Grecian monument with rising female figure to Wilmot Lambert (d.1815) on the south wall of the tower. But perhaps the most engaging

118. Monument to Sir Daniel Lambert at Banstead.

memorial is the oblong tablet on the east wall of the nave to a baby, Paul Tracy (d.1618), showing the small figure in a chrisom robe. A ledger stone in front of the chancel step commemorates Edward Lambert (d.1763 in his 83rd. year) and his wife, Anne (d.1720) and their daughter, Mary (d.1737) who were only 33 and 17 respectively when they died.

On the south side of the communion rail is a brass plate commemorating 'James Read who for 40 years served King Charles ye 1st. King Charles ye 2nd. and King James ye 2nd. with all Loyalty, Courage and Fidelity in ye quality of Captaine both by sea and Lande'; he died in 1691.

BARNES, St Mary

The story starts with the building of a small flint chapel in the first half of the twelfth century which Henry of Northampton, canon of St Paul's Cathedral, gave at the end of the century to St Paul's Hospital. Richard of Northampton who was appointed priest-in- charge immediately enlarged this place of worship both westwards and eastwards, the chancel so formed being dedicated, some say, by Stephen Langton on his way back from Runnymede after the signing of the Magna Carta and which still survives as the Langton Chapel. It is probable that the triple lancet windows in the east wall were installed at this time. The next milestone in construction was the addition of the brick tower in *c.*1480 with a rising stair-turret at the south-west corner; other changes that took place then were the building of an external buttress on the south wall at the junction between nave and chancel, the blocking of the rood-loft staircase (now partially uncovered) and the sealing of the original

Norman door with the introduction of a new entrance slightly to the west. Another long interval elapsed before further structural change but in 1786, after the Hoare family had moved into the parish, they were permitted to remove the north wall of the nave and add a family chapel, vault and gallery. This formed a small north aisle which was extended eastwards in 1838.

The building of the railway from London to Richmond in 1846 had a major impact upon the village, the population of which quadrupled between 1800 and 1870 from 1,000 to over 4,000. Plans were set in train as early as the middle of the nineteenth century to rebuild the entire church but, although substantial extensions and renovations were carried out in 1852 and new churches were opened in Castlenau and Westfields in the latter part of the century, it was not until 1904-06 that a major rebuilding took place, which increased the seating capacity to almost 1,000 places, under Charles Innes. This catered for all major needs until June 1978 when the church was largely gutted by fire. For nearly six years, the building was a ruin but the public responded admirably to the appeal fund and in February 1984 a new church to a most original design by Edward Cullinan was constructed, preserving as much as possible of the parts that had survived the fire.

The impression upon approaching from the south through the lych-gate is that one is about to visit a medieval church, as much of the early twelfth-century place of worship and the Tudor tower survives. A blocked Norman arch to the east of the main entrance reminds one of the original church and two sturdy brick buttresses with very wide pointing support the old south wall. The unblocked triple lancets with vesica above remain at the east end and the tower appears little changed from when it was first built.

A great surprise awaits one on entry. Whilst preserving the old nave and chancel, the architect, Edward Cullinan, has designed a most imaginative new nave stretching north from the old part to a new high wall which contains the stone-traceried east and rose

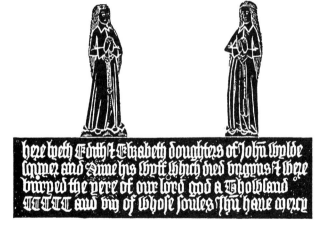

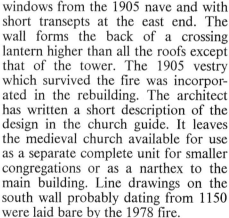

windows from the 1905 nave and with short transepts at the east end. The wall forms the back of a crossing lantern higher than all the roofs except that of the tower. The 1905 vestry which survived the fire was incorporated in the rebuilding. The architect has written a short description of the design in the church guide. It leaves the medieval church available for use as a separate complete unit for smaller congregations or as a narthex to the main building. Line drawings on the south wall probably dating from 1150 were laid bare by the 1978 fire.

This is a reassuring example of what modern architecture can do whilst paying respect to the character of the old in an area which, despite its very large growth in population and proximity to London, still retains much of its village atmosphere.

119.   Brass of Edith & Elizabeth Wylde (1508) at Barnes.

Furnishings

A handsome memorial to a former rector, named Squier, in the shape of an oval with an attractive surround, survives on the south wall of the Langton Chapel. On the opposite wall, a brass plate, 9½ inches high, commemorates two young girls of the Wylde family 'which died virgyns' in 1508. A slab in the new nave floor is in memory of John Moody, an old Member of Drury Lane Theatre (d.1812 at the age of 85), and his wife, Kitty Ann (d.1816 at the age of 83).

A beautifully maintained small churchyard contains one seventeenth-century headstone to an infant, James Barr, dated 1686 situated near the lych-gate and, on the exterior of the south wall between the two buttresses, there is a memorial to Edward Rose (d.1653); unfortunately the rose-bush associated with his name and planted with his bequest is no longer there.

BEDDINGTON, St Mary

A church, probably of wood, was mentioned in Domesday Book. Fragments of a Norman building remain but the structure is basically late fourteenth-century, overlaid with much Victorian alteration. Chancel roofs and nave, decorated with outsize angels, chancel, chancel arch and outer north aisle were all work of the 1850's/1860's whilst the tower was rebuilt earlier in the nineteenth century. The dormer windows date from 1915. The south porch, however, is fifteenth century. St Mary's was closely associated with the Carew family and Nicholas (Lord of the Manor 1354-91) was the main force behind the building; a later Nicholas, the son of the Richard Carew who built the Carew Chapel south of the chancel in 1520, was executed in 1539 on a trumped-up charge of treason. The family connection however was maintained and Charles Hallowell Carew was buried in the family tomb as late as 1872. The Chapel is one of the finest parts of the church with a good parclose screen.

The church with its well-proportioned and commanding tower stands handsomely back from the road in a spacious churchyard with the Carew manor (now a school) behind and, although twentieth-century refacing of the flintwork has removed the original texture, St Mary's has an impressive appearance.

Nineteenth-century restoration is again all too evident in the interior, but the Carew Chapel with its monuments, and the furnishings – especially the organ gallery (*Colour Plate XXX*) by Morris & Co. – give much to enjoy. A fourteenth-century mural painting was discovered during the restoration of the chancel arch.

Furnishings

Installed in 1869, the Morris & Co. organ gallery, screened like a minstrel's gallery, is decorated with a painted dado and a tier of small figures. Pevsner rates it as 'a delightful piece'. There are nine fourteenth-century stalls in the chancel with misericords, which may have come from Merton Abbey. The pulpit with Elizabethan linenfold panelling dates from 1611 and the standard type Purbeck-marble font is thirteenth century. The communion rails date from 1713.

The Carew Chapel contains many brasses and monuments to members of the family and these form one of the best sets in Surrey. The main monuments are to Sir Richard Carew, Governor of Calais (d.1520), who built the chapel and to Sir Francis Carew (d.1611); Sir Richard and his wife lie in a canopied tomb in a fine Perpendicular recess; Sir Francis, who was uncle of Elizabeth Throckmorton who married Sir Walter Raleigh, is carved in alabaster as a recumbent effigy with his head on a rolled-up mat and his family kneeling in relief against the front of the tomb-chest.

BETCHWORTH, St Michael

Nestling in a cul-de-sac off a country road beside a bend of the River Mole, St Michael's is an old foundation, being mentioned in Domesday Book and possessing one of the few Surrey pre-Conquest survivals; although it is a perplexing and not very exciting stone fragment it does indicate that the pre-Conquest church may well have been of stone rather than the more usual wood. This fragment is the capital or base of a pier worked into the south window under the tower which originally was central but was taken down and rebuilt in its present position at the east end of the south aisle in 1851. After the Conquest, this place of worship came unto the powerful hands of Richard of Tonbridge, Lord of Clare, thence to the Warennes, the Earls of Surrey, who, in 1199, presented the living to the Priory of St Mary Overie, Southwark. After the Dissolution, the advowson passed to several laymen in succession until in 1548 it was presented to the Dean and Canons of Windsor with whom it remains. The main fabric of the building dates from the first quarter of the thirteenth century. The aisles were widened in the fourteenth century and many windows date from these periods, but much of what one now sees was affected by major restorations in 1851 and 1870, when most of the windows were renewed in a stone totally different from the original one, and the addition of the north transept in 1879. The very much renewed nave clerestory windows are of dates ranging from the thirteenth century to the seventeenth century. Both west and south porches are also Victorian.

One enters the churchyard from the north through a large lych gate roofed with Horsham slabs; this material is also used for the roofs of the unusually grey-hued, larger-than-average building. The tower now stands in an eccentric position on the south side. The clerestory has irregular circular openings.

The nave arcades are thirteenth century with piers mainly circular but one octagonal. Of this date also are the chancel arches to the south chapel and the two lancets in the chancel north wall. The nave aisles were widened in the fourteenth century. The only parts of the Norman church which remain are the western arch, which was moved with the tower to its present position at the east end of the south aisle and the late twelfth-century arch in the eastern part of the re-built tower. The former, which was once the arch into the crossing tower, is now very cramped, exaggerated by large capitals. Despite these earlier survivals, the interior is strangely lifeless.

Furnishings

The only old furnishings are two medieval brasses and a large ancient dug-out chest made out of the trunk of an oak with seven iron staples. The font is Romanesque in style and tub-shaped, by Eric Kennington (1951). The pulpit (*Colour Plate XXXII*) has five kinds of marble and inlaid mosaic panels of Faith, Hope and Love. There is stained glass by Clayton & Bell in the north transept.

The two medieval brasses consist of one on the south side of the chancel to William Wardysworth (parish vicar who died in 1533), a small figure holding a chalice, and the other on the south side of the south chapel to Thomas Morsted and Alianora, his wife, erected by their son who was Henry V's chief medical officer at the battle of Agincourt. The other monuments are nineteenth-century and not out of the ordinary.

BISLEY, St John the Baptist

Set apart from the village, this church stands isolated in fields. To the south west is the St John Baptist well, mentioned by J. Aubrey, in which at one time all baptisms were carried out. The most attractive feature is the shingled belfry supported on fourteenth-century timber framing inside the nave tying it into the walls. There is a late fourteenth-century timber porch with the external arch fashioned out of one tree-trunk and prominent bargeboarding. The interior has good modern pews and a Jacobean pulpit. The early nineteenth-century chancel replaced a much more attractive timber-framed one and the north aisle dates from 1873.

BLECHINGLEY, St Mary the Virgin

The church lies back from the eastern end of the main A25 road which divides this attractive village in two. Mainly Perpendicular, dating from alterations made about 1460, with Victorian accretions (e.g. north arcade and south aisle windows 1856), there are earlier parts. The chancel is part eleventh-century and part thirteenth-century, the very wide south aisle part thirteenth-century and part fifteenth-century and the north transept or Ham Chapel fourteenth-century. The tower is of varying dates, basically c.1090, but heightened by a belfry in c.1160 and the top added in the seventeenth century; the whole was renewed in 1910. Its walls are five feet thick at the base and it is twenty feet across inside. A spire which existed previously was destroyed by lightning in 1606.

A low-lying building with battlemented west tower, south porch and aisle (the battlements are modern); the chancel and south chapel have twin gables at the east end of equal height to the nave. A prominent feature is the two-storied Perpendicular south porch. The Perpendicular style south-aisle windows date from 1856 (compare with the north arcade). The turret in the south-east corner of the south aisle gives access to the former rood loft whilst the quatrefoil in the south chapel alongside it probably represents the site of the cell of Brother Roger, hermit of Blechingley, who received a grant of a barrel of wheat from Henry III in 1233.

The interior is a mixture of mid-fifteenth-century Perpendicular and mid-nineteenth-century Victorian, with a wide south chapel and towering monument to Sir Robert Clayton. The south doorway is renewed but the richly moulded

120. Bisley – west turret.

121. The hermit's quatrefoil window at Blechingley.

arch is thirteenth-century. The east window was once Perpendicular but, during the restoration by J.L. Pearson in 1870, was replaced by the present three lancet windows. This was a reversion to the original form but the Pearson lancets are different in shape and location.

Furnishings

The Jacobean pulpit, dating from 1630, was thrown out during the 1870 restoration and removed to Orsett in Essex whence it was later recovered. The back, which can be moved forward, conceals the nave altar niche. The hour-glass stand is of the same date. The font is routine Perpendicular with its cover carved in 1906. The reredos by G.E. Street dating from 1870 shows Bishop Wilberforce among the apostles.

St. Mary the Virgin is justly noted for its monument (*see figs. 75 & 76*) to Sir Robert Clayton erected in his lifetime for his wife by Richard Crutcher – his only known work – and has been variously described as 'one of the most splendid early eighteenth-century monuments in the country'[26] and as 'a fearful nightmare'.[27] It is a very large monument, both the main figures being over life-size but these contrast with the pathetic figure of their stillborn son at the foot who died in 1669 (an echo of the memorial to the same child at St Giles', Ickenham, Middlesex), although here he is shown in embroidered clothes whilst, at Ickenham, he is wrapped in swaddling clothes. The table tomb to Sir Thomas Cawarden (d. 1559) on the south side of the chancel is not outstanding but the small brass plate on top (discovered at Loseley in 1836) has beautiful Italic writing. There are various brasses dotted around, most of which have been removed to the walls of the north transept; the oldest is that of an unmarried girl with coifless hair of *c*.1470. On the north side of the chancel floor is a priest in mass vestments (Hugh Hestall *c*.1460). The Warde brass (and unrelated Trinity brass) has been removed from the chancel wall and replaced in its original stone which has been placed in the middle of the tower floor.

Thomas Herring (rector) became Archbishop of Canterbury in 1747. William Wakelyn, whom Sir Thomas Cawarden appointed as rector when he was Lord of the Manor, was married with four children; he had to leave when Mary was on the throne but, when he came back, two more had been added so that presumably whilst he was away 'childer' had not 'ceased bornin'.

BRAMLEY, Holy Trinity

Centrally placed in a large village on the main road between Guildford and Horsham, Holy Trinity was originally a small Norman building of which fragments remain in the head of the west doorway; the west front has been rebuilt in that style. The chancel with triple lancets at the east end and on the north and south walls, and the tower with low, octagonal, shingled spire are thirteenth-century, but the rest is Woodyer work of 1850 and 1876.

122. Ludlow Monument at Bramley.

Furnishings
There is much nineteenth-century stained glass of varying quality and design. A notable furnishing is the monument in the south aisle to Henry Ludlow (d.1730) in the form of a large well-carved urn and flambeau in a Palladian architectural frame.

BROCKHAM, Christ Church

123.   Christ Church seen across Brockham Green.

Christ Church, one of Benjamin Ferrey's main works in Surrey, forms an admirable vignette on the Green with the adjoining houses. It presents a side elevation with plate tracery in the gabled north transept and a combination of firestone walls with limestone dressings, which make an effective colour pattern. Cruciform in shape, the style is thirteenth-century with a seemly and satisfying interior. The indifferent stained glass in the nave is German.

BUCKLAND, St Mary

This is one of Woodyer's best achievements, described by Ian Nairn [28] 'Victorian village-church building at its best', it incorporates the old four-post belfry framing and is built of Surrey's attractive Bargate sandstone. The shingled belfry has delicate windows, with a large curvilinear-headed west window below.

   The interior fittings are not notable except the fourteenth-century stained glass figures of St Peter and St Paul, in dark reds and blues, on the north side of the nave. Nairn considers this glass as 'about the best in the county'. The mid-nineteenth-century gilded reredos is thought to be German.

The church lies on the south side of the busy Guildford to Reigate road facing a pleasant green on which is an unusual black-boarded wooden barn, with a small turret at one end, itself looking like a church.

BURSTOW, St Bartholomew (formerly St Michael the Archangel)

124.   The timber west tower at Burstow.

First mentioned in 1221 when the Archbishop of Canterbury, who held the living by virtue of Burstow Manor being part of the Archbishop's Manor of Wimbledon, granted it to the Cluniac Priory of St Pancras at Lewes. The priory – being alien – probably had to cede it back to the Archbishop at the end of the thirteenth century and, except for a time during the fourteenth century when through 'voidance of the see' the living passed to the Crown, it stayed in Canterbury's hands until 1536. Thereafter, apart from the period of the Commonwealth, it has rested in the hands of the Crown, presentation now being made by the Lord Chancellor, although Burstow remained a peculiar of Canterbury until 1851. Originally consisting only of nave and small chancel, the latter was altered about the middle of the thirteenth century but the fifteenth century (probably during the time of Archbishop Chichele 1413-43) saw the enlargement of the chancel and the addition of the south aisle, whilst the church's outstanding feature – the west tower – was built either in the fifteenth or sixteenth century. Benjamin Ferrey carried out an extensive but not too drastic restoration between 1884 and 1895.

The notable timber tower of a type more common in Essex than in Surrey (but see Great Bookham, and Newdigate) is a separate construction, the church having a west wall of stone. The tower is enlarged below to accommodate three aisles and is weatherboarded, while above there is superlative, possibly eighteenth-century shingling (renewed in 1961) reaching up to the broach-spire and the four delicate corner pinnacles. The upper stage is battered.

The four-light windows are fifteenth-century but restored with stone from a different source than the local stone used originally; the small, square-headed priest's door on the south side however is original. Two Norman windows remain respectively in the nave (blocked) and chancel. There is pretty Victorian bargeboarding to both nave and aisle.

The overall effect in the interior is Perpendicular including the chancel arch, which is framed by a pair of niches; piscinas indicate various medieval altars. Of particular interest is the tower framing.

Furnishings
The font is a cut above the ordinary fifteenth-century octagonal type. The lectern and pulpit are modern, the former dating from 1910. A large chest with a semi-circular, entirely iron-bound top at the west end of the nave appears to be of about 1600. Beneath the sill of

the chancel north-east window is a recess with two trefoiled openings separated by a mullion which may at one time have been used as an Easter sepulchre.

John Flamsteed, the first Astronomer Royal, was rector from 1684 until his death in 1719 and is commemorated in the east window and in a sculptured plaque, presented in 1975 to mark the tercentenary of his appointment as Astronomer Royal. He is buried at Burstow.

BUSBRIDGE, St John the Baptist

This church is another example of a Victorian architect's respect for the vernacular. Built by one of the Scott family (probably G.G. junior) in 1865-67, it is constructed of Bargate stone which was quarried close by. The shingled central tower is the most notable exterior feature. Although there are no transepts, there are gabled 'transept ends', consisting of lancets.

Furnishings
The interior is distinguished by the Burne-Jones stained glass in the east and west windows, made by Morris & Co. in 1909: there is also Morris glass in the south side of the chancel, made in 1905. The west window is particularly notable. More striking, however, is the rood and chancel screen, made in iron by J. Starkie Gardner from designs by Sir Edwin Lutyens and installed in 1899 (*see fig. 102*). The composition is an intricate affair of loops and scrolls supporting the figure of Christ with outstretched arms above two kneeling angels.

The churchyard contains tombs by Lutyens to Gertrude Jekyll, with whom he worked so closely, and to her brother, Sir Herbert Jekyll, and his wife. The tomb slabs have an urn and stone balustrade behind.

BYFLEET, St Mary the Virgin

St. Mary the Virgin, Byfleet is set apart from the village on its southern edge, more easily observed across the River Wey from Wisley than from the village itself. There is a place of worship mentioned in Domesday Book, but the present building of flint and pudding-stone consisted in medieval times of nave and chancel, dating from the late thirteenth century or early fourteenth century, with a splay-footed, shingled spire and belfry of the fifteenth century.

Unfortunately, the illusion of St Mary's being a medieval place of worship has been dispelled by cruel treatment during the nineteenth century, first by the addition of a south aisle in 1841, built of Bargate stone, and then the south transept in 1864, the latter addition by Woodyer. There were further alterations subsequently, especially in 1924, when the chancel was repaved and the nave relaid with wooden blocks.

Before the addition of the south aisle, the main entrance was on the south side through a low wide-gabled porch but now one enters from the north. This has the advantage of seeing first the medieval part of the church unaffected by Victorian alterations, making a pleasant introduction.

One soon becomes aware of the Victorian intrusions which have produced a muddled and inconvenient design. The former galleries and box-pews have disappeared and only the nave and chancel remain from the original building, but with an unattractive chancel arch, having a thick inner order which Woodyer copied with most unfortunate effect in his Victorian transept. The three-light east window has intersecting tracery.

Furnishings

There is much of interest as well as a particularly noteworthy brass (see below). The peripatetic font (it had been moved five times before it was placed in its present position at the west end of the south aisle) is of fifteenth-century date and of typical octagonal form. The pulpit, cut down from a three-decker, dates from 1616 and has the initials R.S. inscribed on it (but it is not known to whom they refer). The sedilia are the original seats in the south-east corner of the chancel and, adjoining them, is an old piscina; another piscina near the vestry door was probably used for a time as a holy-water stoup. Most of the stained glass is modern but there is both old and twentieth-century glass of note. The medieval glass consists of fragments assembled in the north-west window of the chancel. Two are of the early fourteenth century, one of which, representing the head of our Lord with strongly pointed features, is a fine piece of work. The twentieth-century glass is in the east window of the organ chamber which had been almost completely masked, until the 1893 organ with large pipes was replaced in 1968 with the present electronic instrument. The glass was designed on the theme of 'Music' and made by Lawrence Lee, one of the finest of contemporary stained glass artists and formerly head of the Department of Stained Glass at the Royal College of Arts. The guide-book [29] contains a full text of a letter he wrote explaining what he was hoping to express. During the 1864 restoration various murals were uncovered, including a circular Maltese cross and what appears to be a king seated on a throne beneath a canopy of pinnacles and flying buttresses. This has been variously ascribed to King David or to the much less worthy Edward II. A finely carved, stylized Victorian Royal Arms of 1843 is placed above the south door. In a glass case near the main entrance door is a bassoon which was played until 1835, when the first organ (a barrel-organ) was introduced.

The brass (*see fig. 61*), already mentioned, is to Thomas Taylar, rector from 1454 to 1489, a period roughly corresponding to that of the Wars of the Roses. It is affixed to the north wall of the chancel beside the pulpit. He was a major Canon of Lincoln Cathedral which makes his vestments of particular interest; he wears an almice of grey with surplice and cassock. The small brass shaped like a scroll, issuing from his mouth, gives the words of a prayer he is saying. Of larger memorials, there is a marble and alabaster monument in the chancel to Lady Louisa Egerton, daughter of the 7th. Duke of Devonshire and, west of the chancel arch, is an alabaster tablet in memory of one of her sons, Frederick G. Egerton, who was killed at Ladysmith in 1899. The War Memorial takes the form of wooden crosses brought over from the graves on the battlefields of the 1914-18 War and commemorate 22 of the 36 Byfleet men who fell. Their names are recorded on the marble tablet below affixed to the west wall of the south aisle.

Byfleet Manor was a royal hunting-lodge and the name of Edward, the Black Prince, who used it, appears as patron on the list of rectors of Wisley Church. The Manor was given by James I to his wife, Anne of Denmark. St Mary's choir wear red cassocks, allegedly of right because the church was a Chapel Royal. Stephen Duck, a Wiltshire labourer, attracted the attention of Caroline of Anspach, George II's wife, with his poetry and, with the influence of the Rev. Joseph Spence, a literary celebrity, became rector of Byfleet in 1752, only to drown himself four years later in a fit of depression – an ironically melancholy end to a man with such a name. George Smith, who lived from 1824 to 1901, was a publisher who, when he was only 22, accepted the manuscript of 'Jane Eyre' from the then unknown authoress Charlotte Bronte. He is buried in the churchyard. Also in the churchyard is the grave of John Parry Thomas, a noted racing motorist, who was killed on Pendine Sands in March 1927 when attempting to break the land speed record. Opposite the west end of the south aisle is the grave of Mrs. Elizabeth Ayres who, when she died in 1760, had been 'mother, grandmother and great-grandmother of 125 children'. (In comparison, Hannah Choat at Wisley easily exceeded this number with 160 such descendants.)

CAMBERLEY, St Michael

St. Michael's is in York Town, the oldest part of the town, which owed its origin to the removal of the Royal Military College to Sandhurst in 1809. It is just in Surrey near the meeting point of the county with its neighbours, Hampshire and Berkshire. The church stands up well above the old A30 main road to Southampton and is set amidst tall conifers. Built by Henry Woodyer in 1849-51, the exterior is given character by the forceful Bargate stone tower and broach-spire, erected in 1891, although the dormers are a distraction. The interior, however, is unimpressive and not helped by the medallions in the spandrels of the five-bay nave arcade added in 1864. Although Camberley has been much spoilt by insensitive development, St Michael's – because of its dominant position – is likely to remain a commanding feature of the townscape.

CAMBERLEY, St Paul, Church Hill

Set in a newer and more prosperous part of Camberley, St Paul's by Caröe (1902) is of completely different style, resembling with its built-up stages a Norwegian stave church rather than anything else. It has an unexpectedly roomy interior.

CAPEL, St John the Baptist
(formerly called St Lawrence)

First mentioned during the episcopate of Henry de Blois at Winchester (1129-1171), when he granted the spiritualities to the Cluniac Priory of St Pancras at Lewes, the chapel (it did not rank as an *ecclesia*) was built *c*.1240 to serve a group of people as a chapel of ease in the sparsely-populated parish of Dorking which then became known as the parish of *Dorking cum Capella*. In 1334, the powerful Warenne family transferred the living to their new foundation for Augustinian Canons at Reigate – the Priory of the Holy Cross – where it remained until the Dissolution. The living was granted to Lord Howard of Effingham, father of Charles Howard who defeated the Armada, and then passed through a succession of private hands until 1922 when it came under the Crown and appointments were made by the Lord Chancellor. It is not known when the church received parochial status.

Although basically of thirteenth-century date, including the roof, the character of the present

125. St. John the Baptist's Church, Capel from the south east.

building was set by Henry Woodyer who restored it in 1864/5, removed the north transept, added a north aisle with his typical square-headed windows and a set of columns inside, and substituted a stone pulpit for the previous one of oak. The pretty shingled bell-turret with spire was renewed and the south porch of 1838 reconstructed. The south and west doorways, however, retain their good dog-tooth moulding.

Furnishings
An unusual if not very elegant feature is the spiral staircase of *c*.1860 which leads to the belfry, but the most notable furnishing is the font of 1865, a fine example with an octagonal bowl of polished brown marble, incised with gilt ornament, on a circular stem.

CARSHALTON, All Saints

All Saints is mentioned in Domesday Book and, after the Conquest, was passed to the Lords of the Manor, one of whom Pharamus de Bolonia, Count Bolonia, granted the living in the mid-twelfth century to the Priory and Convent of Merton with whom it remained until the Dissolution of the Monasteries. About 1550, it passed to private hands. The medieval church is still visible in the Lady Chapel (formerly the chancel), the square space under the axial tower (there were no transepts) and part of the south arcade. About 1200, the chancel/sanctuary, which consisted originally of the part under the tower, was extended and a south aisle added to the nave with Norman octagonal piers and carved leaf-crocket capitals of note. Earlier in the mid-twelfth century, a north aisle had been built but this disappeared with the Blomfield alterations at the end of the nineteenth century. In the fifteenth century, the chancel was further lengthened. Nothing further happened until the early part of the eighteenth century when the south aisle was raised and new windows inserted. At the same time the chancel (now Lady Chapel) was furnished with a reredos (*Colour Plate XXII*) (gilded and painted by Sir Ninian Comper in 1936) and the upper part of the tower built or rebuilt; the north aisle was also raised. Galleries may have been added but the records indicate 1811-15 as the period when they were inserted (possibly as replacements).

A major alteration was carried out between *c*.1893 and 1914 when Sir Arthur Blomfield (son of a Bishop of London) and his nephew, Reginald, completely changed the appearance of All Saints. Sir Arthur took down the north aisle and north nave arcade, building a new nave in their place with a north aisle beyond; he also added a chancel next to, but shorter than, the old one. He worked in a fifteenth-century Perpendicular style. In 1913, the west end, including an agreeable half-octagonal belfry, was built.

Approaching from the pond, the nineteenth-century work in front dwarfs the older part behind. The tower with its eighteenth-century spike is prominent, but not improved by its surface of flint, brick and drab-coloured stucco. From the far side, the old part is over-shadowed by Blomfield's work, although neither the nave nor the chancel extends to the same length as that of the old. The south aisle wall retains its medieval buttresses (restored in the eighteenth century) but the surface texture is unattractive.

Furnishings
The interior is confused but, for Comper devotees, there are about thirteen different works by him. The medieval crown-post roof of the Lady Chapel is estimated to be fourteenth-century or fifteenth-century, whilst the fine wrought-iron communion rail dates from the eighteenth century. G.F. Bodley is believed to have designed the triptych reredos in the new chancel, the chancel screen with rood and the font but the main influence in the furnishings

was provided by Sir Ninian. Other furnishings include the Georgian pulpit in the new nave, thought to have been part of a three-decker, but with modern stem and the Comper sounding-board and stairs. There is also an early thirteenth-century piscina in the old chancel with two credence niches.

Inside the communion rail is the altar tomb of Nicholas Gaynesford (d.1497) and his family and this may have been used as an Easter Sepulchre; the brasses above were formerly enamelled – an unusual treatment. Other large monuments are to Sir William Scawen (d.1722), a reclining effigy with sarcophagus above (*see fig. 84*), and to Sir John Fellowes (d.1724), a tall, standing wall-monument, without figures, and large, fluted sarcophagus. These are at opposite ends of the south aisle. Sir John Fellowes was one of the directors of the South Sea Bubble financial speculation of 1720 which crashed. Under the eastern arch of the tower is a fine early eighteenth-century railing from the Scawen tomb and next to it a large framed painting of the seventeenth century attributed to Rubens or Jordaens, although more probably by a Rubens pupil. A monument of 1751 to John Braddyll is by the renowned Rysbrack.

126. The monument to Sir John Fellowes at Carshalton.

CATERHAM, St Lawrence

Estimated to have been under construction as far back as the late eleventh century, the original Norman building consisting of nave and chancel was enlarged by the addition of a south aisle or chapel in the twelfth century. This, for reasons unknown but possibly fire, has disappeared, but a north chapel which was added at the same time remains. The north aisle was added about 1220-30. The east end was originally apsed and the beginning of the apsidal curve can be seen by the south wall of the chancel before the latter was extended in the thirteenth century. Being near to collapse, the east wall had to be rebuilt *c.*1790, using clunch and brick, but it was not possible to straighten the roof timbers which lean steeply towards the east.

This is an interesting example of what a simple downland church looked like without nineteenth-century interference. A small timber turret enhances the effect. The church now consists of nave, chancel, north aisle, vestry and porch. The early thirteenth-century priest's door on the south wall of the chancel should also be mentioned. Not in service since 1866 and only occasionally used since refitting in 1927, the church has a somewhat forlorn appearance but, being free of Victorian restoration, gives a good impression of a pre-nineteenth-century village church.

Now redundant, the interior has been swept clear of furnishings. On the central circular pier of the nave arcade is a thirteenth-century stone bracket supported by a monster head which may represent one of the seven deadly sins. The mid-thirteenth-century chancel arch replacing the narrow Norman arch has no capitals, the arches dying into the imposts. The roofs are varied but were improved by the removal of matchboarding in the nave in 1927. One monument of interest is a kneeling figure of Elizabeth Legrew (d.1825) carved by her son.

127.   *St. Lawrence's, Caterham from the south east.*

CATERHAM, St Mary

St. Mary's was built in 1866 by W. & C.A. Bassett Smith opposite the old church of St. Lawrence to cater for the increased population. The church was enlarged and a 126-ft. spire added in 1883; it was further extended in 1916.

Furnishings
The reredos and an iron screen in the chancel are by Comper. The thirteenth-century font came from the old church.

CHALDON, St Peter & St Paul

Chaldon Church is mentioned in Domesday Book. The present building dates mainly from the late twelfth or early thirteenth century and consists of a plain nave and chancel with aisles having round piers (the north being the Lady Chapel and the south a chapel dedicated to St Kateryn). A pleasing south-west tower with shingled broach spire was added in 1843 and there was an overall restoration in 1869-70. Made of flint, St Peter and St Paul's presents a typical Surrey village church exterior set off by the south-west tower.

For such a small and secluded place of worship, this church has unusual features, one of which is of more than local importance. This is the wall-painting (not a fresco but painted on the plaster) on the west wall, discovered during the 1869/70 restoration (*Colour Plate IV*). Dating from *c*.1200 and measuring 17 feet 2 inches by 11 feet 2 inches, it depicts a rare subject, being a mixture of the Ladder of Salvation – a theme of Eastern European origin – and the Last Judgment. Silhouetted on a background of dark red ochre, the small figures are shown trying to climb the ladder in order to reach the heavenly regions above. The iconography of the detailed composition is clearly explained in the church guide.[30] This unassuming village church is rightly noted for its wall-painting which gives such a clear idea of what these pictorial sermons may have meant to an unlettered peasant mind.

Furnishings and bell
The pulpit is made of lizard oak and is a rare example of one dating from the Common-wealth period (1657); it is octagonal in shape and the name Patience Lambert is inscribed on it. The font consists of a monolithic bowl set on an octagonal shaft – a rare type for Surrey. The plaster copy of a bell, hanging in the south aisle, commemorates one that used to hang in the porch until it was stolen. It was of flower-pot shape and was claimed to date from not later than 1250 and, as such, was reputed to be the oldest in England. It was inscribed CAPANA BEATI PAULI. An early Renaissance tablet in the north wall of the chancel dated 1562 has an inscription of rhythmical construction admonishing people to be good to the poor and needy. The remains of a tomb and partially preserved arch in the chancel may have been an Easter Sepulchre. A small lozenge of old glass can be seen in a window of the side chapel.

CHARLWOOD, St Nicholas

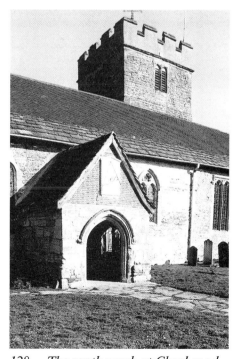

A Norman church was built about 1080, consisting of the present north aisle and the lower part of the tower. To this was added *c*.1280 a south aisle which was expanded to the present nave and chancel *c*.1480, the latter having been built as a chapel in memory of Richard Saunders. Prior to this, a chancel had been constructed *c*.1330 to take the place of what was probably a small apse with altar. The late fifteenth century is also the date of the chancel screen, the finest in Surrey. During restoration in 1858 by William Burges, the wall paintings on the south wall of the nave were discovered.

A typically slow-growth medieval church with an off-centre north tower sited awkwardly between the original and the extended old chancel. The two gables of equal height stretching the full length of the church do not compose well although the lower courses of Horsham slates on the south roof help to relieve the monotony of the hard machine-made tiles. The fifteenth-century south porch has an attractive sundial of 1791.

The windows are of varying dates; they include

128.   The south porch at Charlwood.

a Norman example, which survives on the north side of the nave but the most striking window is the one cut *c*.1300 through the north wall to the west of the old chancel arch; it has two cusped lights supporting an ogee quatrefoil. There are pleasant crown-post roofs.

Furnishings
The outstanding feature – although modest by Devon or East Anglian standards – is the chancel screen of 1480 (*see fig. 45*) which consists of narrow bays with trefoiled heads; above is a vine trail below a repeated motif of winged gryphons holding the initials RS (Richard Saunders who died in 1480). He was related to the Carew family of Beddington and Blechingley and his mother was a Carew heiress. In the centre, angels hold IHS and a crowned M of the Virgin Mary. The cornice may originally have been around the Saunders pew in the chapel and, after being hidden, placed in its present position in the eighteenth century. This hypothesis is supported by the fact that it is in three pieces, which do not fit accurately on the screen.

The wall-paintings on the south side of the nave include the story of St Margaret in three tiers of *c*.1350, and the Three Living and Three Dead of the late fourteenth century. After the Black Death this was a favourite allegory on the inevitability of death, in which three kings meet three skeletons who warn them that, as the skeletons now are, the kings will one day be. The octagonal font may be seventeenth-century and the pulpit is part Tudor/part Jacobean with both linenfold panelling and Jacobean strapwork; the texts all have reference to the 'Word of God'. A muniments chest, with three locks, under the tower, dates from the seventeenth century.

Sir Thomas Saunders, King's Remembrancer of the Exchequer, erected a brass south of the altar in 1553 in memory of his parents, Nicholas and Alys. They are shown in kneeling posture with ten sons and daughters behind.

CHEAM, St Dunstan

This is a large church, built by G.A. Pownall in 1862-64, with a north-west tower and broach spire; the east end is apsed. It took the place of an older church of which the flint chancel, called the Lumley Chapel, survives. There is a blocked thirteenth-century arch to a former south chapel, while in the north wall are two round-headed windows, often attributed to the late Anglo-Saxon period. The roof of the chapel is a most attractive remodelling of 1592 (*see fig. 57*). Along the top of the walls is a plaster frieze whilst the tie-beams are also plastered with a fruit trail. The ceiling is tunnel-vaulted.

The chapel contains the monuments of John, Lord Lumley, who died in 1608, and his two wives, Jane and Elizabeth. That to Lord Lumley consists of a tablet of his pedigree of 16 generations, flanked by two columns and surmounted by strapwork and his coat of arms. Jane, Lady Lumley, who died in 1577 but whose monument was not designed until 1590, kneels in an alabaster panel, while below in front of a tomb-chest are two further panels of kneeling children, all with fanciful architectural backgrounds (*see fig. 70*). Elizabeth, Lady Lumley lived until 1603, although her monument, with a reclining alabaster effigy, was carved in 1592. Lord Lumley was the son-in-law of the Earl of Arundel who completed Nonsuch Palace in 1556 and sold it in 1592 to Queen Elizabeth.

There are six brasses: two of civilians, dating from *c*.1390, one about 3 ft. 6 in. high and one about 12 in. high; one to John Yarde and wife, engraved *c*.1475, with figures less than 7 in. high; one to John Compton and wife of 1458, demi-figures only 9½ in. high; one to William Woodward (d.1459), about 7 in. high, and a palimpsest brass to Thomas Fromonde (d.1542), his wife and eleven children. This has kneeling figures plus St John Evangelist dating from *c*.1420 on one side and a scroll, heart etc., dated 1500 on the other.

An early nineteenth-century monument by Henry Westmacott commemorates Philip Antrobus who died in 1816.

Five of St Dunstan's rectors between the years 1581 and 1662 were later consecrated bishops. The most notable was Lancelot Andrewes (1555-1626) of Winchester, the great scholar, administrator and preacher who supported King James I in his stand against Roman Catholicism. With others, by their sound scholarship combined with their courage and the purity and sanctity of their lives, the Church of England was saved from destruction during the religious strife of the seventeenth century. Bishop Andrewes will also always be remembered for his prayers. His monument is in Southwark Cathedral.

CHELSHAM, St Leonard

The living was presented by William de Wateville to the Prior of Bermondsey in 1158 together with Warlingham, although Chelsham was only a chapel, the benefice today being known as 'United Benefice of Warlingham with Chelsham and Farleigh'. There is no village, the church being built to serve three large houses (almost completely disappeared), and scattered smaller houses and farms in the area. The parish, however, covers about 3,000 acres.

Part of the chancel and south wall go back to the end of the twelfth century but the main structure is thirteenth-century, heavily restored in 1870/71, when a chancel arch, a new east window, new roofs and a new tower top with pierced parapet were added. The 'Sussex cap' (small pyramidal top), shown in the Cracklow drawing, was replaced with a spire. The exterior, with flint walls, is much restored. The interior is aisleless. One two-light window of Reigate stone with quatrefoil in the head and Geometrical tracery on the north side and the two-light square-headed Perpendicular window in the south wall are, however, genuine. The latter's hood-mould has diamond-shaped stops – unusual in the Home Counties. In the south-east corner of the chancel is a single angle shaft which may have been part of sedilia or wall arcading and, opposite, is another with stiff-leaf capital possibly used as an image bracket; next to the latter is a piscina with triangular head. The base of the tower and the tower arch date from the fifteenth century.

Furnishings
The chancel screen of *c*.1530 which originally acted as a parclose to a chantry chapel was cut down in 1871 to half its height (now no more than 3 feet 10 inches) and consists only of the balustrading, capped by a modern cornice, but the iron H-scroll hinges of the doors are original. Some of the bottom panels now form the oak chest which stands in the chancel. A copy of the original complete screen acts as a reredos to the altar. The thirteenth-century font is of Bethersden marble and tapers upwards with central stem and four modern angle shafts. The attractive Royal Arms by Marjorie Wratton commemorate the Coronation of Queen Elizabeth II (*Colour Plate XLIII*). The stained glass is modern glass except for fifteenth-century and seventeenth-century fragments in the north chancel window. The south-west window of the chancel depicts St Leonard holding manacles and St Francis holding a rabbit.

The 'Kelly' Bible and Prayer Book (in a glass case below the tower) are a reminder of Thomas Kelly. After tending his father's sheep, he went to London in 1786, made his fortune as a publisher and became Lord Mayor of London. There are many graveboards (sometimes familiarly called 'bed- heads') in the churchyard.

CHERTSEY, St Peter with All Saints

The church goes back to about 1300 when it probably served as an *ecclesia ante portas* of the great Benedictine Abbey in whose shadow it lay. It was then known as the Church of All Saints, the Abbey itself being dedicated to St Peter. Today, the only medieval parts are the chancel with a fine crown-post roof, the fourteenth-century chancel and tower arch plus the base of the tower. Most of what one now sees dates from the rebuilding of 1806 in a peculiarly unattractive form of Gothic. The original builder contracted to complete and cover the nave roof for £ 6,000. He did this by framing and slating the roof first, supporting it on wooden pillars, but then decamped to America with the money and without having begun the walls. The parish had to find a further £ 6,000 to have these completed by another builder. At the same time, the tower was raised and given a brick top. In 1869, the interior was renewed and in 1878 the chancel walls were strengthened by encasing them in a softer stone than sarsen but similar in appearance.

Situated at the head of the 'T'-junction where Chertsey's three main roads meet, St. Peter's is in the very centre of the town. The tower is an agreeable mixture of rubble freestone and puddingstone patched with brick, but the outer walls of the chancel have been renewed so that, with the later nave faced with Sarsen stone, there is not much medieval texture left. Most unusually, the buttresses are hollow and contain the wooden pillars which the first builder used to support his roof. The path beside the east end used to lead to the Abbey, of which only fragments plus two barns survive.

The muddled work of 1806 has left the church with an unprepossessing nave consisting of square wooden piers, with four small shafts attached at each corner; the piers support amateurish vaults. The nave is of hall type with the side aisles as high as the nave and therefore without clerestories. The chancel with its arch is much better, the arch having two orders of shafts with foliage capitals. Unusual two-bay arcades, as at Chipstead and Merton, decorate the chancel walls. The reredos dates from 1869. The galleries which once ran the whole length of the church were shortened in 1963. At the east end of the south aisle is a Memorial Chapel to those killed in the two World Wars, in the sanctuary of which are some of the Abbey tiles, although not very good examples. In medieval times, Chertsey tiles were famous throughout the country.

Furnishings
The Royal Arms high up on the west wall date from 1811-14. The octagonal font of Caen stone dates from 1845. There are several monuments, but none notable, although they include a Flaxman bas-relief to Emily Mawbey (d. 1819), depicting the raising of Jairus's daughter, and a Westmacott to Sir John Mawbey (d. 1798). There is a tablet in the south aisle to Charles James Fox, the Whig statesman who lived on St Ann's Hill. At the east end of the north aisle is a tablet – 'In the Memory of Nathaniel Rowe of Chertsey Esq. who was the One and Thirtieth Child of His Father John Rowe Esq, a Magistrate'. He died on the '16th Day of December 1778 in the 65th Year of his Age'. Below in another tablet, Mrs. Ann Rowe – presumably the mother of this formidable progeny – is commemorated with others. She died on 18th November 1783, aged 65 years.

Although bells are normally outside the scope of this book, those at St Peter's are of such interest as to warrant an exception. There are eight, the peal being completed in 1859. The oldest is the fifth, cast in 1310 and re-cast in 1380. It came to the church from the abbey at the Dissolution. The Armada Bell is so named as it was cast in 1588. The Curfew is still rung every night from Michaelmas to Lady Day, by the fourth bell. A bell (probably the fifth) is said to have tolled for Henry VI when his body was brought secretly to Chertsey after his murder in the Tower of London. There is also a carillon which plays different tunes after the clock strikes at 8 am, 1, 5 and 10 pm. The Abbey bell (the fifth) is associated with the legend of Blanche Heriot, whose lover (Neville, the nephew of Warwick the Kingmaker), was imprisoned at Chertsey during the Wars of the Roses. As a Lancastrian, he was condemned by the Yorkists to die on the ringing of the curfew. There was a hope of reprieve if he could send his ring as a token to the king (Edward IV). It was sent but the messenger returning with the pardon was delayed so Blanche climbed the curfew tower and heroically clung to the clapper of the bell to prevent it sounding until her lover was reprieved.

To save extensive repair bills, the Anglican, Methodist and United Reformed Churches have agreed to share St Peter's Church and have contributed jointly towards a Church Hall built north-west of the church.

CHESSINGTON, St Mary

Situated in an unpromising area, St Mary's nevertheless retains a village atmosphere together with some medieval features (early thirteenth-century lancets, early south doorway and base of font). Enlarged in the nineteenth century, the spire was restored by Hesketh in 1854 and the south aisle added by Sir Thomas Jackson in 1870.

Furnishings
The sedilia in the chancel south wall consist merely of two blank arches. The furnishings include a fifteenth-century Nottinghamshire alabaster of the Annunciation on the south wall.

129.   *Nottingham alabaster carving at Chessington.*

CHIDDINGFOLD, St Mary

Records go back to the twelfth century when, as a chapelry of Godalming, the church of St. Mary was tranferred *c.*1115 by Henry I from the Crown to Sarum (Salisbury). It was not until 1846 that Winchester took over but, curiously between 1852 and 1873, the patronage passed to distant Lichfield before finally coming to rest with the Crown through the Lord Chancellor.

The main building periods were the thirteenth century and the fifteenth century, with the tower (before it was heightened) started in the fifteenth century but mainly mid-sixteenth. The medieval atmosphere has, however, been seriously compromised by an all-embracing restoration by Henry Woodyer in 1869-70 during which the tower was raised by 14 feet to provide for a ringers' chamber. The effect of this can be compared with the tower as shown in Cracklow's drawing, and the Hassell watercolours of 1828/30.

One enters the churchyard through a lych-gate (1888) roofed with Horsham slabs and with a central oak rest for the coffin-bearers to lay down their burden until the vicar arrived. The church is well situated at the focal point of the village at the bottom of the irregular green, next to a pond and opposite the ancient but much gentrified Crown Inn. On reaching the church, one passes by one of the most interesting features – five thirteenth-century long and deep lancets (three together at the east end and two in the south wall of the chancel, one slightly shorter and one extended downwards to make a low side-window). There is also a thirteenth-century priest's door and, in the south aisle, two low segmented sepulchral recesses which may have been intended for the founders of the extension.

Entering through the rebuilt early fourteenth-century porch and its thirteenth-century doorway, one is struck by the height of the four-bay nave with its long, slender piers. It is a mixture of thirteenth-century and fifteenth-century work and lends distinction to the interior. The chancel is thirteenth-century; so too is the chancel arch which gives added scale, and the north chapel arcade of two bays. The chancel has a crown-post roof of chestnut formerly extending over the chantry chapel. A west gallery for musicians and singers was removed in 1860.

Furnishings
Between 1226 and 1617, Chiddingfold was a centre of the glass-making industry although foreign experts were required to make coloured glass. A reminder of this industry is the window at the west end of the south aisle where 427 fragments of fourteenth-century to sixteenth-century Chiddingfold glass, including 224 coloured pieces, have been leaded together. They were all found on the sites of the glass-working furnaces in the parish – one of the largest in England. A plaque below describes the glass. There is fifteenth-century Dutch glass in the two small windows opposite the organ console, telling the story of Tobias and the Angel. There are piscinas, fourteenth-century in south aisle, thirteenth-century and *c*.1300 in the chancel of which the earlier was converted to an aumbry when, shortly after 1300, a Papal Bull decreed that the celebrant should consume the rinsings. The two chandeliers in the chancel came from a City of London church and are older than the larger one in the nave dated 1786; all are hand-made. The sanctuary lamp from Palestine is about 200 years old. The 1867 font has an unusual pyramidal counterweight-balanced cover. Although Victorian restoration removed most of the old woodwork, seven seventeenth-century benches, including a child's bench, and three exceptionally fine seventeenth-century chairs survive. The oldest is the early seventeenth-century Sussex oak Bishop's chair given by Archbishop Laud; the others, dating from the second half of the century, are of walnut. (The chairs are not on display.) Two hatchments of the Winterton family of Shillinglee hang beside the tower arch.

On the west wall is a memorial to Sir William Bragg, who invented a prototype of the iron lung. There are several small late eighteenth-century tablets with tasteful inscriptions in gold on black marble. On the east wall is a tablet recording the overnight resting-place of Bishop Samuel Wilberforce's body on his last journey to Lavington in July 1873. In the churchyard are several eighteenth-century arched graves, constructed of wedge shaped bricks.

CHILWORTH, St Martha on the Hill

Although not specifically mentioned in Domesday Book, St Martha's must have been one of the three churches attached to Bramley, which was included, for it is known that a Saxon church existed on the site of the nave (with a large tower outside the west door). To this was added early in the thirteenth century a chancel and transepts, when St Martha's was joined to Newark Priory, with which it remained until the Dissolution, when it became Crown property. Eventually, it came under the owners of Chilworth Manor.

An explosion from the nearby gunpowder works in the eighteenth century wrecked the tower and possibly brought down the nave roof, but services continued to be held in the chancel until the roof of that too fell down in 1846. Henry Woodyer carried out a praiseworthy restoration, not copying what was there before but creating a church which blended well with the lonely hilltop site where it stands. Using dark Bargate stone with other sandstone dressings, he built a cruciform place of worship with a low central tower and an interior which is fully in keeping. He started work in 1848 and St Martha's was re-opened in 1850. The benefice was united with that of Albury in 1904. The church has a most romantic setting 573 feet up, about a mile from Chilworth village. Near the east gate of the churchyard there is a memorial tablet to Yvonne Arnaud, the actress whose name lives on in Guildford's theatre. Inside the four, pointed, crossing arches of the tower echo the original arches of *c*.1170 and the archway into which the west doorway was placed.

Furnishings
The tub twelfth-century font came from Hambledon. Two stone coffin lids of unknown origin are to be seen in the chancel. There are several twentieth-century contributions.

CHIPSTEAD, St Margaret

130.   The triangular-headed lancet windows on the north side of the chancel at Chipstead.

St. Margaret's is one of 250 churches in England dedicated to this saint, who was held in great veneration during the Middle Ages. Pleasantly situated, high up and standing alone by a triangular green, this is one of Surrey's best churches, generally Early English in style both without and within. The notable cruciform building dates from the end of the twelfth or the beginning of the thirteenth century, to which period belong the chancel, nave, south aisle

131.   Sir Edward Banks memorial at Chipstead.

and lower storey of the central tower. The windows and doorway of the south aisle are fifteenth-century. It was owned by Chertsey Abbey from Saxon times until the Dissolution. The upper part of the tower dates from 1631. Various alterations were made in the nineteenth century before 1860, including the rebuilding of the south transept by the rector, acting as his own architect. (The old transept had been destroyed by fire in the seventeenth century.) In 1882, a major re-ordering to the designs of R. Norman Shaw took place and this greatly altered the church's appearance. The north aisle was added and the west window, plus the old doorway with dog-tooth moulding of *c*.1175, were replaced by the present ones. The old doorway was re-set in the north wall but is much worn. The main fabric is built of flints with Reigate stone for the dressings. Practically nothing – if anything – remains from the earlier Norman church. The nave roofs sweep down over the aisles preventing the clerestory windows from being seen from outside (*cf.* Merstham). The main attractions are the rows of lancets in the chancel (five recessed) and in the north transept, those in the north wall of the latter having a quatrefoiled oculus above. The lancets on the south wall are renewed.

The interior is as impressive as the exterior. The nave has well-proportioned Early English arcades with circular piers and clerestories of small quatrefoil windows. The lancets in the chancel and transepts, also the door in the north transept, have the unusual feature of being triangular-headed. Stone seats are ranged along part of the north and south chancel walls; they were an early form of seating and have decorated curved arms at each end. Good vaulting, with a lively central boss, is to be seen under the tower. The supporting piers lean outwards, possibly under the increased weight of the tower. The north aisle (rebuilt in 1883) was the work of Norman Shaw who also designed the attractive west doorway and window in neo-Perpendicular style. The roofs are nineteenth-century in date. The advowson went with the Manor except for a period between the sixteenth and the nineteenth centuries. In 1937, it passed to the Archbishop of Canterbury.

Furnishings

The font is a rare Surrey example of Decorated work, octagonal in shape with various tracery patterns; the circular base dates from 1827. Pulpit and reading-desk are Jacobean, the chancel screen fifteenth-century with an early nineteenth-century (probably George III) Royal Arms above. The east window is a replica of one destroyed in the 1939-45 War. St Margaret's suffered considerable air-raid damage in the war. The glass consists of medieval fragments collected by the rector and his wife from elsewhere in the church, except for the four figures in the upper part, which date from 1851. He also executed and leaded windows in the south aisle using several other medieval pieces and in the south side of the chancel. The finest glass, however, is in the high window of the south transept consisting of early fourteenth-century and later fragments with mainly thirteenth-century glass in the centre panels of the three lancets below; the glass is richly coloured. A brass commemorates Lucie Roper (d.1614). The stone monuments include one commemorating the Rev. James Tattershall (d.1784), in the form of an urn placed before an obelisk, by R. Westmacott Senior and, on the south wall of the south aisle, one to Sir Edward Banks (d.1835) who built the former London, Waterloo and Southwark bridges. The three bridges are represented on the memorial, in the centre of which is a bust in a niche.

CHOBHAM, St Lawrence

This is one of the oldest and most interesting churches in the north-west of the county but, like many others in Surrey, has suffered from the attentions of the Victorians. The structure goes back to about 1080 when an aisleless church was built, of which the splays of the Norman windows in the spandrels remain. The south wall was cut through to provide the south arcade and the curiously roofed south aisle in *c.* 1170, but the chancel arch of this building phase has been renewed. The north aisle is a Victorian addition of 1866 and the chancel and south transept followed in 1898. The 52-foot high tower, built of heath or sarsen stone with a lead-sheathed spirelet, dates from about 1400 and the west porch (probably reset) from the fifteenth or sixteenth century.

The main features of the exterior are the tower, the huge roof covering the nave and south aisle sweeping down to eight feet above the ground and the variety of materials used in construction. The deficiency of good stone was overcome by using what was to hand or could be obtained – heathstone for the tower, lead for the spirelet employed in a herring-bone fashion, Horsham slabs and tiles on the catslide roof and a chequerboard of pudding-stone, brick and heathstone on the aisle south wall (*Colour Plate I*).

132. The wooden font at Chobham.

The contrast between the 1170 south and the 1866 north arcades make for an uneven interior but the four-bay south arcade looks well (*see fig.7*). The west bay has heavy square piers, the others being circular with square multi-scalloped capitals. The arches are all pointed with a slight chamfer. The roofing of the south aisle, referred to earlier, consists of detached upright timbers resting on corbels which protrude from the wall and are linked to the rafters of the lean-to roof. There are wind-braces between the wall-plate and the purlin. East of the aisle is the attractive Lady Chapel restored in 1951.

Furnishings
The lead font bowl is panelled in oak and the shaft is of stone; it dates from the sixteenth century although the cover is later. At the foot is a small piece of green marble brought from St Columba's Bay in the Island of Iona. It is one of two fonts in the county using wood for the construction, the other being at Ash. The chest with three locks dates from the thirteenth century. The chandelier over the font was given to the church in 1737. The pulpit was carved by an amateur class of Chobham boys in a shed behind the baker's shop opposite the church in 1893. The oak pews were given as thank-offerings or memorials to relations and the plaques on the ends record their work or hobbies, ranging from those of a stockbroker to those of a housemaid. One with a drum and gate on it commemorates a boy living on a farm locally who became a drummer boy at the age of sixteen in the 1914-18 War and was killed on his first day in France. The War Memorial Screen, erected in 1950, was given by the village as a tribute to their dead from the two World Wars.

In the chancel under an uninscribed blue stone lies Nicholas Heath who was deprived of his office as Bishop of Worcester by Edward VI but returned to favour under Queen Mary when he became Lord Chancellor. He was deprived again both of this office and as Archbishop of York under Elizabeth and was sent to the Tower, but Elizabeth treated him leniently 'believing his mistaken Piety sincere'. She even visited him in his retirement at Chobham Park.

Admirably sited at the bend of the High Street and the focal point of the whole village, St Lawrence is beautifully framed in a spacious and well-kept churchyard. It was not, however, until 1215 that the parish was allowed by Pope Honorius to bury their dead in their own churchyard. Previously, they had to be taken to Chertsey Abbey and, to obtain the concession, 10 lb. of beeswax a year was paid to the Abbey, this being the origin of 'Bee Farm' on Chobham Common. The outward calm one experiences today was not always such, as in 1800, a new vicar found the parish 'sunk in the depths of ignorance and immorality'. So much for looking back with undue nostalgia to the past !

COBHAM, St Andrew

The parish of Cobham (known at the time as *Cofa's Ham*) was granted to Chertsey Abbey shortly after the abbey was founded in 666 and remained under it until the Dissolution. The present church was begun *c*.1150 during the reign of King Stephen and the tower, tower arch and south door date from this period. The first Rector was Aymer de Fureth appointed in 1166. In *c*.1200 the chancel was extended eastwards and a chantry chapel added at the north-east corner. In 1406 Chertsey appropriated the rectory and instituted a vicarage. St Andrew's was originally aisleless with a two-bay arcade between the chancel and chantry chapel. In 1826 a north and in 1854 a south aisle were added when the south doorway and the fifteenth-century windows were moved to their present positions. The Victorians were not content with that, however, and there was further work in 1872 and 1886, and an immediate post-Victorian restoration in 1902, so that the church has been greatly affected by this activity.

The Norman west tower built of carstone and flint, with west door and window above inserted into the tower, both of *c*.1450, and the Victorian north aisle faced entirely with flints, make a pleasing introduction. The north (once chantry) chapel is roofed with Horsham slabs, whilst the south side, where the fifteenth-century windows and Norman south door were reset when the south aisle was built, are rendered with roughcast. The door with inner roll-moulding and prominent zig-zag and an outer hood-mould is much renewed, but still makes a powerful impact. With one exception the four fifteenth-century south windows are original and there is a blocked twelfth-century lancet on the north wall of the chancel.

The interior is virtually all Victorian with modern roofs and four-bay arcades. The piers on the north side are of clustered circular form with circular abaci; those on the south are octagonal with octagonal abaci. The chapel, which was truncated when the north aisle was built, was restored in 1919 and converted into a War Memorial Chapel with stone screen. The tower arch is Norman.

133. Tombstone in Cobham churchyard.

Furnishings

At the west end of the north aisle there is a very colourful pair of stained glass windows, recently restored, depicting the Annunciation and the Nativity. The Annunciation was from a design by Sir Edward Burne-Jones. The seventeenth-century chair behind the altar was given to the church in 1838. The brass chandelier in the middle of the chancel, on a gilded and painted scrollwork pendant, dates from 1730 and has fourteen sconces. A triangular-headed piscina is to be seen in the south-east corner of the north chapel.

There are memorials to Matthew Arnold, the poet (south-east corner of south aisle), to Aminadab Cooper (d.1618) and various ones to members of the Combe family. But St. Andrew's chief attractions are the brasses, one on the south side of the chancel approximately 6 x 4 inches dating from *c*.1550, which is a rare representation on a brass of the Nativity with animals and shepherds – part of a larger composition the remainder of which is lost (*see fig. 63*). The other is a palimpsest on the south jamb of the arch between the chancel and the south aisle. This is conveniently mounted so that one can turn it and see on one side the original figure which is a priest in eucharistic vestments of *c*.1500 and on the other a novel bearded figure of *c*.1550 in armour, possibly James Sutton, a bailiff of the manor. The palimpsest is approximately 18 inches high (*see fig. 65*).

There is a very large mausoleum on the north side of the church to Harvey Christian Combe and family, with a sarcophagus under a canopy. He was a brewer (Watney Combe & Reid) who became Lord Mayor of London: he purchased Cobham Park (then Down Place) in 1806 and died in 1818. Two headstones are of intriguing interest: one, near the west doorway, to the oddly named Karenhappuch Jelly (*see fig. 133*) and the other, at the north-east corner of the church, to David Archibald who died on the '31st February 1880' ! They are much worn and now hard to decipher.

COMPTON, St Nicholas

If, as many believe, the tower of St Nicholas is pre-Conquest, this is one of the most notable Anglo-Saxon survivals in the county. Made of Bargate stone, the masonry and notably the quoins are of high quality. The south-west corner of the nave and the chancel walls appear to be of the same date, but the main fabric is late Norman. This consists of a nave with three-bay arcade, aisles, chancel, tower arch, north and south transepts, south doorway and the extraordinary double sanctuary. Apart from late thirteenth-century lancet windows in the chancel, the fourteenth-century splay-footed shingled spire and the raising of the south aisle in the fifteenth century, there were few other alterations and Woodyer carried out a responsible restoration in the nineteenth century.

One approaches up a slope to the south door, with the ground near the tower raised from the number of burials in this area. The roof sweeps down over the aisle in a catslide (*cf.* Chobham) with three dormers to light the clerestory. The unbuttressed tower is a fine feature.

In the interior there are many signs of restoration especially in the chancel arch, where a plaster moulding replaces the original stone work and crimped decoration is used to provide ornament. (This Surrey feature will be found in Worplesdon and other churches of the county.) Twelfth-century painted murals of lozenge pattern have recently been discovered above the arch. The chancel is long, but the eye is immediately drawn by the very rare feature of the double sanctuary at the east end (*see fig. 15*). A vaulted chamber below is surmounted by a separate chapel above, open to the chancel but protected by a guard-rail of nine arches with thin stems cut from a single plank and this must be some of the oldest woodwork in the country. The purpose of the upper chapel is not known. Contemporary with the sanctuary is a small room to the south with a Norman window which may have been a cell or oratory. On the south side of the chancel arch, the figure of a knight (of end-twelfth-century date) is scratched on the stonework. The nave arcade piers with scalloped capitals are made of clunch (chalkstone) giving a very white appearance to the interior.

Furnishings
The square-bowled font is early Norman and is in the form of an arcade capital. Altar rails, pulpit with tester and tower screen, formerly in the chancel, are all of c.1620. In the east window of the lower sanctuary is a charming tiny panel of twelfth- or thirteenth-century glass, very dark, showing the Virgin and Child. The Virgin holds in her hand the flowering sceptre whilst the Child is in a green robe. Near the font in the west wall of the south aisle is a replica of sixteenth-century Dutch glass depicting the baptism of Christ, the original having been destroyed by bomb damage. The work of Sir Ninian Comper is represented by a window at the east end of the north aisle.

Edward Fulham (d.1694) and family are commemorated by a satisfying late Palladian marble tablet in the porch; this was erected in 1778. There is a canopied fifteenth-century tomb in the sanctuary and part of an early sixteenth-century brass to the Jenyn family in the nave. In the north wall of the north aisle are two Decorated fourteenth-century arches of sophisticated form, part of tombs which have disappeared.

COMPTON, Watts Cemetery Chapel

The Watts cemetery chapel was designed in 1896 by Mrs. G.F. Watts as a memorial to her husband, the late Victorian painter who lived at Limnerslease in Compton. He died in 1904 and is buried in the churchyard in a cloister also designed by Mrs. Watts. The whole structure is a confection of different styles (*Colour Plate XL*) in an attempt by the artist to grope her way to *Art Nouveau*. The Plan is that of a Greek cross with four carved walls between the arms and, inside, a circle with four deep embrasures representing the arms of the cross. By the time that the inside was designed in 1901, *Art Nouveau* forms had been developed, but the effect in the Watts Chapel is far from pleasing to many.

The Chapel is a curiosity to find in the Surrey countryside but provides an opportunity to see what motivated artists at the end of the nineteenth century.

COULSDON, St John the Evangelist

The church is about a mile up from the main Brighton road and is, therefore, away from the town and railway station making a pleasant contrast to the bustle below. Attractively sited on the east side of a large green, although in the midst of suburban development, the mainly thirteenth-century old church has been overtaken by a much larger brick nave and sanctuary added on the south side in 1958 by J.S. Comper and does not amount now to more than an anteroom to the new building. The old church, however, is unrestored. The fifteenth-century west tower of stone and flint culminating in a later truncated pyramid roof with a spike on top, all shingled, gives St John's an individual look and the new church is screened by the old, although the north aisle was rebuilt and enlarged in 1898. In the interior the thirteenth-century features include the west lancets of the north and south aisles, plus attractive blank north and south arcading, resting on circular shafts in the chancel. But the outstanding survival is the very fine sedilia and piscina on the south side of the chancel with detached circular colonettes and richly moulded trefoiled arches. This feature is of more than local importance (*see fig. 20*).

Furnishings
There is a window by C.E. Kempe in the north aisle of *c*.1899. A notable tablet in the south aisle commemorates Grace Rowed (d.1631) in the form of a diptych with segmental pediment. Out of her mouth comes a scroll with writing and there are other emblematical inscriptions.

CRANLEIGH, St Nicolas

Cranleigh was not a separate parish when Domesday Book was compiled but was included in the Manor of Shere; records do not start until 1244 when the living was granted by Roger de Clare to John Fitz-Geoffrey. Whilst there is evidence of an earlier church, possibly late twelfth-century, built in a different (buff) stone, the main building period was the first quarter of the fourteenth century and so St Nicolas is a rare example of a Surrey place of worship constructed in the Decorated style, although this has been much obscured by the heavy hand of William Butterfield in his restoration of 1864-6. The building material used at St Nicolas is carstone, a rough-textured gritty sandstone, and the plan consists of nave with aisles, clerestory without windows, chancel without aisles, western tower and transepts, the last being extended by Butterfield who also added the south porch. An unusual feature of the bulky squat tower, which has a clasping stair-turret at the north-west corner, is the survival of the putlog or scaffold holes. The character is heavy Wealden, similar to that of many Sussex churches.

The interior is spacious with two very wide and high bays on each side of the nave, an effect which is echoed by the wide and high tower and chancel arches. A pair of piers west of the chancel arch now support figures of St John the Evangelist and St Nicolas: they may have been intended for the west arch of a former crossing. The most noteworthy features are the bases of the piers with claw decoration. Other features of interest are the arch above the pulpit, the carved head below the south transept and the corresponding head on the north side in the form of a cat, which many people like to think was the inspiration for Lewis Carroll's Cheshire Cat.

Furnishings

These include large restored fourteenth-century trefoil-headed sedilia, separated by shafts of Sussex marble, and a simple screen in the south transept (once the private chapel of Baynards Park). Fragments of the north transept screen have been worked into the new pulpit. The lectern is a pleasing, perhaps German or Dutch, late sixteenth-century furnishing with a large twisted column for a stem and a strapwork base. The fourteenth-century font is supported on nine octagonal shafts. All the older stained glass was blown out by bomb blast on 27th August 1944. A 1928 window above the font depicts heraldically the history of the church by including the arms of the various patrons of the living from the earliest times. Below the window on the north side of the chancel are fragments of a medieval brass depicting the Resurrection of Christ, all that remains of the brass belonging to the tomb of Robert Harding (Master of the Goldsmiths' Company in 1489), erected in 1504. The figure of our Lord stepping out of the tomb indicates that this monument was part of the Easter Sepulchre. On the opposite side of the chancel on the floor is the brass half-effigy of a priest – probably Richard Carynton, who became rector in 1489 and died in 1507. Further brasses dated 1565 are to be seen in the six arches of the reredos behind the altar and thought to be Flemish work.

The lychgate of 1880 with stone bows underneath a timber roof is a work of distinction, possibly by G.E. Street. In the churchyard a reproduction of an old cross recalls pathetically his first wife, who died only eight weeks after they were married.

CROWHURST, St George

Crowhurst is not mentioned in Domesday Book but the original church may have been built soon after the miraculous intervention of St George in aid of the Crusaders at Antioch in 1098 and therefore dedicated to him. The earliest documentary reference is in a taxation return of 1291: in June 1304, the appropriation of the rectory is recorded after the advowson of the church had been granted by Henry de Guldeford to the Prior and Convent of Tandridge which had been founded as a hospital for three priests, and lay brethren. The church consists of chancel, nave, south aisle and south porch plus a timber steeple, the south aisle being added towards the end of the twelfth century. The chancel was reconstructed with new lancet windows early in the thirteenth century and the east end rebuilt in the early fifteenth century. The latter century also saw the erection of the timber steeple but it had to be rebuilt after a fire in 1947. According to parish register records the church, 'which had lien in heaps a long time', was 'made plain and repaired' in 1652. The damage may have arisen from a Civil War skirmish some few years earlier. Fairly gentle restoration was carried out in the 1860s. The exterior forms a harmonious composition of Wealden stone and Horsham slate roof with a fine vertical emphasis in the weatherboarded belfry and tall and shingled splay-footed spire. With minor exceptions, the windows are all medieval, ranging from the thirteenth century to the sixteenth.

The interior is simple, with a through vista to the fifteenth-century east window, due to the removal of the chancel arch (at a date unknown), and unaisled except for a single-bay south aisle entered through a pointed arch of *c*.1190. The roofs of the nave and chancel are of collar-and-rafter type, the chancel roof dating from the early fifteenth century and the nave roof possibly earlier.

Furnishings
The font is an awkward thirteenth-century design, square at base changing to octagonal top with the aid of broaches, on a central stem with four shafts at the corners. The pulpit was made of sixteenth-century panels and replacing an earlier one. Fragments of medieval glass remain, consisting of fifteenth-century glass in the tracery of the east window, depicting angels and seraphim under canopies, and heraldic sixteenth-century glass in the main lights of this window and in the middle window on the north side of the nave.

St. George's is well-known for its Gainsford monuments although these are not remarkable artistically. Three medieval tomb-chests in the chancel include two to members of the family – John Gainsford the elder (d.1450) and John the younger (d.1460). The former of Purbeck marble is without canopy and the chest has panelled sides containing plain shields within quatrefoils; the latter with battlemented canopy is a more elaborate affair, decorated with the badge of a grapnel or four-fluked anchor, grotesques and even an otter. The third, although canopied, is unnamed. All three tomb-chests have brasses on top, the one of the younger Gainsford being a lively composition. Nicholas Gainsford, commemorated on the north wall of the nave, belonged to the Carshalton branch of the family (q.v. Carshalton). Perhaps, however, the most interesting monument is the cast-iron slab on the chancel floor to Anne Forster (d.1591), a reminder of the Wealden iron works. As well as the inscription, there is a figure enveloped in a shroud between panels showing Anne's two sons and two of the five daughters. Symbolic of the Resurrection, this macabre fashion in monuments was beginning to become popular.

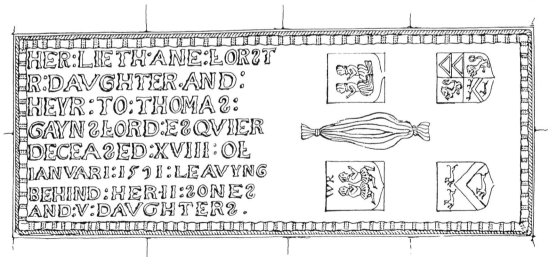

134.   Iron tomb-slab to Anne Forster at Crowhurst.

The churchyard contains several old headstones, probably of the late seventeenth century, near the east end of the church, but is most famous for its huge yew-tree – 33 feet in circumference. The hollowed trunk was fitted with seats in the early nineteenth century.

CROYDON, St John the Baptist

Domesday Book says of Croydon – 'Here is a Church' – and an Anglo-Saxon will of 960 was witnessed by Elfsies the Priest of Croydon. The church was founded in the tenth century, rebuilt in the Perpendicular style at the end of the fourteenth or the first half of the fifteenth century and was almost completely destroyed by fire on the night of 5th January 1867 during a gale and blinding snowstorm. Only the 124-foot west tower, the two-storeyed south porch and charred walls remained standing. The size of St John the Baptist Church – the largest parish church in Surrey – was undoubtedly due to generous contributions by successive Archbishops of Canterbury who, until 1780, had a favourite summer residence at Croydon and, only as recently as 1985, did Croydon cease to be a peculiar of Canterbury. The Archbishop's Palace is now the Palace School. Sir George Gilbert Scott rebuilt the damaged church to the original design except for adding outsize pinnacles to the tower and it was re-consecrated on 5th January 1870, three years to the day after the disaster.

The medieval aspect of the exterior – although much restored – is retained and, despite the complete transformation of the surroundings, still imposes with its lofty tower and the size of the building. The Scott pinnacles, however, are not as pleasing as those shown in Cracklow's drawing.

By contrast, the interior, whilst retaining the plan and style of the pre-fire building is – with its expensive furnishings – that of a Victorian town church. The six-bay (originally five) arcade has tall piers with four shafts and four hollows supporting moulded arches: the windows both in the clerestory and aisle have three lights. The two chantry chapels, one dedicated to St Mary probably of *c.*1400, at the east end of the north aisle and the other to St Nicholas founded about 1443, at the east end of the south aisle, were dissolved in the reign of Edward VI. The latter was reconstituted in 1912 when the present reredos and panelling were dedicated and the former was refurnished in 1951. The lower storey of the south porch is vaulted. Among survivals are two large fourteenth-century corbels at the west end of the south aisle.

Furnishings

Inevitably most of the furnishings are Victorian but a notable exception, to which pride of place must go, is the fine fifteenth-century brass lectern with eagle on a robust stem and resting on three small lions (*Colour Plate XIV*). A fifteenth-century stoup also survived the fire; it has a crocketed gable and a cusped arch. The Victorian octagonal font is made of alabaster with a cover which is adorned with carved figures of St John the Baptist and three of the Croydon archbishops. The pulpit is finely carved with statuettes of Christ and six saints, including the four evangelists who bear their symbols on plaques. The choir stalls have various carvings on the finials including grotesques. The reredos is made of coloured alabaster. The most interesting, however, of the Victorian furnishings is the screen separating St Nicholas Chapel from the chancel, as incorporated in the carvings are 34 birds known as 'The Hovering Birds', a very rare form of decoration. A wall-painting on the north wall of the chancel is a fresco of the Feeding of the Five Thousand and dates from 1885.

Of the six archbishops buried in the church, the best known is Archbishop Whitgift (d.1604) who was a great benefactor of the town. His monument in St Nicholas Chapel was badly damaged during the fire but was restored in 1888. It is of alabaster with recumbent effigy in prayer and decorated with many diocesan and college coats of arms. The stained glass behind the tomb illustrates the Hospital Almshouses and the Trinity School building which were founded and endowed by the archbishop. The monument in the south aisle to Archbishop Sheldon (d.1677), who endowed the Sheldonian Theatre in Oxford, was the most ornate and was approached by a flight of four steps; he reclines on a pillow. Unfortunately it has been sadly mutilated although the effigy and sarcophagus were restored in 1959.   Of the others, all that remains is a badly damaged marble tablet commemorating Archbishop Grindall (d.1583).

Among secular people, there is a tomb-chest in the St Nicholas Chapel thought to commemorate Thomas Warham (d.1478); the brasses on the rear panel of the tomb recesses were probably torn out during the Reformation period. In the south-west corner of the south aisle are fragments in a recess tomb of a monument to Nicholas Heron (d.1568) with herons figuring in the coat of arms. On the other side in the north aisle is a late fifteenth-century tomb discovered during restoration in 1859 and re-erected when the new church was built. A thirteenth-century double piscina, one of the stones salvaged from the fire, rests on the tomb. A Grecian portrait tablet in the north aisle commemorates the American artist, J.S. Copley, who died in Croydon in 1815. Brasses include an oblong one to Elis Davy (d.1455), in the south aisle, one to Gabriel Silvester (d.1512), shown as a priest in vestments on the south pier of the chancel arch and, on the opposite pier, two brasses of William Heron (d.1562) and his wife Alse. In the south aisle, a small brass depicts the seven daughters of William Heron (d.1544) and, facing the Sheldon monument, is an inscription – the oldest in the church – to the memory of Giles Seymore (d.1390).

CROYDON, St Michael and All Angels, with St James

A short step from modern twentieth-century Croydon, with its tall office blocks, lies one of Surrey's finest nineteenth-century places of worship, designed by John Loughborough Pearson and built in 1880-3. The church is large but the intended tower and spire, as at Pearson's other notable buildings in the South of London (St Peter's, Vauxhall and St John the Evangelist, Upper Norwood) were never built. At St Michael's, only the base of the south-west tower was constructed. The building material is red brick outside and light brown inside. In the exterior the absence of vertical emphasis detracts from the overall visual pleasure of this building. French influence is apparent in the apse clasped by turrets with pyramidal caps and in the copper flèche over the crossing. There are transepts and a south-east Lady Chapel.

The interior, however, is a tour de force described by Sir Nikolaus Pevsner as 'one of the most satisfying of its date anywhere',[31] without chancel arch and dominated by the huge Hanging Rood designed in 1924 by Cecil Hare. Mostly of brick with high wide stone-ribbed vaults, the strong vertical emphasis and the exquisite proportions make a noble place in which to worship, with furnishings living up to the architecture. The apse is enclosed with acutely pointed stone arches between which are finely wrought iron grilles; a tiny ambulatory runs behind. A particularly attractive part is the Lady Chapel, which has its own nave and aisles of equal height separated by the slenderest of shafts. It is entered through a beautiful arcade and is built of stone with intricate vaulting over the altar. Decoration and furnishings were by Sir Ninian Comper.

Furnishings
The font with canopy, the pulpit also with canopy and the richly gilded organ case, and the clock in the north transept are all by G.F. Bodley, except for the font cover which is the work of J.L. Pearson's son (F.L.). The choir stalls were by Temple L. Moore, and C.E. Kempe made some of the stained glass from 1895 onwards (east window, north chapel and east end).

CUDDINGTON, St Mary

Cuddington is a small parish two miles north-east of Ewell. The ancient church, together with its manor house and village, were swept away by Henry VIII to make room for Nonsuch Palace. The present church (St Mary) was built by A. Thomas in 1894/5.

DORKING, St Martin

Dorking parish church was mentioned in Domesday Book. Prior to the present place of worship there was a medieval one dating from the fourteenth century and a later undistinguished structure of 1835-36. The present place of worship was built during the ten years 1868 to 1877. The south chancel chapel did not follow until 1912. The tall west tower and spire is an arresting sight from wherever one looks at it and nowhere better than in descending the road from Ranmore Common to the town. The steeple is 210 feet high (*see fig. 95*), built in memory of Bishop Samuel Wilberforce who was killed in a riding accident near Dorking in 1875. The Bishop acquired the nickname of 'Soapy Sam' at one point in his career when he gained an unfair reputation for being evasive.

Internally, the excellent proportions, the acutely pointed arches and the richly shafted chancel arch all combine to create a satisfying vertical emphasis.

135. St. Martin sharing his cloak with the beggar as depicted on the pulpit at Dorking.

Furnishings
The pulpit, which is thought to have come from the Netherlands about 1857, incorporates a panel, which is probably seventeenth-century, depicting St Martin cutting his cloak in half to share it with a beggar who stood shivering in the cold. The altar fittings are very seemly consisting of two large candlesticks and a corona of suspended oil lamps only one of which is left. There is a mosaic by Powell of the Crucifixion over the chancel arch dating from c.1890. The frequently rebuilt organ was last reconstructed by Hill, Norman and Beard in 1933. Historically interesting are the large stone slabs near the west end, containing lists of the Archbishops of Canterbury and Bishops of Winchester and Guildford. St Martin's can well claim to be Woodyer's finest and largest church in Surrey. The church has been shared with the Methodists since January 1973.

DUNSFOLD, St Mary and All Saints

St. Mary and All Saints is not mentioned in Domesday Book as it was part of the manor of Bramley in the parish of Shalford. Mainly built between 1260 and 1290, the church is first referred to in the 1291 tax return and the first rector was presented in 1294. In 1305, the right of presentation of Shalford with Duntesfeld (Dunsfold) was granted by Edward I to the Hospital of St Mary at Spital without Bishopsgate, a priory of Augustinian Canons. At the Dissolution of the Monasteries, the advowson reverted to the Crown and still today rests with the Lord Chancellor.

Situated on high ground about half a mile from Dunsfold village, St Mary and All Saints is a notable example of a Surrey village church of the late thirteenth century, transitional between the Early English and Decorated styles. The masonry shows a sophistication which puts it above the average of such churches in the county and this is probably due to it being under the patronage of the Rector of Shalford, a Crown living, at the time of the main building work and thus benefiting from the skill of royal masons. It is exceptional in the harmony of style, its main fittings being the old oak pews, the double piscina and sedilia, and the ironwork of the south door with its 12½-inch key. William Morris – with what must be regarded as hyperbole – called St Mary and All Saints 'The most beautiful country church in all England'.[32] The remoteness of the site may be due to the need to build above the flood level of a tributary of the River Arun, plus the fact that it may well have been a pre-Christian burial ground, the mound on which the church stands being thought to be artificial: it is also near a holy well with a reputation for miraculous cures of eye diseases.

The windows, except for the slightly later west window of three lights intersected and cusped, have late Geometrical bar tracery, the east window being raised in the nineteenth century. The outer walls are made of Bargate stone (Surrey's best building material) which is galleted (ironstone chips inserted in the mortar). The fifteenth-century shingled bell-turret together with the west window and wall were all rebuilt in 1892. The south porch may be as early as the thirteenth century, but the outer doorway is Tudor.

The interior is cruciform with transepts at different levels, both containing piscinas and the south used as a Lady Chapel. There are no aisles but there are indications that a south aisle may have been contemplated. The deep splays of the windows result in an uneven wall surface. A string course runs right round with delicate mouldings in the chancel. The chancel arch was heightened and widened in the nineteenth century and now has no capitals.

Furnishings

Dunsfold church is famous for its thirteenth-century pews (*see fig. 30*), probably the oldest in the country although the seats have been widened and the backs filled in. The ends are carved into delicate whorls with cusps below and pricket holes for candles above. At floor level, holes were cut in the walls to enable water to be sluiced through for cleaning and three of the ducts can be seen externally beside the south door; although blocked up on the inside, the old wooden plugs secured by chains are still in place. The double-piscina with aumbry shelf above and three stepped sedilia seats are of particular interest. The mouldings are delicately carved and the seats are separated by colonettes of Sussex marble ('winkle stone'). The south door has long plain iron strap-hinges, closing ring, key escutcheon and large oak lock-case; there is also an arched fillet of iron strengthening the top, a rare feature. Protracted use of the 12½-inch key (kept by the Rector) has caused the wards to turn almost at right angles to the stem. The Sussex marble font is of uncertain date with a seventeenth-century cover. The well preserved George IV Royal Arms date from 1828.

EAST CLANDON, St Thomas of Canterbury

This is the only church in Surrey dedicated to Thomas à Becket although he was a very popular saint in medieval England. Its history, however, goes back much further than the martyrdom (29th December 1170) and it is not on the line of the so-called Pilgrims' Way. It is probable that the original charter of Chertsey Abbey included the Manor of *Clanedune* and a church at this place was mentioned in Domesday Book. It remained under the Abbey until the Dissolution and its influence in the medieval church is very evident with the monks using the chancel for worship and the parishioners an altar in the north aisle. Construction goes back to 1110 when the broad nave was built and much of this work remains in the fabric today. The chancel with its widely spaced and deeply splayed twin lancets was extended, four other lancets inserted and the two-bayed north aisle (not the present one) added in the early part of the thirteenth century, but it was not until the fourteenth century that Chertsey's greatest abbot (John Rutherwyk) restored and consolidated the whole structure. From the low-side window on the north side of the chancel, dating from this time, a bell would probably be rung at the elevation of the host so that workers in the field could stop for a moment in silent prayer. The chancel arch is also fourteenth-century and there are traces on it of stonework and timbers which would have supported the rood screen.

136.   Church of St Thomas of Canterbury, East Clandon from the east.

After the Dissolution, St Thomas's passed into the care of Sir Anthony Browne, Master of the King's Horse, who converted the monastic building into a parish church. The living was vacant during the Civil War. Today patronage rests – as at West Clandon with which the benefice is now united – alternately between the Bishop of Guildford and the Earl of Onslow. During the eighteenth century and nineteenth century St Thomas's fell into a bad state of repair but, in 1900, restoration, including re-erection of the bell-turret with retention of part of the fifteenth-century framing, was undertaken by Sir Thomas Jackson, who also added a new north aisle with an attractive mock-Jacobean plaster ceiling designed by H.S. Goodhart-Rendel.

The church forms an attractive accompaniment to one of the few real villages in this part of Surrey. Material comprises flint, local chalkstone and brick infilling. There is a late thirteenth-century doorway on the north side with a shouldered lintel. Underneath the bell-turret is a blocked doorway which may at one time have been the entrance to the church.

Within the interior the authentic early medieval fabric has Perpendicular details and good fifteenth-century roofs of crown-post type at the east end. A Tudor-bricked arch is to be seen in the tower. One wide single arch on sturdy cylindrical piers with circular capitals (their size gives some indication of the magnitude of the old north aisle) leads into the north aisle where there are remains of what may have been a chantry chapel; a doorway and steps lead down from what was probably a rood loft. It was clearly the intention to extend the arcade westwards. The delicate plasterwork in the north aisle by Goodhart-Rendel is centered on Thomas à Becket, who is in bishop's robes, flanked on each side by the four patron saints of the British Isles (St. Andrew, St David, St George and St Patrick). Above Bishop Thomas, the Holy Spirit is represented in the form of a dove and below is a pelican on her nest; at the base a small fishing boat can be seen and the whole is bordered by a rich design of grapes and vine leaves. The ceiling was designed as a memorial to Lord Rendel, at one time the patron of the living and the owner of Hatchlands. Beneath it also lies his tomb, a Neo-Jacobean tomb-chest with canopy to Stuart, Lord Rendel (d.1913) by Goodhart-Rendel. The Rendels were descendants of Admiral Boscawen (1711-61) who built Hatchlands.

Furnishings
The plain eighteenth-century font with bulging baluster stem near the altar has a pleasing cover designed in 1948 by Goodhart-Rendel. Six hatchments to members of the Aungier family (patrons in the seventeenth century), who were ennobled to become Earls of Longford, are raised up on the west and east ends of the nave. The communion rail is a plain late seventeenth-century example with modern top-rail. Royal Arms, probably of early eighteenth-century date, are placed at the western end under the hatchments. A damaged thirteenth-century piscina lies at the entrance to the north aisle, which is now used as a Lady Chapel.

EAST HORSLEY, St Martin

At the south end of the long straggling village of East Horsley lies the parish church of St. Martin. It is possible that the lower stages of the west tower go back to pre-Conquest times, but most of the building one sees today stems from a comprehensive renewal by H. Woodyer in 1869 and one has to look hard to find anything medieval in the fabric. However the latest extension of a north transept by Raymond Syms completed in 1982 has been carried out with sensitivity and adds to the visual pleasure of the interior.

The west tower lies close to the road and is, therefore, immediately dominant. The removal of stucco from the lower two stages has exposed what appears to be Saxon flintwork. Above these is a third stage added or rebuilt in brick with a battlemented parapet but unfortunately still stuccoed. The middle stage is lit on three sides by single lancets which date from the twelfth century, but those on the north and south sides have eighteenth-century brickwork lining the stone window frames. The west doorway of the late twelfth century has an almost complete round-headed Saxon window above it. The clock dates from the early seventeenth century although the single hand may be older. Horsham slabs which once covered the roof and the south porch have been replaced by tiles.

137.   East Horsley Church from the south west.

Apart from the brasses and monuments, medieval features of the interior are confined to the thirteenth-century chancel arch with original capitals, but jambs with attached half-columns were retooled in 1869. The two westernmost bays of the north aisle are also probably original thirteenth-century work retooled. A new tower arch has been inserted containing the remains of the twelfth-century arch. The rest is by Woodyer or later but by raising the chancel arch and in other ways he has produced an interior of unexpectedly good proportions. The addition of the north transept by Raymond Syms has further enhanced its appearance. East of these lay a chantry chapel, but this was absorbed in 1869 into the aisle and the south wall of the chapel replaced by a two-bay extension of the arcade. Apart from the two fifteenth-century windows with cinquefoil lights in the north aisle, most of the other windows are nineteenth-century lancet windows. Three of these in the east wall of the rebuilt chancel were subsequently blocked and above the altar stand two pleasing effigies of St Elizabeth of Hungary and St Martin of Tours.

Furnishings
Pulpit and font date from the 1869 renewal and the only medieval glass consists of the fragments of sixteenth-century and possibly earlier glass in the north aisle windows. Above the tower arch is a mourning hatchment to William Currie. The alabaster table-tomb in the north aisle to Thomas Cornwallis, groom porter to Queen Elizabeth, (d.1596) and his wife Katherine, who was married to him for 30 years and survived him for the same period until her death in 1626 at the age of 85, immediately claims one's attention. Although the effigies are stiff and lack vitality, the work is well executed. Miniature figures representing their two

sons, Robert who died as a young man and Henry as a child, kneel beside their father; an achievement (coat of arms) is affixed to the wall behind. A well-executed Rococo cartouche commemorates James ffox (d.1753).

The brasses consist of a fourteenth-century half-figure, 13 inches high, beside the chancel arch to Robert, the brother of Thomas de Brentyngham, Bishop of Exeter, a fifteenth-century example in the north aisle to John and Alys Snellying (dated 1498), whose six sons and five daughters are shown on a separate brass panel below the inscription, and to Thomas and Jone Snellinge (dated 1504) in an incomplete floor slab on the south side of the nave. The figures are missing but those of their eight sons and five daughters remain. But the most interesting brass is the fifteenth-century one on the north-east side of the sanctuary to John Bowthe, Bishop of Exeter, an unusual design showing him kneeling in mass vestments with mitre and crozier. Below him is an inscription stating that he died in 1478 and was buried in the church (*see fig. 60*). The see owned a manor at Bishopsmead in the parish which Bishop Bowthe left for the benefit of the poor of the parish.

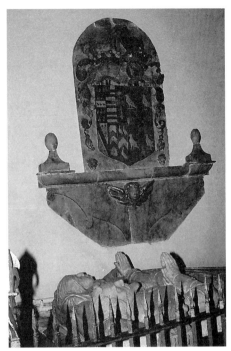

138. The achievement of Thomas Cornwallis in East Horsley Church.

In the north-east corner of the churchyard is a mausoleum where William, Earl of Lovelace, was buried in 1893 and, in the south-west corner, a gazebo where the youngest choir boy was posted to watch for the Lovelaces approaching the church so that the rector would know when to start the service (*Colour Plate XXXI*).

EAST MOLESEY, St Mary the Virgin

The first mention of a church in Molesey was in 1190 when Gilbert the Norman endowed Merton Priory with the church at Kingston and the chapelry of Molesey. Neither the priory nor the church seems to have taken much interest in the building at Molesey as it frequently fell into a bad state of repair. In the latter half of the eighteenth century, the living of East Molesey was made independent and constituted a perpetual curacy. The old church with bell tower and splay-footed spirelet was damaged by fire in December 1863 and, although reparable, the growth in the village made it desirable to build a larger church – a project which had been under consideration even before the fire – and in 1864-65 a new place of worship to the design of Talbot Bury was constructed, a tower being added shortly after. North and south aisles were built in 1862 and 1883, that to the south by Charles Bury Jun., and the chancel extended by about 24 feet in 1926.

Furnishings
Brasses and monuments from the old church can be seen in the tower whilst, next to the lectern, is a brass plate to Anthonie Standen (d.1611), 'cup-bearer to the King of Scotland sometime Lord Darnley, father to King James now of England and also sworn servant to

His Majestie'. A window in the south aisle commemorates Alfred Gillott, whose father was the inventor of the steel pen nib which followed the quill. The carved wooden screen and pulpit were erected in memory of his wife by Mr. Claude Staniforth, a churchwarden for many years.

EAST MOLESEY, St Paul

Built by Salter and Laforest in 1854, a tower was added in 1888. There are Kempe windows in the baptistry (1891) and a north aisle window, dated 1899, by him of the Crucifixion.

EAST SHEEN, Christ Church

The spread of population in the southern part of the parish of Mortlake in the mid-nine-teenth century created a need for a new church in the area and Arthur William Blomfield (son of a former Bishop of London, then only 33 and living in East Sheen) was engaged to build it. He based his design on thirteenth-century Northern French style using Bargate stone, with Bath stone quoins and dressings. The foundation stone was laid on 17th June 1862. All was ready for consecration in March 1863 when, the day after the workmen had left, Blomfield had the mortification of learning that the 92-ft tower which had just been completed had collapsed owing to a fault in the foundations. Blomfield was exonerated but the rebuilding of the tower delayed consecration until 13th January 1864. The tower has a pyramid roof and the aisles are cross-gabled. The north aisle was added in 1887. This place of worship is of interest as being one of Sir Arthur Blomfield's first works, although it has been criticised for over-ornateness and his use of side gables to the aisle. The nave contains four bays and the arcade columns and smaller shafts are of Whitehaven stone, slate and serpentine. Incised black and white plaster decorates the arches – an unusual feature. Considerable restoration and repair has been carried out since, especially that caused by incendiary and bomb damage during the 1939-45 War.

Furnishings
Of the furnishings, the dwarf chancel screen and the pulpit are of alabaster and the font is supported on four columns of Devonshire marble with a central shaft bearing eight angels; the carved bowl is inlaid with Devonshire spar.
   Christ Church has had close associations with members of the Royal Family living in East Sheen Lodge and White Lodge, strengthened in 1889 by the marriage of the Earl of Fife with Princess Louise, daughter of Edward VII, whose favourite home became East Sheen Lodge.

EFFINGHAM, St Lawrence

The church of St Lawrence is first mentioned by John of Salisbury as having been given by the Bishop of Winchester in about 1147 to the monks of Merton Priory, but it appears that at first they were deprived of the gift and it was not until John had interceded with the Pope (Adrian IV) that they were confirmed in their living. In 1388, the Priory was ordered by the Bishop of Winchester, William of Wykeham, to repair the chancel which had been allowed to fall into a state of neglect. At the Dissolution, the patronage was assumed by Henry VIII and remained with the Crown until 1866. It now rests with Keble College, Oxford. The church was sweepingly restored in 1887, losing most of its medieval character. Externally the restoration has left the church featureless, the brick tower of 1759 having been replaced by an unattractive stone one, but it is possible that the right-hand head on the hood mould of the north-west chancel window represents a prior of Merton.

Although restoration has given the interior a nineteenth-century look, there was some compensation later in 1933 when the crown-post roof of the south transept dating from *c.*1250 was uncovered. The transept which is larger than the chancel was probably built originally by Merton Priory at that time. The two modern lancets replace a single lancet. The early fourteenth-century east window of the chancel retains its original tracery and the north-west window is probably also of this date.

Furnishings
High up under the tower is a well-executed reclining effigy and mourning figure commemorating Maria Parratt (d.1844). In the churchyard to the south of the porch is a headstone to Sir Barnes Wallis, inventor of the bouncing bomb which was used to such destructive effect on the Möhne Dam during the 1939-45 War.

EGHAM, St John the Baptist

This late Georgian church, evoking mixed reactions, was built of brick in 1817-20 by Henry Rhodes to take the place of one in a bad state of repair and too small. The latter had succeeded a Norman predecessor of the early twelfth century which came under Chertsey Abbey. The fifteenth-century lych-gate with attractive spandrels (the former porch) and a tablet of 1327 with beautiful Roman and Saxon type lettering recording the rebuilding of the chancel by Chertsey's famous Abbot Rutherwyk are the only reminders of the old church. Rhodes' building is classical in design, depending for its effect entirely on straight lines, with rounded corners, and the minimum of ornamentation. The square shape is relieved by the west tower composed of belfry, then an oval stage, followed by a pyramidal cap and finally a small tempietto on top.

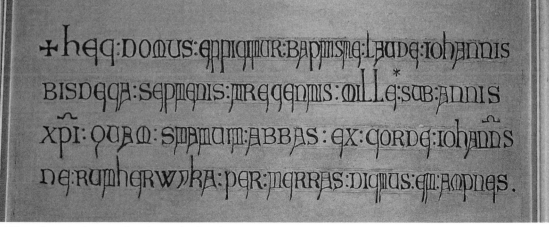

139.   *Inscription in the chancel of Egham Church recording the rebuilding of the chancel of its predecessor by Abbot Rutherwyk in 1327.*

140.   Egham Church – exterior from the south west.

Its interior is noteworthy for its large unsupported ceiling, segmental chancel arch and sweeping gallery. At the west end there is a smaller and more elegant gallery with the organ in the middle. The sanctuary is narrow with a mural altar-piece by Hans Feibusch of 1951 which took the place of an earlier painting by Westall, largely destroyed by arson in 1949. The gallery carries replicas of the coats of arms of the 25 barons chosen as sureties to defend Magna Carta signed on 15th June 1215 on nearby Runnymede.

Furnishings
Sanctuary tablets bear the Commandments and are made in marble with excellent gilded lettering. The simply designed pulpit, although known to be over 200 years old, is of uncertain date, with a fine inlaid tester and double door, still with original latch and catch. It was placed in the church in 1948 but was previously at Little Livermere Church in Suffolk. The Royal Arms on the north side are an excellent 1660 example (Charles II). The pews are ill-designed and set up on platforms. The south-east chapel, dedicated in 1948, contains a most interesting collection of chairs given in honour of famous names in English church history. English oak doors to the tower commemorate the Coronation in 1952 and bear the Royal Arms above with those of Canterbury and Guildford on the doors.

The outstanding features of the church are the monuments, especially that to Sir John Denham, probably by Maximilian Colt. Sir John was Chief Baron of the Exchequer under James I and died in 1638. It is of the Resurrection type and shows him rising from the grave in his winding-sheet on Judgment Day, whilst his wife languishes in the charnel house below in which lie 'skeletons and bodies gruesomely hugger-mugger' (Nairn).[33] This type of monument was made fashionable by that to John Donne (dating from 1631) by Nicholas Stone in St Paul's Cathedral. The Denham monument is on the staircase in the vestibule to the west gallery; on the other side is a monument to Lady Cecile Denham (d.1612), his first wife, and Lady Eleanor Denham, his second. This is a very naturalistic painted representation of the two women, the second holding her eldest son, the future poet.

In the body of the church at the east end there is a frontal marble demi-figure of Sir Robert Foster (d.1663) in a circular frame and, at the east end of the side aisle, a large memorial to a young officer who distinguished himself as the right-hand man of the Duke of Wellington at Waterloo. In the gallery is a memorial to the Duke's sister, Lady Anne Culling Smith, and in the same aisle is an Elizabethan monument in veined alabaster to Richard Kellifet, an official in the Queen's Household. Various Grecian tablets in the chancel of early nineteenth-century date to the Gostlings are not of particular note. A brass plate of 1596 commemorates Anthony Bond. Near the western entrance to the churchyard lies a flat grave stone to the last man – a Frenchman – to be killed in a duel in England. Press reports in the church describe the incident in detail.

141.   Elstead Church – bellcote.

ELSTEAD, St James

The original church was built *c.*1138 on two acres of land given by the Bishop of Winchester to the monks of Waverley Abbey, under whom it remained until the Dissolution when it became a chapelry in the care of the rectors of Farnham. The first resident priest came to Elstead in 1829. Despite the bellcote, the north porch, the nave roof and the graceful three-light east window (the best feature), the church generally has a much restored appearance. The south aisle was added by Henry Garling in 1872 when the remains of a gallery beneath the bellcote were removed. The nineteenth century is also responsible for the unsightly window with plate tracery in the otherwise attractive west end. The lancet windows east of the porch in the nave and another in the chancel are of interest.

Furnishings
There is little of note but among the curiosities are the bellcote stair which is constructed of a solid baulk of timber cut into steps and the pointed wooden arch above the door into the church. The panelled chest is either Elizabethan or Jacobean and there is a fragment of old glass in the window by the pulpit. The font dates from 1845.

ENGLEFIELD GREEN, St Simon and St Jude

This church is the product of an architect whose desire to be original outstripped his architectural maturity – Edward Buckton Lamb (1806-69), who also built at Addiscombe. The foundation stone was laid on 28th October 1858 and the building was completed in eight months, dedication being on 5th July 1859. The building materials were Kentish rag with Bath stone dressings outside, and the use of these stones plus brick in alternate polychrome bands inside gave rise to the contemporary comment that the church was 'notoriously harlequinized' and that 'gaudy and variegated colours and workmanship' had been 'displayed'.[15] The style is mid-fourteenth-century. Although of cruciform design, the placing of the tower on the south transept and the longer arm of the nave away from the road produces a muddled composition. The font is of Caen stone.

The two curious little brick Gothic gabled mausolea in the churchyard next to the road are to the Fitzroy Somerset family and are probably also by Lamb (*see fig. 99*).

EPSOM, St Martin

St. Martin's, the parish church of Epsom, is almost entirely a building of the nineteenth and early twentieth centuries, apart from the fifteenth-century Perpendicular north-west tower, with higher stair turret, taking the place of an earlier church which had fallen into disrepair. The flint-and-stucco west end in Commissioners' Gothic and the nave, with thin piers and aisles of nearly the same height, were built in the 1820s to the designs of Charles Hatchard of Pimlico. It was opened in September 1825. The east end with crossing and transepts was begun by Sir Charles Nicholson in 1907 and is in quite a different style. The latter uses stone of a brown-brick colour but also flint chequer.

Furnishings
The fifteenth-century font is octagonal, with quatrefoil panels. Among the monuments is a notable tablet to Elisabeth Evelyn (d.1691) with barley-sugar Corinthian columns and a predella, splendidly carved. She was the first to claim the right for a market and two fairs to be held in Epsom. Other monuments include two by Flaxman: John Brathwaite (d.1800), and J.H. Warre (d.1801), both with a standing woman and an urn; one by Chantrey to Susan Warre (d.1821), a kneeling figure holding a baby, and one to John Rowe (d.1810) by John Bacon Jun. with two women, an urn and a pedestal. St Martin's has a copy of the 'Vinegar' Bible dated 1717. These bibles mistakenly used the word 'vinegar' instead of 'vineyard' in the heading to chapter 20 of St Luke's Gospel.

EPSOM, Christ Church, Epsom Common

Christ Church was founded in 1843 as a Chapel of Ease to St Martin's. The population of Epsom was then only 3,500 but, as many cottages were being built in the locality and as it was a long walk to the parish church, it was decided to build a church to provide for the inhabitants of the area.

This church was soon found to be inadequate and a new Christ Church was consecrated by the Bishop of Winchester on 18th October 1876, the architect being Sir Arthur Blomfield. Of flint and stone with a square north-west tower and fine chancel, it occupies a prominent position on the Common. It is provided with a fine rood screen.

ESHER, St George

St. George's is a rare example of a church built during the Reformation period, probably in Edward VI's reign (1548). Although Esher is mentioned in Domesday Book there is no reference to a church and the first indication of a patron and rector is not until 1292. Nothing remains of St George's predecessor other than the doorway on the south side of the nave and the priest's door (now walled in) on the north side of the chancel, both fifteenth-century. Most of the present structure is Tudor.

The history of St George's is closely bound up with that of the nearby mansion of Claremont, built at the beginning of the eighteenth century by Sir John Vanbrugh and successively occupied by Thomas Pelham, Duke of Newcastle, whose brother lived at Esher Place, Clive of India for whom the present house was built, and later the much loved Princess Charlotte, who died in childbirth in 1817. Subsequently, Victoria both as Princess and Queen used to stay at Claremont until in 1848 it became the home of the exiled royal family of France.

After Christ Church was built on Esher Common in 1853/4 to accommodate the expanding population, St George's fell into a state of neglect from which happily it was later restored without Victorian 'improvement'. As a result we see today an unspoilt church with many attractive Georgian furnishings. It is now cared for by the Churches Conservation Trust.

An appealing, homely building, the church is set back from the heart of Esher, contrasting sharply with the bustle of the nearby traffic. There is a small oaken bell-turret with pyramid

142. Esher, St. George – interior looking east, showing Newcastle pew on the right and fine, arch-braced roof.

spire and, on the south side, a brick building with slate roof and its own exterior entrance, which was the Newcastle pew. The dun-red brick north aisle with castellated gables does not spoil the general effect. Apart from brick, the building materials include clunch (a hard form of chalk), undressed flints from the North Downs and ironstone rubble from further afield.

The interior is a charming, largely Georgian, period piece and has the Newcastle pew on the south side, an eighteenth-century three-decker pulpit, a reredos of 1722 with good carving and original Tudor open roof, with tie and collar-beams, arch braces and side-purlins. The north arcade separating the nave from the north aisle has tall round oak piers.

Furnishings
The Newcastle pew was erected by Sir John Vanbrugh for the Duke of Newcastle in 1725/6, the four fluted Corinthian white piers in front being surmounted by a pediment of pine (*see fig. 83*). Later the pew was divided, the eastern half being reserved for Esher Place and the western for Claremont. The Royal Arms above the three-decker pulpit are those of George II. Over the entrance is the west gallery (early seventeenth-century) and above this an upper gallery added in 1842. The box pews were removed in 1908. The font with a marble bowl and oak baluster stem dates from 1829.

The best-known memorial is that on the west wall of the north aisle to Princess Charlotte; it shows her and her husband, Prince Leopold, in different scenes. Above it is a painting by A.W. Devis showing the princess being received into Heaven. On the chancel north wall are monuments to Lady Lynch of 1702, kneeling at a prayer-desk, and to Lady Fowler

143. Richard Drake's monument at Christ Church, Esher.

(d.1738), in the form of a marble cartouche with three delightful cherub faces at its base by Sir Henry Cheere. On the south wall there are three memorials, two by Flaxman, to Elizabeth Ellis (d. 1803), her mother Lady Hervey and her daughter also named Elizabeth (both d.1820).

ESHER, Christ Church

Built by Benjamin Ferrey in 1853/4 of buff stone with a broach spire, this church has transepts plus clerestory. Impressively set on the east side of the green, it imposes more by its air of consequence and its spire than by its architectural qualities.

Furnishings
The east window of 1909 is by Sir Ninian Comper and there are monuments in the south aisle to Prince Leopold, Duke of Albany (d.1884), in the form of a marble bust with alabaster surround, and a large marble memorial of 1867 to Leopold, King of the Belgians: also – moved from the old church – to Richard Drake (d.1603), brother of Sir Francis, with kneeling effigy.

EWELL, St Mary the Virgin

There may have been at least two churches at Ewell before the present one built in 1847-48. Of the old building the fifteenth-century tower, to which a brick parapet and a fine wrought- iron weathervane were added in 1789, remains despite bomb damage and vandalism. This church consisted of nave, south aisle of flint and Bargate stone – mainly of thirteenth-century construction – a slightly higher fourteenth-century chancel and chantry chapel built in 1529 by Richard Bray. During demolition traces of earlier work were found. In the medieval period, the right of presentation to the living of Ewell belonged to Chertsey Abbey until 1415 when Henry V transferred the advowson to Newark Priory who held it until the Dissolution. It was near this church that William Holman Hunt painted 'The Light of the World', the doorway in the painting being an abandoned hut used by gunpowder workers.

The present church, designed by Henry Clutton in 1847 in Early English style with a north aisle (later widened) and west gallery, is not architecturally important, but several monuments and fittings were removed to it from the old church. A factor in its present location is that Sir George Glyn (patron and rector) offered a new site, provided a right-of-way to the old church, which passed close to the windows of the rectory, was moved. He also contributed £ 500 to the cost of the new building. St Mary the Virgin suffered greatly from arson in 1973 but has been fully restored: the Lewen monument survived intact.

Furnishings

These include a fifteenth-century font decorated with quatrefoil panels, a rood-screen (much renewed), an ornate alabaster and marble pulpit of 1897, a communion table of 1612 with Tudor bulbous legs and a reredos dating from the end of the nineteenth century, depicting the Last Supper.

There is a very fine standing wall-monument to Sir William Lewen (d.1721). He was Lord Mayor of London in 1717 and is shown semi-reclining in wig, mayoral robes and chain with a background of Corinthian pilasters and open segmental pediment. Old brasses are grouped at the west end of the south aisle including Lady Iwarby (d.1519), kneeling and wearing her heraldic mantle and triangular head-dress, Margerina Treglistan (d.1521), standing, and Lady Dorothy Taylare (d.1527), with effigies of her five sons and five daughters.

EWHURST, St Peter and St Paul

The recorded history of the church of St Peter and St Paul starts with the founding, thought to be in *c*.1140, of a chapelry by the Priory of Merton. The monks may have held a forest retreat here, where they seem to have indulged their love of the chase, as they were reprimanded for spending too much time in hunting. The chapelry became a parish church in 1307 although the list of incumbents gives 1291 as the date. There was extensive rebuilding *c*.1250 resulting in a Norman cruciform structure without aisles, but the cruciform shape is now obscured by the insertion of a modern organ in the north transept. Local Wealden stone of an attractive honey-coloured hue was used and the mortar was galleted (chips of stone inserted when the mortar was wet, probably for ornamental rather than structural reasons). Subsequently, later windows were introduced but the next major building phase was in 1838/9, after the eccentric, outsize shingled tower and spire (in Cracklow's drawing they are wreathed in creeper) had collapsed in 1837. This necessitated the rebuilding not only of the tower but also the chancel and north transept and the work was done by Robert Ebbels who, despite his poor effort at St Nicolas, Guildford, performed an excellent job. The neo-Norman tower with shingled splay-footed spire was a great improvement on the old one and blends well with the rest of the church. The removal of the tip of the spire in 1954 gives it, however, a slightly foreshortened look. Ebbels inserted a Perpendicular east window in the new chancel and rebuilt the transept in its original form; later restoration was gentle.

The exterior is solid but reassuring with liberal use of Horsham slabs for roofing. These, combined with the attractive stone, create a most agreeable ensemble. Clunch (hard chalkstone), however, was used in the fifteenth-century west porch and doorway. The outstanding feature is the south doorway (*see fig. 10*), described by Ian Nairn as 'the best piece of Norman decoration in Surrey'.[34] Large jamb-shafts, curiously uneven in height, are topped by cushion capitals, but the arch, with double roll-moulding resting outside the capitals on imposts (large, flat stones) of different material, may have been partly rebuilt in the nineteenth century. At one time there were five doorways, a surprisingly large number for a small church; they were possibly for the use of parish Guilds maintaining side-altars and chantry chapels.

One of the pleasures of the exterior is the immaculately kept churchyard, in which there are many graveboards, an object lesson to many others where alien marbles, granites and unsuitable memorials have been introduced into God's acre.

The interior is unassuming and satisfying with attractive furnishings. Many of the windows have been changed, but three lancets on the south wall of the south transept remain. Over the west porch is a large three-light, fifteenth-century window whilst there are segmental-headed Perpendicular windows in the nave and south transept. The east window is also fifteenth-century and the small panes of slightly tinted glass in it have been attributed to the Chiddingfold glass works. The south transept has a roof of this date with finely moulded tie-beam and crown-post.

144.   *The altar rails and altar at Ewhurst.*

Furnishings
The mid-seventeenth-century altar rails with spiral balusters which unusually enclose the altar on three sides are beautifully carved. These and the attractive frames of the Commandments and Beatitudes came from the private chapel of Baynards, an historic house on the borders of Ewhurst and Cranleigh. The altar is a late seventeenth-century table with fluted legs and inlaid top, in the centre of which is a cross. The pulpit is also late seventeenth-century and the parclose screen across the north transept is believed to incorporate panels from a second pulpit. The font, partly thirteenth- or fourteenth-century, has a tapering bowl decorated with St Andrew's crosses and chevons. The two chairs in the sanctuary are of about the same date as the altar and pulpit and are of foreign workmanship.

FARLEIGH, St Mary the Virgin

Although less than five miles from Croydon, St Mary's is one of a trio of Norman village churches (the others are Wisley, dedication lost, and St Nicholas, Pyrford) which, despite the surge of commuter traffic in the nineteenth century, have come down to us structurally largely unaltered. There have been changes but no addition of aisles or large transepts. Not mentioned in Domesday Book, the nave and chancel of St Mary's date from *c.* 1100, but the chancel was extended by ten feet in *c*.1250 and the lancets are also from this time, including the unusual combination of two lancets in the east wall, of which one is round-headed and the other slightly pointed. The nave windows are Norman. Other alterations are the west porch of possibly sixteenth-century date and the bell-turret of the nineteenth century (it does not appear in Cracklow's drawing). The west doorway, however, the window above and the priest's door on the south side are Norman. Victorian 'improvement' was fairly restrained but included the insertion of the chancel arch. The modern roofs of both nave and chancel are poor. The exterior is stuccoed.

Since 1956, St Mary's has formed part of the 'United Benefice of Warlingham, Chelsham and Farleigh' and the presentation to the living belongs to Merton College, Oxford, to whom it was granted in 1264 by Walter de Merton, Bishop of Rochester and Lord Chancellor of England.

145.   *Farleigh Church from the west.*

Furnishings

These are of no especial interest, nineteenth-century pews and pulpit, font somewhat older. On the south wall of the chancel there is a brass in a ledger slab to John Brook (d.1495), citizen and poulterer of London, and his wife plus four sons and one daughter; his wife wears the high linen headdress fashionable in her day. On the opposite wall is a marble ledger to Dr. Samuel Barnard, a former rector (d.1657), and his wife Elizabeth who died nearly 50 years later in 1705.

FARNCOMBE, St John the Evangelist

Farncombe has been on a main line of communication from the middle of the eighteenth century, first the road from London to Portsmouth, converted into a turnpike in 1749, then the Wey Navigation, extended to Godalming in 1760, and much later the railway, completed to Farncombe in 1849, but not extended to Godalming until ten years later. As a result and particularly since the coming of the railway the population grew to rival that of Godalming, only one mile away. A simple chapel was built in 1846-9 by George Gilbert Scott (then in his thirties) which received high praise from *The Ecclesiologist*. As the need for accommodation in the church grew, a north aisle was added in 1860 and a south one in 1874 in very contrasting styles. The central sanctuary of Portland stone was completed in 1971. The exterior shows an agreeable three-gabled west front with lancets and oval windows plus a typical Surrey bellcote over the central gable. The building material is Bargate stone with warm brown tints and there is some galleting. The churchyard is enhanced by trees which, however, mask the west front.

The interior is bright and uncluttered in thirteenth-century lancet style with excellent stonework. The north arcade of arches dying into the piers is very different from the south with its octagonal piers and capitals. In the north aisle, shafts with annulets are set against the piers, possibly for extra strength, but giving a rather awkward appearance. Heads in stone of Queen Victoria and a bishop are to be seen above the chancel arch. In the Lady Chapel beyond the south aisle Purbeck marble is used for a column.

Furnishings
Behind the high altar is a fine reredos by Gambier Perry, included in the 1971 exhibition of Victorian Church Art at the Victoria & Albert Museum; the mosaic of the reredos and of the floor in front were executed by Italian workmen. A sixteenth- or seventeenth-century chest in the north aisle has good woodwork. The west window has colourful stained glass depicting St John the Divine being inspired to write the Book of Revelation and there is good thirteenth-century glass in the pair of lancets at the east end of the south aisle. A particularly interesting feature is the carved and painted crucifix, reputedly seventeenth-century Russian, in the Lady Chapel where there is also a painted and carved nineteenth-century Madonna and Child, which came from the Community of St Peter at Woking. Two panels of St John and St Peter are of interest in the north aisle, where there is also a painting on boards of the Holy Family, thought to be sixteenth-century Italian work.

A most evocative memorial is the brass plate in the north aisle recording the action of one of Farncombe's most heroic sons, the description of which reads:

In memory of
John George Phillips
Aged 26 years
formerly a Chorister of this Church
Chief Wireless Operator on
R.M.S. Titanic
Which Sank at Sea on April 15, 1912.

———————————————

Faithful To His Duty Till The Last

He is remembered in more substantial form by the Phillips Memorial Cloister of 1913 on the north side of Godalming churchyard.

FARNHAM, St Andrew

Situated to the south of the town near the river in a pleasant churchyard, St Andrew's has grown from a small cruciform Norman place of worship with central tower and transepts to the substantial town church which it is today, rather dull from Victorian attentions until David Nye brought some lightness and brightness to it in his 1959 restoration. The Norman church dates from *c.*1130 to which, in *c.*1180, north and south chapels were added to the chancel which was vaulted. The south aisle was added in the first half of the fourteenth century whilst a new and lengthened chancel was completed and dedicated in 1399. In the fifteenth century the nave was rebuilt, possibly as a result of a fire having burned down the earlier nave, and a large north aisle was constructed. It was then that the central tower must have been pulled down. This was replaced in the early sixteenth century by a tower of four stages at the west end. During the nineteenth century, the church received more than the normal dose of Victorian restoration, particularly in the early Victorian period by Benjamin Ferrey, which resulted in the outer walls being refaced throughout and in producing a rather colourless interior but, on the plus side, the heightening of the west tower (previously rather a puny affair) by Ewan Christian in 1865/6 created a steeple of great distinction and one of the finest in the county (*see fig. 48*).

146. The Norman capitals of the former central tower at Farnham.

The approach from Upper Church Lane with the Somerset-quality tower of St Andrew's at the far end is a beautiful piece of townscape. Closer inspection reveals the complete renewal of the exterior and one is soon conscious of the absence of clerestories. Ewan Christian, in addition to heightening the tower, added the pinnacles, upper windows and battlements giving it the stately appearance it has today. The buttresses are polygonal, always a mark of importance.

The lack of clerestories and the equal height of the nave and aisles create a hall-type interior which, despite David Nye's work, is rather plain. The five-bay nave, with octagonal piers and capitals, contrasts with the later chancel arcades which have moulded and scalloped capitals. The modern nave roof is of modified hammer-beam type. The chancel arch was heightened by about six feet and the capitals renewed in 1841 and the chancel itself restored in 1848, but the large tower arch with a single attached shaft is unrestored. The west vaulting shafts of the Norman chancel remain, one with a palmette leaf capital.

Furnishings
The finest furnishings are the sedilia and piscina of fourteenth- or fifteenth-century date in the fourteenth-century extension of the chancel. They consist of four bays with ogee arches and pleasing tracery under square heads. The next of note are the late seventeenth-century altar rails decorated with complex floral panels – re-sited in 1959 close to the St James's altar. The fifteenth-century font in the south transept, a good octagonal example, is carved with sacred monograms and the symbols of the four Evangelists; it has an attractive modern ogee cover. Eleven eighteenth- and nineteenth-century hatchments decorate the north and south aisle walls. Later work includes the stained glass east window of St James's Chapel by Pugin, shown in the 1851 Exhibition – rather anaemic compared with his usual richly

147.   The font at Farnham.

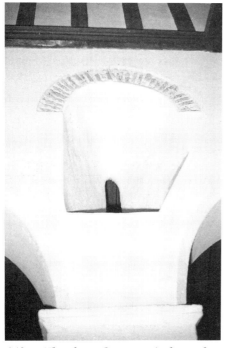

*148.   The late Saxon window above
the south arcade at Fetcham, with an
arch of Roman bricks.*

coloured glass. Both the statuette of St Andrew and the reredos of the Lady Chapel are by a parishioner, the late Eleanor Price.

There are a number of eighteenth- and nineteenth-century tablets but none of particular note except for four wall cartouches in the Lady Chapel and a Westmacott memorial to Sir Nicholas Rycroft (d.1827) in the same chapel depicting a pilgrim resting on his journey. In the tower, a medallion bust commemorates William Cobbett. One of Farnham's most famous, forthright and controversial characters, he was born a short step to the south of the church in what is now the public house bearing his name and is buried even closer to St Andrew's outside its north door beneath a marble altar tomb. In the Lady Chapel, a memorial of Sussex marble or 'winklestone' remembers the Marson brothers, who were locksmiths. In addition, however, mention should be made of four brasses from the sixteenth and seventeenth centuries. One to Sir George Vernon (d.1692) is on the floor of the Lady Chapel, partly concealed by the modern communion rails. The other three are inscribed on plates and affixed to the south wall of the same chapel. They include Benedict and Elizabeth Jay, shown with their three boys and three girls behind their parents all kneeling; Benedict was buried in 1586 and carried the interesting title of 'Sergeant of the Woodyard to Queen Elizabeth'. Nearby is the kneeling figure of Sibyl Jay, with three daughters before and two daughters and one son behind her; she died in 1597. Finally, there is the brass to Henry Vernon, who was host to King Charles I for a night in December 1648 when he was being taken by an armed Parliamentarian escort to London before his execution in the following month. Henry Vernon appears to have been a man of exemplary character. Among modern brasses there is one erected early this century to the Revd. Augustus Montague Toplady, author of the hymn 'Rock of Ages', who was born nearby in a West-Street cottage.

FETCHAM, St Mary

The history of St Mary's (the dedication is uncertain as, prior to 1899, it was simply referred to as Fetcham Church) reaches back into pre-Conquest times. There was a Saxon cemetery nearby on Hawkes Hill and, although the burials were pagan, this indicates that there was a considerable Saxon community living here which later may have become Christian. The blocked window above the north arcade with Roman brick dressings is very probably pre-Conquest and is contemporary with the west quoins of the formerly aisleless nave. The church structure grew slowly. The south aisle was originally added in the mid-twelfth century and the base of the tower to the south at the end of the century. In the early thirteenth century the chancel was extended and the north aisle built with its beautifully shaped arches. At the same time, the north transept, which may once have been a manorial chapel, was added. St Mary's is cruciform in shape with the tower taking the place of the south transept. The tower was completed in the early eighteenth century with a brick upper stage. The church lies in a leafy setting under the shadow of the formidable Fetcham Park. The south aisle had to be rebuilt in the mid-nineteenth century.

Inside, the chancel is much renewed but retains a thirteenth-century arch opening out into it from the tower. The east wall of the north transept is noteworthy with two lancets flanking a lower and broader recess, enriched by dog-tooth ornamentation, for an altar. The two-light north window of the transept probably dates from about 1320-30. The highlights of the interior are, however, the two nave arcades, especially the north one which is original Decorated work and consists of two delightfully-proportioned large arches (suitable for a much larger church) and the faithfully reproduced late Norman south arcade in the style of c.1150. These give this place of worship much distinction.[6] The east window is Perpendicular.

Furnishings
Except for a font dating from 1632, returned from a school at Alton run by the Wantage Sisters, (now installed in front of the congregation) and a triple sedilia with Purbeck marble shafts, one circular and one octagonal, there is not much to note. The pulpit is modern and there is another font of 1868 at the rear of the church. The 1852 restoration obliterated the wall paintings in the north transept but coloured drawings of these are preserved at Castle Arch in Guildford.

Of interest are the monuments to Antony Rous (d.1631), carved as a corpse with hourglass underneath; to Henry Vincent (d. the same year), in the form of a frontal bust shown praying, both in the chancel, and, in the side chapel, to John Bolland (d.1820), an early nineteenth-century Grecian tablet, and Robert Sherson (d.1821).

In the churchyard, the memorials include one to Admiral Sir George Henry Richardson, the hydrographer and promoter of submarine telegraphy, who, as a young Commander, went on an expedition in search of the ill-fated Arctic explorer, Sir John Franklin; and another to Sir Francis Graham Moon, printer and publisher, who was Lord Mayor of London in 1854.

FRENSHAM, St Mary

This goes back to 1239 when, according to the Annals of Waverley Abbey, the church was moved to a new site probably because access to the old church was cut off when a bridge over the River Wey was made unusable by storm damage. The sanctuary walls, the oldest part of the building, date from this time. This is underlined by the lancet window in the north and the piscina/aumbry in the opposite wall. From the fourteenth century the south wall of the nave largely survives, also the remains of an early tomb in the north wall of the sanctuary, probably used at one time as an Easter Sepulchre. In the same century, the building of the tower was begun and, as the west window is in the Perpendicular style, this must be one of the earliest such windows in the country. There are no signs of later medieval work, but in the sixteenth century the chancel roof was rebuilt and covered with plaster. The north aisle was added in 1827. Later in 1868, St Mary's was subjected to an insensitive restoration – mainly in neo-Decorated style – which removed much of its medieval character as well as the Georgian furnishings. A mediocre chancel arch was inserted, and the nave given an 'Early-English' north arcade with lavishly decorated naturalistic capitals, whilst the flooring of gravestones was replaced by tiles and the floor level of the sanctuary raised, which effectively spoiled the east end.

Attractively sited behind a low wall and externally appealing, St Mary's like so many other Surrey churches has felt the heavy hand of the Victorian restorer – in this case an architect named Hähn. The exterior is dominated by the fourteenth-century west tower of sandstone rubble with massive diagonal buttresses; this was restored by W.D. Caröe in 1929. The churchyard is a model of a well-tended burial ground with headstones generally of local material and few kerbs. The interior is an unfortunate example of unsympathetic Victorian restoration during which the poor chancel arch referred to earlier was inserted and the character of the building drastically changed. The nave, however, has an old crown-post roof.

149.   'Mother Ludlam's cauldron' at Frensham.

Furnishings
The font in Purbeck marble on modern shafts is of uncertain origin, but seemingly Norman and at one time elaborately carved, but now much worn. A curiosity is the huge round copper cauldron in the north aisle standing on a trivet. It measures about three feet in diameter and is 1 ft. 7 in. deep. It is familiarly known as Mother Ludlam's cauldron; she is supposed to have lived in a cave near Waverley Abbey. It was used to contain the ale drunk at the parochial festivities known as 'Church Ales'.

I.   The 'Macedoine' of stonework at Chobham Church south aisle.

II.   Saxon window at Thursley.

III.   Norman window at Tandridge.

IV.   The wall painting at Chaldon.

V.   The wall painting at Pyrford.

VI.   *Godalming Church from the south.*

VII. The east end at Addington. *VIII. Glass at West Horsley.*

IX. Glass at Oxted. *X. Glass at Buckland.*

XI.   Glass at Worplesdon.

XII.   Glass at Worplesdon.

XIII.   Glass at Wimbledon.

XIV.   The fifteenth-century lecturn at Croydon.

XV.   Sir Anthony Benn's monument at Kingston upon Thames.

XVI.   John Ownstead's monument at Sanderstead.

XVII.   John Goodison's monument at Horne.

XVIII.   The Leigh monuments at Addington.

XIX.   The Vincent monuments at Stoke d'Abernon.

XX.   Pulpit at Petersham.

XXI.   Pulpit at Holy Trinity, Guildford.

XXII.   The reredos at Carshalton, later decorated by Ninian Comper.

XXIII.   The Royal Arms of George III at Wisley.

XXIV.   The Cranston Library at Reigate.

XXV.   Glass at Stoke d'Abernon.   *XXVI.   Glass at Ashtead.*

XXVII.   Glass at Great Bookham.   *XXVIII.   Pulpit at Mickleham.*

XXIX.   The Lady Chapel at Woking Convent.

XXX.   The organ case at Beddington.

XXXI.   The look-out at East Horsley.

XXXII. Pulpit at Betchworth.

XXXIII. Font at Okewood.

XXXIV. Pulpit at Ranmore.

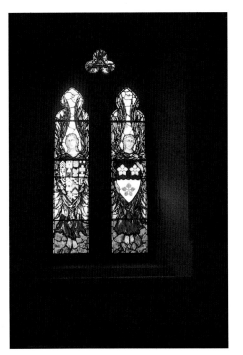 

XXXV.   *Glass at Lyne.*   *XXXVI.*   *Glass at Titsey.*

XXXVII.   *The Cyclists' window at Ripley.*

XXXVIII.   The Chancel at Lower Kingswood.

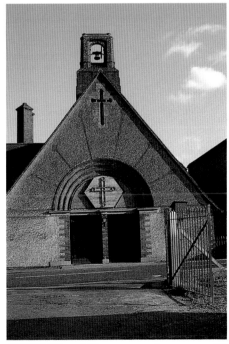

XXXIX.   The west front at Pixham.

XL.   Watts' Chapel, Compton.

XLI.   An altar frontal at Ockham.

XLII.   Glass at Abinger by Lawrence Lee.

XLIII.   The Royal Arms of Elizabeth II at Chelsham.

FRIMLEY, St Peter

Frimley was formerly a chapelry of Ash until it was made into a separate parish in 1866. Cracklow shows a half-timbered chapel dating from 1606 at Frimley (*see fig. 4*). This was replaced by the present Commissioners' type building, by J.T. Parkinson in fifteenth-century style, dating from 1825 (*see fig. 91*). The church has since been frequently enlarged, a major alteration taking place in 1881.

The exterior is in the form of a rectangular box of freestone throughout, with a small west tower and projecting east end. The interior has an institutional look, although not deserving of Ian Nairn's epithet – 'awful'.[35] Galleries were installed later.

Furnishings
These are of little account with a particularly anaemic Burne-Jones-type window at the east end. Francis Brett Harte, the American poet and writer of tales of the California gold rush, who died at Camberley in 1902 and Admiral Frederick Charles Doveton Sturdee of Falkland Islands fame (d.1925) are buried on the north side of Frimley churchyard.

GATTON, St Andrew

A church at Gatton is mentioned in Domesday Book, but little is known of its medieval history. Later, when John Aubrey visited the church in the 1680s, he was not impressed and Sir James Colebrooke, a wealthy banker, when he acquired the estate in 1751, decided – for reasons unclear – to empty the church of all its monuments and for the next eighty years the building, which was then without transepts, was much neglected. However, it underwent a sea-change when Lord Monson acquired Gatton Park in 1830. He gothicised the fabric with the aid of his architect, E. Webb, and filled the church with furnishings he had obtained during a Grand Tour which he made in 1834. They make an interesting collection, imported mainly from the Low Countries and France.

Until 1763 the churchyard was on the south side of the church, but this was appropriated by the owner of the Hall (Sir George Colebrooke), who gave land on the north side in exchange. This was consecrated in 1778 and, as a consequence, there is no grave earlier than 1799 in the churchyard. Set in park-like surroundings, the exterior has recently been greatly improved by the removal of most of the pebbledash rendering. The west tower and shingled spire, however, are rather skimpy and not helped by the brick porch, backed by a tall gable. Until 1834 the tower had stood at the north-west corner.

The interior is a Pandora's box of interesting furnishings which have been fitted in cleverly, with stalls set in college style, to give the impression of having been there for some time and to create a harmonious interior. The wagon roof is plastered and transepts were added during the Monson alterations of the 1830s: these are now filled with galleries, a family pew, pulpit and stairs. The thirteenth-century font and piscina remain from the old church but, apart from the family pew, the fine screen at the west end which came from an unknown English church and possibly two of the easternmost choir stalls, all the other furnishings came from the Continent. Near the font is a plaque listing the rectors of Gatton, starting with Adam de Essire in 1306.

Furnishings
Starting from the west end, the furnishings are as follows:

An octagonal font, with plain bowl, resting on a central pillar with four attached shafts: below the bowl there is a band of good thirteenth-century carved foliage.

Carved nave stalls in Flemish Baroque style came from a Benedictine monastery at Ghent. Each arm rest ends in a cherub's head and the seats all have misericords, decorated with differing heads. The panelling behind has delicate tracery heads set against it (seen to better advantage in front of the open family pew). The cornice of the coving has a moulded top-member with an inscription in Gothic lettering in the form of a prayer. The panelling and coving came from Aarschot Cathedral near Louvain.

The communion rails, thickly detailed with clustered shafts leading to ogee heads under quatrefoils, came from Tongres in Flanders.

The carved chancel panelling came from Burgundy and in the tracery can be seen the briquets and flames (flint and steel) from the Burgundy arms.

The two chancel chairs on each side of the altar, dating from 1515, may be Flemish.

The high pulpit above on the south side forms part of the south transept gallery front. The fine carved work on the panels, together with that in front of the communion table, were once contained in a reredos depicting the descent from the Cross, to a design attributed to the great German engraver, Albrecht Dürer.

Linenfold doors below the pulpit lead to the south gallery; the door on the left has spirited carving in the top panels on either side of a chalice. The doors came from Rouen.

Opposite in the north transept is the family pew, containing the original furniture with restored upholstery; the seats and overmantel are panelled. There was separate access from the Hall to the family pew, by a covered way – with a Victorian fireplace – enabling the family to worship in comfort and undisturbed. On the rear wall of the pew are tablets commemorating the mustard king, Jeremiah Colman (1859-1942) and Mary, his wife (1864-1954). The seventh Lord Monson sold Gatton Hall to Jeremiah in 1888.

150. The Royal Arms of Henry VII in stained glass of c.1830 in the west window at Gatton.

Of the stained glass, the west window has rich glazing, probably of *c.*1830, showing the arms of Henry VII, the south nave window contains French glass dating from 1580, and the south transept one has armorial bearings. The east window contains glass of about 1500, depicting the eating of the Passover as prescribed in Chapter 12 of the Book of Exodus; this came from an old conventual church near Louvain. The east window in the north transept is thought to be fifteenth-century in origin. Nineteenth-century glass is represented by the south chancel window by C.E. Kempe, dating from 1879, and the most recent glass is a memorial window of hand-painted glass by Jane Gray placed on the west side of the porch in 1980.

In the churchyard, near the east end of the church, is the outline of an octagonal mausoleum, in which the bodies of Lord Monson and his mother, the Countess of Warwick, rested before removal to their ancestral home. The successor of the Monsons, Jeremiah Colman and members of his family are buried nearer the entrance to the churchyard, the place being marked by an elaborate memorial capped by an object, not unlike a mustard pot.

This is a unique Surrey museum piece, interest lying in the contents rather than in the architecture, but still used as a place of worship by the few remaining parishioners.

GODALMING, St Peter and St Paul

This place of worship is a slow-growth, basically medieval, building going back to Saxon times. Surprisingly, the living was in the gift of the Dean and Chapter of Salisbury from 1155 until 1846: we are reminded of this by the names Deanery Place, Dean Lodge, etc. in Godalming. The Saxon church embraced the two eastern bays of the nave plus a chancel on the site of the base of the tower. Of this, only two blocked double-splayed, circular windows in the west wall of the tower remain and these are only visible from inside the ringing chamber. To the Saxon church was added in the twelfth century the Norman chancel and later in the same century the north and south transepts. The blocked windows of this chancel were exposed above the arcades in Sir George Gilbert Scott's restoration of 1879; also the base of a door-jamb of a priest's door on the north side of the south chapel. A Norman window can be seen above the arch on the west side of the south transept, but the corresponding window in the north transept is hidden by the organ.

The tower of attractive Bargate stone is also Norman. It was heightened in the thirteenth century and the timber-framed, lead-covered spire added in the fourteenth (*Colour Plate VI*). The church thus became a cruciform building with the chancel longer than the nave but, in the thirteenth century, this form was obscured by the construction of the nave aisles (widened in the nineteenth century) and the addition of the chancel-aisle chapels, which have short circular piers. Further medieval alterations included lengthening the chancel, extending the nave by a bay and incorporating Perpendicular windows in the two transepts (although that on the north side was moved outwards in the nineteenth century).

Apart from the insertion of galleries (now removed) in the seventeenth and eighteenth centuries, there were no further structural alterations until 1840, when the organ gallery was moved to the north transept, and a further and final bay added to the nave. The nave ceiling was raised to its present shape, with fifty bosses, carved into heraldic shields, many collected from the south chapel and the north aisle. In 1879, very drastic changes were made to earlier designs by Sir George Gilbert Scott (he died in 1878). The aisles were extended to the lengthened nave, the west chancel arch removed and the east chancel arch heightened by four to five feet. Finally, the south porch was built in 1911.

The exterior is dominated by the tall and noble lead spire, rarely found in this part of England. The cruciform design is largely lost under later additions, but the interesting intersecting tracery of the east window (inserted *c.*1850) and the Geometrical tracery of the south chapel east window, with the Perpendicular doorway below (moved from the west end) are notable features. The north, south and west walls of the nave are all nineteenth-century work.

The Scott alterations have created a rather lifeless interior but, on the credit side, must be set the finding of the Norman chancel windows and, more importantly, the opening to view of the whole of the fine east window. The north and south chancel arcades are thirteenth-century, also the east window – one of the best examples of Geometrical tracery in the county – and the south-east window of three lancets, with detached inner shafts of Sussex marble, in the south chapel. The square-headed windows in the same chapel, with ogee heads to the lights, date from the fourteenth century.

Furnishings
These include sedilia in the chancel with restored Decorated hoods and a thirteenth-century piscina in the south chancel chapel of interesting design, with two aumbries above

and two piscinas below. The pulpit is a cut-down largely Elizabethan example of monotonous panel design. There is also a brass candelabrum of 1722 with two tiers of brackets and eight sconces on each in the chancel, a thirteenth-century pin-hinge chest in the south transept and a sixteenth-century altar in the south chapel. On the Westbrook tomb-chest (of 1513) in the south chapel are some Saxon remains in the form of worn stone fragments. These have recently been dated by the British Museum as *c*.820-840.

151.   Saxon carved stone in Godalming Church.

Monuments in the church include a kneeling figure on a memorial to Judeth Elliott (d.1615) and two late brasses, to Thomas Parvoche (d.1509) and his wife, in civilian dress, and to John Barlow (d.1595), in plate armour. Above the sanctuary is a mural tablet to the Rev. Owen Manning (d.1801), joint author with William Bray of *The History and Antiquities of the County of Surrey*; he was vicar of Godalming for 37 years. A memorial stone in the floor of the south transept commemorates John Coston, who was appointed sexton of the parish in the fifteenth year of his age and held the office for 59 years. He was 74 years old when he died suddenly on 9th May 1741. His inscription records that 'he was the King of Humours and the best of husbands to his well beloved wife IANE who now is in great sorrow and grief for her loss of him'.

Godalming's most famous citizen, James Edward Oglethorpe, succeeded to the Manor of Westbrook in 1718. In June 1732, with twenty associates, he obtained a charter for settling the colony of Georgia in the U.S.A. Four months later he embarked with 120 settlers and for the next ten years devoted all his energies to the new foundation, including the choice of a site for the town and supervising the cultivation of the land. The clerical staff of the colony included the young John and Charles Wesley, the former being succeeded later by the youthful George Whitefield. Outside the Westbrook Chapel, a plaque of 1982 commemorates the 250th. Anniversary of the founding of Georgia; the flag of the State hangs above. A character far from deserving admiration was Mary Toft, who claimed in

1726 to have given birth to some seventeen rabbits. The hoax was exposed by George I's physician and others, after examination.

GODSTONE, St Nicholas

Godstone was probably one of perhaps ten minsters in Surrey, Chertsey being the first. These were set up, before the ninth century, by kings or bishops under royal patronage, in important administrative centres to serve the religious needs of surrounding areas. This place of worship is set about half a mile to the east of Godstone Green, in a separate hamlet known as Church Town and away from the main roads. Of the church founded in the twelfth century, only the base of the early thirteenth-century tower and Norman window fragments in the west wall remain. The north aisle dates from 1845. Sir Gilbert Scott, who lived nearby at Rooksnest, almost entirely rebuilt St Nicholas in 1872/3, adding a south aisle, heightening the shingled spire, opening the nave roof and refitting the interior. He also built in 1872 immediately south of the church, St Mary's Homes, a picturesque timber-framed one- and two-storied group with a charming chapel.

Apart from the attractive south-east tower with shingled clock and bell-opening stages, the exterior effect is entirely nineteenth-century. This also applies to the interior which, apart from the north aisle, is almost all Scott.

Furnishings
The octagonal fifteenth-century font, with pointed quatrefoil panels, is an attractive feature. Sir John Evelyn (d.1641) and Dame Thomasin, his wife, are commemorated in a black and white marble monument with recumbent effigies. He was half-brother to the father of John, the diarist, who lived at Wotton. His father, George Evelyn (1530-1603), manufactured gunpowder at Long Ditton and Wotton and Sir John, who inherited the family monopoly in this business, established another factory at Godstone. There is also a monument to James Evelyn (d.1793) by John Bingley, with a standing, mourning woman, and to Mrs. Smith (d.1794), an urn with a garland. In the churchyard, a sarsen stone marks the grave of 'Walker Miles' (E.S. Taylor, d.1908), one of the earliest organisers of rambling.

GREAT BOOKHAM, St Nicolas

The church of St Nicolas at Great Bookham, one of 413 Anglican churches in England dedicated to this popular saint, has a long history and is mentioned in Domesday Book. Two Norman (possibly Saxon) windows were discovered above the north nave arcade in 1913. The nave dates from the twelfth century, the Norman south arcade of *c.*1140 being earlier than the north (of *c.*1180), with its slightly-pointed arches indicating that it is Transitional in style. The Decorated chancel was rebuilt in 1341 by the illustrious Abbot Rutherwyk of Chertsey Abbey, as recorded in the stone slab, containing some of the finest flowing, deeply-cut Lombardic writing to survive (*see fig. 17*). The church came under the Abbey from pre-Conquest times to the Dissolution. The flint base of the tower dates from the twelfth century, but the attractive timber upper stages are fifteenth-century. In the same century – about 1440 – the aisles were widened and the eastern part of the south aisle formed into the Slyfield Chapel. The north aisle was rebuilt during major alterations by R.C. Carpenter in 1841-45. Later in 1885, William Butterfield made extensive changes whilst further work was carried out by P.M. Johnston between 1913 and 1922: he added the present outer porch and it was he who discovered the Norman windows above the north arcade.

The exterior makes a pleasing ensemble when viewed from the lych-gate, with the west end mainly medieval. The most striking feature is the weatherboarded west tower (*see fig. 42*) – one of the few in Surrey of the Essex type, completely built up from the ground (but compare with Burstow, with its more sophisticated shingling and the much-restored Newdigate tower). The western angle buttresses are fifteenth-century with brick patching of 1788. The south aisle and the porch are roofed with Horsham slates. The three-light Perpendicular windows of the south aisle and Slyfield Chapel are of good proportions, whilst the four-light side windows (one blocked) above the nave arcades are attractive Decorated examples. At the east end, outside the chancel east window, are two corbels familiarly referred to as 'the Parson' and 'the Clerk'.

The Norman/Transitional nave has scalloped capitals on the piers, which are sturdy round cylindrical columns on the south side and octagonal (except for a central hexagonal one) on the north. The roof is original. The chancel, however, was given a new roof in 1872 and the chancel arch rebuilt during the Carpenter alterations of the mid-nineteenth century, but the arch from the chancel into the Slyfield Chapel is fifteenth-century. This chapel has an ancient piscina and a fine east window, but with glass of crude colour by O'Connor, completed in 1859. The east window of the chancel was renewed in 1841 to the same design as the old one of 500 years earlier. A parclose screen of *c*.1500 separates the chancel from the Slyfield Chapel, at the entrance to which from the south aisle there are remains of a fine early fifteenth-century rood screen.

Furnishings
The font is twelfth century (*c*.1190) of Sussex marble, but with a new base and stem. The pulpit and choir stalls date from 1885. The only old stained glass (in the east window) consists of six panels, of episodes from the life of Our Lord, and reputedly fifteenth-century Flemish. These were acquired in 1954 from a set of forty smuggled out of a French church during the French Revolution and bought for the chapel of Costessey Hall, Norfolk. When the Hall closed down, the panels were split up; some are in Stoke D'Abernon church and others in the U.S.A. A clear explanation of the various scenes is given nearby.

There are many memorials of interest, notably brasses to Elizabeth Slyfield (d.1433) – the oldest – beside the pulpit, to Henry Slyfield (d.1598) and his wife, on the chancel arch respond, and to Robert Shiers (d.1669) on the floor of the south aisle immediately in front of the chapel. This shows him dressed as a member bencher of the Inner Temple. Robert Shiers together with his wife (d.1700) and his son (d.1685) are also commemorated in a stone monument in the north aisle, where they appear in three busts within a large architectural surround. There are also fine ledger slabs to the Shiers family in the floor of the south aisle. Another monument in the north aisle commemorates Colonel Thomas Moore (d.1735), Overseas Paymaster, depicted in a reclining martial attitude 'in the full uniform of the commanding officer of a regiment of foot in the reign of Queen Anne'. The Moores lived at Polesden Lacey. The best, however, of the monuments is in the south aisle to Cornet Geary who died in 1776 in the American War of Independence. This is an admirable composition with a relief showing how he died in an ambush (*see fig. 86*). The most curious is the Gothic tablet in the chancel to Elizabeth Andrews (d.1816) and several relations, probably erected about 1830. The background consists of a weeping willow in low relief, which extends to the whole height of the chancel, with an iron railing round its foot. On an inscribed paving stone in the south aisle a member of the Howard family, Francis, who died at the age of 18 months in 1633, is touchingly described as 'this rosecheeked child'.

GUILDFORD, Holy Trinity

No reliable evidence exists as to the building of the first church. The list of rectors goes back to 1304, but there is reason to believe that a place of worship existed here well over a century before that date and that originally it may have been a Norman foundation. The gift of the living in medieval times from the early twelfth century to the Dissolution is believed to have been granted by Henry I to Merton Priory.

The decay that was allowed to overtake so many of England's churches in the eighteenth century reached a point at Holy Trinity when, on 23rd April 1740, the tower of the present church's predecessor collapsed and reduced it to a state of ruin. Apathy prevailed after the disaster and it took seven years to raise enough money to pay for the demolition of the walls, and, even after work had started on the present church, it came to a halt a year later for lack of funds. Finally, it was completed in 1763 to the designs of James Horne. In 1869, Henry Woodyer skilfully changed the double tier of round-headed windows into a single tier and later, in 1888, with the growth of population, Sir Arthur Blomfield designed a new chancel, transepts and apse, transforming the building into a single room but

152.   The chancel, the apse and the screen at Holy Trinity, Guildford.

retaining the west gallery. After the diocese of Guildford was created in 1927, Holy Trinity became the pro-cathedral from 1927 to 1961.

Holy Trinity is Surrey's only considerable eighteenth-century place of worship. Built of red brick with a battlemented west tower, supporting an ornate wrought-iron flagpole, it is a harmonious composition (*see fig. 80*) and this makes it a handsome focal feature at the top of Guildford's much admired High Street. The fine railings, decorated with the initials of the contemporary churchwardens, remain from the earlier church, the central iron gates and piers dating from 1712, the others 1813. On the south side the flint and freestone chequerboard Weston Chapel, with three-light windows, is a survival from 1540. The west end is pedimented and the east is the apsed extension of Sir Arthur Blomfield. The interior is in the form of a large room with tripartite openings at the east end. The most striking feature is the apse, the central feature of the decoration of which is 'the Presence of the Crucified in the Church of all ages'. The central figure of Christ upon the Cross is flanked on the north side by Aaron, David and Isaiah, representing the Priests, Kings and Prophets of the Jewish Church and on the south side by St Paul, St Stephen and St Augustine of Hippo, representing the Apostles, Martyrs and Bishops of the Christian Church. The paintings below the text were completed on 27th October 1891 and the vault paintings dedicated on 3rd November 1898.

Furnishings
The pulpit dating from 1770 is of impressive size with a canopy on two large fluted columns (*Colour Plate XXI*). The impressive wrought-iron choir screen, stretching across the church,

dates from 1927 when Holy Trinity became the pro-cathedral. Two monuments, which survived in a battered state from the collapse of the tower, are to be seen in the west porch. They are to Sir Robert Parkhurst (d.1637), a lifeless figure lying on its side with headless figure of his wife kneeling beside him under a canopy. The other, on the opposite side, is a similar tomb of an unknown female figure lying above skulls placed hugger-mugger, which can be viewed through the side of the chest containing them. In the body of the church on the south wall, a more substantial memorial commemorates Arthur Onslow (d.1778), speaker of the House of Commons for 33 years: he is shown as a semi-reclining figure in Roman dress on a plain inscribed base (*see fig. 85*). The most impressive monument, however, is the elaborate memorial (*see fig. 71*) erected in the south transept of the old church in 1640 (and now in the south chapel) to George Abbot, Archbishop of Canterbury (d.1633) who preceded William Laud. It is signed by Matthew and John Christmas and is full of allegory. Below the archbishop is a mass of sculptured bones and skulls in relief, and above him a six-column canopy with profuse carving. The columns are of polychrome marble and rest on pedestals built up of books. Near the place on the south wall where the monument used to stand, a charming brass with kneeling figures marks the burial site of his parents, both of whom died in 1606 within ten days of each other after 58 years of marriage. Although of humble stock, five of their sons rose to eminence in their particular spheres. One became Bishop of Salisbury and another Lord Mayor of London.

GUILDFORD, Chapel of the Hospital of the Blessed Trinity (Abbot's Hospital)

153 & 154.   The north window and the almsbox at Abbot's Hospital Chapel, Guildford.

The chapel occupies a small space at the north-east corner of the ground floor of the Hospital erected by George Abbot, Archbishop of Canterbury for twelve men and eight (later ten) women. It measures about 32 feet by 24 feet and is a highly individual building.

Despite its small size there are large windows on the east and north walls. The glass is enamel painted in the Flemish style, showing Esau and Jacob in what Nairn [36] describes as 'crowded compositions'. It has been suggested that it may have come from the Dominican Friary in Guildford, but there is no proof of this. A curious feature is the wooden Jacobean almsbox, shaped like a mace.

There is much to be seen in the Hospital including fine Jacobean woodwork and ironwork and the Monmouth Room, where the rebel Duke, pretender to the throne of James II, spent the last night of his journey as a captive on the way to execution on Tower Hill after his defeat at Sedgemoor in 1685.

GUILDFORD, St Mary the Virgin

St. Mary's is the middle of the three Guildford churches on or near the north side of the High Street and affords a complete contrast to the Georgian Holy Trinity at the top and the High Victorian St Nicolas at the foot. It is believed that St Mary's was the original parish church, but there is no evidence that, when the Castle was used by the Court, the dignitaries living there worshipped in the church. There was, in any case, the King's own chapel of St. Stephen in the Castle. The beginnings of the church are wrapped in obscurity, but it is generally agreed that the tower (probably originally western) is partly pre-Conquest, with its double-splayed windows inside and pilaster strips of plastered flint, which once reached down on the north and south sides to the ground; the battlements are later. St. Mary's is made particularly interesting by the upward ascent from west to east, due to the natural rise of the ground. The chancel appears to be early Norman work which was followed by the transepts. In the twelfth century (c.1175) there was largely a rebuilding, in the Transitional style which included the nave arcades and the chapels of St John and St Mary north and south of the chancel; the narrow nave aisles were widened in the early and mid-thirteenth century. The chapels are apsed (see fig. 18) and, from the disposition of altars, it seems that at one time there were seven apses. In c.1220 the chancel was

155. St. Mary's, Guildford – looking west into the nave from the chancel, showing the fall in levels.

156. St. Mary's, Guildford - passage way from south chapel to chancel.

given a good rib-vault with two piers of dog-tooth decoration in the first bay and piers of three clustered shafts similarly decorated to support it. Later windows have been added of which the three-light Decorated window of *c*.1315 in the north chapel has good tracery. The east end is an attractive network of squints and diagonal passages. The gift of the living in medieval times from the early twelfth century to the Dissolution is believed to have been granted by Henry I to Merton Priory. In 1715, the benefices of St. Mary and Holy Trinity up the High Street were combined. In 1825, Quarry Street was widened cutting off the chancel apse, allegedly to permit George IV's coach and four to proceed more easily on its way from Windsor to Brighton. In 1863, St Mary's underwent a severe restoration.

The exterior is mostly renewed, but the flint tower makes for an interesting elevation. The north doorway is an attractive feature: its arch mouldings, Purbeck marble shafts and capitals are all delicate thirteenth-century work. This is one of the best town church interiors in Surrey with its unusual ascent from west to east, rib-vaulted chancel and chapels and its Transitional arcades of the late twelfth century. The arcades have round columns, pointed arches and, except for one round capital on the north side, much-scalloped square capitals. There is a low, square window at the west end of the north aisle. Tradition says that this was for a light to guide travellers across the river. The nave and aisle roofs retain all their fifteenth-century timbers and some of those in the aisles are embellished with corbels of grotesques. The earlier north chapel roof has scissor-braced rafters but these are difficult to see above the collars. The west end bay has been converted into a bookshop.

The Rev. Charles Dodgson – 'Lewis Carroll' – sometimes preached at St Mary's when staying with his sisters at The Chestnuts nearby. He died there in 1898 (a plaque on the house records this) and is buried in the Mount Cemetery across the river.

Furnishings
The west window of the north aisle has Munich stained glass of *c*.1850, with predominantly blue colouring; all the other glass is Victorian. There is an early seventeenth-century armchair in the space under the tower and a Royal Arms of Queen Anne over the north door. The recently installed organ by Saxon Aldred, at the west end of the south aisle, is a fine example of modern workmanship. Unfortunately, the murals in the apse of St John's Chapel, probably thirteenth century, are no longer visible, but drawings exist at Castle Arch and details are given in the church guide. Set into the floor against the north wall of St. John's Chapel and moved from their original position are two brasses showing a couple dressed in the costume of around 1500, but nothing is known of them.

GUILDFORD, St Nicolas

Although the origins are unknown, there has been a church here since the early Middle Ages, but recent excavations have failed to reveal the date of this or whether there was an even earlier pre-Conquest church. Cracklow's drawing of the 1820s shows a typical homely Surrey building with tower clasped by two gables. This medieval church lay near the narrowest point of the Wey Gap, where the medieval bridge was built. The heavy masonry of the bridge led to frequent flooding and resultant weakening of the fabric. The medieval church was demolished in 1836, except for the Loseley Chapel, which had been owned by the More and More-Molyneux family since 1508. But this was not the predecessor of the present church as, in between, a badly-built Commissioners' Gothic place of worship, designed by Robert Ebbels, was in use between 1837 and 1875. The present church was designed by the insensitive S.S.Teulon, who died before building began so that the work, in neo-thirteenth-century style, was executed and tempered by the prolific but less able Ewan

Christian. It was thoroughly re-furbished and brightened by David Nye in his restoration begun in 1968 and today is an interesting example of High Victorianism.

Situated where the High Street comes to an abrupt stop beyond the bridge and still subject to flooding, as plaques on the wall indicate, the main entrance is in the south-west corner and follows the curve of the road. It has a somewhat forbidding exterior with aluminium roofs and large imposing central tower. The Bargate stone of the south aisle contrasts with the rough flint of the medieval Loseley Chapel (a private chapel until 1983) of 1540 in the south-east angle and the newer flint of the well-designed and discreet Parish Centre, south of the church.

The interior is bright and cheerful, with a spacious and welcoming west end, separated from the main body of the church. This area is divided into two sections, the southern part leading to the Loseley Chapel. The nave has a tiled floor and is of five bays, terminating in a central sanctuary with a new Carrara marble altar, the table of which is supported on five points. Bath stone is employed on the arches, windows and doorways of the nave. The east end is apsidal with lower walls lined with marble, and there are two aisles. The gabled east end of the south aisle was formed into St George's Chapel as a war memorial in 1921 and the north aisle into a Lady Chapel in 1912.

Furnishings
St. Nicolas is famous for its font by Thomas Earp and for its painted and gilded towering canopy of 1891, carved by Henry Woodyer, which completely encloses the font (*see fig. 101*). It is just inside the porch and, under the cover, there is a carved wooden dove. Woodyer also executed the fine wrought-iron screens. The pulpit was made by Thomas Earp and the hanging rood was designed by Charles Nicholson in 1920. The organ was originally built by 'Father' Henry Willis, but with subsequent additions and alterations. A particular feature is the stained glass which is mostly by Clayton & Bell, one of the better Victorian glass-makers. It is especially successful in the west end and the apse. The richly coloured main west window is in memory of Dr. Monsell, the hymn-writer and rector from 1870 to 1875, who was killed by falling stone when surveying building operations. The reredos of the old altar is also by Clayton & Bell. The paintings on the west wall, dating from 1900, are by Joseph Aloysius Pippit, who worked for this firm.

In the south aisle, there is a Rococo cartouche to John Knowles (d.1741). The Loseley Chapel, deep down on the south side, has a memorial to Arnold Brocas, rector from 1387 to 1395, in the form of a recumbent effigy under a three-arched canopy with lierne vaulting; it was moved from the north aisle. A large monument on the west wall records the union of the Mores with the Molyneux family and, on the east wall, there is a memorial to Sir William More (d.1600) and Dame Margaret, his wife, lying side by side; it is full size but dull sculpturally. There are also two small kneeler monuments and several seventeenth-century and eighteenth-century tablets. To the west of the door is the brass in memory of Caleb Lovejoy (d.1677) who provided for the building of the four stone almshouses close to the church (rebuilt in 1840-41).

GUILDFORD, St Catherine's Chapel

High above the road from Guildford to Godalming lie the ruins of this early fourteenth-century chapel. This pleasing small construction is one of the few ecclesiastical places of worship in the county to demonstrate the Decorated style, which, although now stripped of ornament, is not unlike a casket which once contained an article of value.

Across the valley to the east lies St Martha's Chapel, also once a ruin (see the entry above), but well rebuilt by Woodyer in 1848-50 using the old materials where possible. An appealing legend (also told of Putney and Fulham churches!) is that when the chapels were built by St Catherine and St Martha, who were sisters, there was only one hammer available between them and they hurled it high over the valley one to another, St Martha catching it from St Catherine, driving in a nail and hurling it back again.

HAMBLEDON, St Peter

Although there has long been a church on this site (the earliest recorded incumbent lived at the end of the thirteenth century and the living was in the gift of the Lords of the Manor from the fourteenth to the mid-seventeenth centuries), the present building was almost entirely reconstructed, except for the fourteenth-century north arcade and chancel arch, between 1840 and 1846. There is a view of the previous church in Cracklow's drawings of the 1820s, which shows a wooden bell-turret rising through the roof near the middle of the nave. Despite the style being local vernacular with shingled bellcote and erected of Bargate Stone quarried nearby, this place of worship to a certain extent lacks charm and the interior has a rather scrubbed look. It stands out well, however, on an elevated site and there are two splendid yew trees in the churchyard. A feature which is likely to be overlooked is a collection of minute carvings of heads on the cornice of the exterior of the south wall of the chancel. The shingled bell-turret was designed by Alban Caröe of the famous family of architects to replace in 1951 an unattractive one added when the church was rebuilt.

Furnishings
The main furnishings and monuments were lost or destroyed when the church was rebuilt, except for a slate tablet on the north wall commemorating Edward Eliot, who died in 1644; the Eliots were at one time Lords of the Manor. The marble font was given by a Mrs. Weguelin, the original twelfth-century Norman tub font having been taken to St Martha's on the Hill at Chilworth, when St Peter's was rebuilt by Woodyer in the middle of the nineteenth century. Of later date (1933) are the east windows by A.K. Nicholson, representing Faith, Hope and Love, given in memory of his wife by Eric Parker (author of *Highways and Byways in Surrey*). He lived at the house named Feathercombe in the village. He also gave two small windows in the chancel, commemorating two sons killed in the 1939-45 War.

HASCOMBE, St Peter

It is believed that the old church was built *c*.1220. The first mention appears in a list of churches of Guildford *c*.1283, where it is described as 'Ecclesia de Escumbe'. The first known rector of Hascombe died in 1316.

When Canon Vernon Musgrave became rector in 1862 (he remained so until 1906) he found the old church, with a little central bellcote, in a lamentable state of decay, windows being filled up with bricks and mortar. Under his inspiration, demolition started in 1863 and the new church, in late thirteenth-century style, to the designs of Henry Woodyer (one of his finest achievements and costing £ 3,100), was consecrated in June 1864. It consisted of nave, apse (the old church was also apsed) and separately roofed Lady Chapel (*see fig. 94*). It would appear that the original intention was that a plain nave should lead into a riot of colour and decoration in the apse and Lady Chapel; in fact the nave itself was not decorated until 1890.

Attractively sited at the junction of two small valleys, St Peter's respects the Surrey vernacular in having a small, shingled bellcote, with splay-footed spire, at the west end and is fortunate in being built of the county's best stone – Bargate – which happened to be available locally. Much of the old fourteenth-century oak timber was used in the porch and the massive mid-Victorian lock on the door was made to fit the ancient key.

The interior is almost Byzantine in its lavish decoration. All the roof rafters in the apse are cusped and gilded, providing a continuous interplay of highlights and the old fifteenth-century chancel screen has been covered with rich decoration in green, brown, gold and red. The central east window appears perkily through a buttress and the surrounding wall is stencilled to create, with carved angel candle-holders, a kind of reredos. The connection with the church's patron saint is underlined by the nave walls being decorated with the post-Resurrection haul of fish. The Rev. B.F.L. Clarke [37] has described St. Peter's as 'A Tractarian Work of Art' and there is no doubt that, at Hascombe, Henry Woodyer has created a highly individual village church and one which is a pleasure to visit.

Furnishings

The stained glass, except for the west window in the Lady Chapel by Clayton & Bell, is by Hardman & Powell, who also painted the screen. In the south-west corner of the nave is a spiral staircase leading to the belfry. The old Petworth marble font, a curious square bowl of 1690 on a square stem, has been retained. On the west wall a large tablet, slightly rough-hewn, commemorates William Diddlesfold (d.1785). There is a brass of 1906 in the chancel floor to Canon Vernon Musgrave, designed by his brother-in-law, Dr. Edwin Freshfield.

HASLEMERE, St Bartholomew

After the area served by St Bartholomew had been made into a separate parish, the old church – formerly a chapel of Chiddingfold – was taken down with the exception of the tower (probably thirteenth century with post-Reformation top) and a small part of the north aisle wall. The old church was noteworthy for its timber arcade separating nave from north aisle. The new church built in 1871 by J.W. Penfold in Early English style has little to commend it architecturally. A south aisle was added in 1888.

Furnishings

There are two Flemish seventeenth-century panels in the west window and the Burne-Jones window of 1899 in the north aisle in memory of Tennyson. There is a tapestry by Morris & Co. in front of the organ. The Victorian font of 1870 is in rich black and red marble with a fawn base, and there is a portable wood and copper font of 1960. The oak pulpit dates from 1930.

An epigram on a tombstone reads:

> 'Death little warning to me gave
> And quickly brought me to my grave.
> I from my friends did quickly part,
> I lost my life by a horse and cart.'

HASLEMERE, St Christopher

St.Christopher's was built in 1902-03 as the population spread westwards. The well proportioned exterior has a low attached south tower and a long nave roof without clerestory. The building material is galleted Bargate stone with occasional chequerboard patterns.

HEADLEY, St Mary the Virgin

St. Mary's stands 600 feet up on the North Downs and replaces an older church, which had fallen into a ruinous state and had become too small for local needs. It is the work of two Victorian architects: Anthony Salvin who built the nave and chancel in 1855, with an exterior faced with coursed cobbles (round flints), and George Edmund Street who erected the tower with splay-footed spire in 1859.

   The list of rectors goes back to 1317 and the living was owned by Westminster Abbey from the beginning of the fourteenth century to the Dissolution. The old church had a low tower with pyramidal cap and a bare south wall. It was made considerably more attractive in 1666 by Mary Stydolf, patroness of the living, who 'new ceiled and beautified the church throughout'.

Furnishings
The east window, replacing an earlier one, dates from 1894 and the altar triptych from 1895. The bowl and cover of the font and the Charles II Royal Arms were preserved from the old church.

157.   St. Peter's Church, Hersham from the north west.

HERSHAM, St Peter

At Queen Victoria's accession the population of Hersham was only about five hundred and there was no church, but in 1839 a place of worship, dedicated to the Holy Trinity, was built as a chapel of ease to St Peter's, Walton-on-Thames. By 1851, Hersham had become a separate parish and the numbers of people living there were such that Holy Trinity was found to be too small and was demolished in 1889. The site of its altar is marked by a commemorative stone near the north wall of the churchyard. To take its place, the present church – designed by the eminent John Loughborough Pearson (architect of the much earlier St James's, Weybridge) – was built in 1886/7 of Bath and Bargate rockfaced stone. Cruciform in plan, it is Early English in style, with lancets and plate tracery. Openly sited, the north-west tower and splay-footed spire rise to 92 feet, topped with a copper weather-vane in the form of a cockerel.

The interior is orthodox, but not spectacular. Inside, yellow brick from Claygate was used, whitened in 1931. Nave piers are alternately octagonal and circular and the aisles extend into the chancel, the walls of which were plastered in 1906 and painted with a design on the theme of the Te Deum. The east window consists of three stepped lancets. A screened Lady Chapel has been adapted and furnished in the north transept. The nave is separated from the chancel by a low Purbeck marble wall on which is erected a screen and gate.

Furnishings
There is a reredos of alabaster, richly carved, dating from the early twentieth century. The font is of Caen stone, also elaborately carved and supported on columns of red and green Devonshire marble. The pulpit is an attractive furnishing of carved oak with perforated panels, supported on columns of polished oak. Most of the stained glass is by Clayton and Bell. A large painting of the Annunciation (of *c.*1800) hangs in the south transept. A memorial commemorating Hersham men who died in the 1914-18 War and measuring 12 feet by 6 feet, made of Bere (Devon) stone and richly carved, is placed below the west window.

HOLMBURY ST. MARY, St Mary the Virgin

George Edmund Street came on a visit to Holmbury in 1872 with his first wife, who was so taken with the place, exclaiming 'This is Heaven's Gate', that Street decided to build a house there, where he was to live for the remainder of his life. It was the beginning of a sad period for the architect because, after losing his first wife shortly afterwards, his second wife died in 1876 eight months after their wedding. Street decided to build Holmbury Church in her memory and her tomb is to be found on the outside wall of the chancel facing south. It was erected in 1879 whilst he was building the Law Courts. Two years later in 1881, Street himself died at the age of 57 and was buried in Westminster Abbey. Consisting of nave, aisles, chancel or sanctuary and upper north chapel, the style is generally Early English to Decorated, using local stone, with Bath stone for the dressings. Owing to the site sloping steeply down to the east, Street raised the chancel and side chapel and positioned the vestries underneath. The west end is capped by a typical shingled belfry – low with short splay-footed spire – with a catslide roof sweeping down from the ridge over the north aisle, the aisle windows finishing high under the eaves. Seen from the road, the gabled east-end chancel and chapel wall is lofty and gives the impression of a larger church, but the composition is awkward, although the Rev. B.F.L. Clarke [38] describes it as 'a model village church'.
  Despite Street's skill as an architect, the interior is dark, due to the stained glass and the heavy but impressive roof unlit by any clerestory, and in consequence is somewhat lifeless. A western narthex is separated from the nave by a glazed screen. The blue Pennant (a carboniferous sandstone from the Bristol area) piers of the nave arcades each have four polished red marble shafts. The aisles have lean-to roofs and a screen divides the nave from the chancel/sanctuary.

Furnishings
Street believed strongly that painting and sculpture should enhance church buildings and, being his own patron at Holmbury, he endowed St Mary's with some notable works of art. He practised this to the extent of himself giving a reredos formed by a Florentine triptych of *c.*1400, depicting in its centre panel the Virgin and Child; he also gave the twelfth-century crucifix of Limoges enamel on the high altar. The Virgin and Child is complemented by a

second Virgin and Child in the narthex on the west wall, portrayed on a Della Robbia bas-relief; this was given by J.R. Clayton of Clayton & Bell. Street also designed most of the stained glass, made by the same firm, of which there is a large quantity in the sanctuary. The font, with a hanging dove (brought from Venice) above, is at the west end whilst the pulpit is decorated with coloured and stencilled designs in red, green, gold and black. In the sanctuary there are richly carved sedilia and piscina and in the choir and sanctuary are hung two pairs of brass candelabra of eighteenth-century Flemish design. Between the choir and the sanctuary is a copy of Fra Angelico's Annunciation. The north wall of the north chapel is decorated with a painting in a 12-sided frame thought to be by Jacopo del Sellaio (fifteenth-century) and the chapel altar has the east window as a reredos. There are two other reproduction paintings in the chapel, one of which is the Adoration of the Lamb by the van Eyck brothers (original in St Bavo's Cathedral, Ghent). There is also a late fifteenth-century Italian Madonna statue in the chapel.

HORLEY, St Bartholomew

In 1313 the church was appropriated by Chertsey Abbey, but the list of vicars starts about a hundred years before, indicating an earlier church – possibly wooden. The present building goes back to c.1310, when it consisted only of the north aisle, and in c.1350 a nave and chancel were added and the steeple erected. At the Reformation, the dedication was changed from St Mary the Virgin to St Bartholomew. The Victorians laid heavy hands on the church in 1881/2 (Sir Arthur Blomfield) and 1900/01, when the south aisle was added and the medieval character largely overlaid.

The generally Victorian appearance is relieved by the unusual and notable steeple (*see fig. 41*), with both bell-chamber and thin graceful spire beautifully shingled, probably by the same man who carried out the exquisite work at nearby Burstow. Although the tower is built up from the ground, the base, unlike those of the similar towers at Burstow, Great Bookham and Newdigate, rises from inside the church and thrusts up through the roof. The unrestored and delicate north doorway, with two small shafts having joined capitals, is an attractive feature. The west front has three gables of equal height, a central porch and Perpendicular windows.

The interior is largely spoilt by Victorian restorations although the fourteenth-century arcade of the nave is original and the arch between the chancel and the north chapel may be of the same period. The posts supporting the steeple are large and rugged with much original timber similar to that found in the nave roof. In 1970, a steel lining was inserted in the tower to carry the weight of extra bells. The north aisle windows have Kentish tracery.

Furnishings
At the east end of the north aisle there is a fine recumbent effigy of Ralph Salaman (d.1315) bearing the double-headed eagle family arms and, on his armour, the leopard motif which is repeated in the trefoils of the north wall windows. The effigy is life-size with uncrossed legs, head on a cushion and feet on a lion. On the north side of the chancel is a large brass showing a female figure of c.1400 with an 'S' collar round her neck, indicating that she was a member of the Lancastrian party. The full-faced figure is less elaborate than the finely-executed canopy. The caption beneath describes her as Joan, wife of John Fenner (d.1517), but the clothes show that she lived much earlier than this; it is probable that she was a member of the Salaman family. Opposite is an appealing small brass figure of a late fourteenth-century civilian.

HORNE, St Mary

St. Mary's, situated almost away from the village, was harshly restored in 1880 and its attractions, which included a timber bell-tower rising from the ground apart from the nave, have largely disappeared. It was originally a chapel of ease to Blechingley and did not become a separate parish until 1705. The oldest portion is the south doorway of *c.*1250, which was moved westwards when the nave was lengthened in 1880. Medieval windows have been scattered around in a haphazard manner and the earlier tower replaced by a bell tower with splay-footed spire, the base of which is engaged in the body of the church, but which is not unattractive. The trussed rafter roof with tie-beams of the nave and the battlemented tie-beams of the chancel are, however, medieval. Other such features are an original fifteenth-century window with rere-arch on the south side of the nave and a square-headed example with three trefoiled lights and good detail, on the north side reset when the aisle was built. East of the chancel step is the doorway to the rood stairway, which is blocked at the tenth riser.

Furnishings
These include an octagonal fifteenth-century chalkstone font and a Perpendicular-type screen with narrow bays and trefoiled heads, which has been moved from the chancel step to the west end. The most interesting feature is the monument to John Goodwine (d.1618) and his wife (*Colour Plate XVII*), on the north side of the chancel, as much of the original dark red and green colouring remains. They are shown as small kneeling black figures.

HORSELL, St Mary the Virgin

Horsell was originally a hamlet of Woking but has taken the brunt of the expansion of the town north-westwards. Nevertheless the village manages to retain some of its separate identity. St Mary's history goes back a long way and the advowson (or right to choose the incumbent) was sold in 1258 together with that of St Nicholas, Pyrford by Westminster Abbey to Newark Priory for forty marks (£ 26 13s. 4d.) for the two. After the Dissolution, the advowson of St Mary's passed to the Crown and then to lay patrons until 1868, when the perpetual curacy was converted to a vicarage by Act of Parliament. The church is nicely located on a hillock. Dating from the late fourteenth century, the diagonal-buttressed tower of the church is built of flint, chalk and local sandstone with some admixture of tiles. It has a battlemented crown with stair-turret rising above the north-east corner.

St. Mary's was considerably altered and enlarged in 1890. The late eighteenth-century chancel was taken down and a new larger one constructed of Bargate stone, while both the nave and south aisle (the latter built mainly of

158.   Horsell Church.

pudding-stone at the end of the fifteenth century) were extended eastwards by another bay. The restoration and alterations, partly by W.F. Unsworth, who also built Christ Church, Woking and All Saints, Woodham, have removed most of the medieval character of the church. Further additions were made in 1909, when the north aisle and vestries were built. A year later, as thanksgiving for deliverance of the vicar's wife from what might have been a fatal accident due to a runaway horse, the sanctuary at the end of the south aisle was provided. The baptistry, the last major structural contribution, was built of Bargate stone in 1921. The materials used in construction give a pleasant tweedy texture to the church.

Furnishings
The pulpit is hexagonal and made of oak with lozenge-shaped decoration on the panels. It dates from 1602, just before the edict of James I's reign stating that each church should be provided with 'a decent and comely pulpit', at a time when increasing emphasis was being placed upon the sermon. The sounding board, although not in position, is still in the church. A candelabrum, thought to date from the first half of the eighteenth century, with eight sconces (others are missing), is worth noting in the chancel. There are medieval chests in the porch and against the west wall. An attractive sanctuary chair is to be seen in the sanctuary. The Royal Arms above the main door are those of Queen Victoria, dated 1842. The heads of the two northern bays of the screen separating the south chapel from the south aisle are original and may have formed part of the former rood screen. By way of contrast to the main furnishings there is a charming and spirited wood carving by a local trader on the sill of the south-west window. The figures are extraordinarily vivid and the articles on the table (platters, rolls and cups) are handled with great skill. A curiosity is the iron spit,11 ft. 7 in. long, in the south-west corner – probably used on the occasion of a parish festival to roast an ox. An inventory of 1553 refers to two 'broches' (the old name) and a 'caudron'. There are two monuments of interest, one on the west wall to Sir John Rose (d.1803) and his wife. The two figures lean on an urn, but in contemporary dress and striking Baroque attitudes; it is by the younger Bacon. The other on the east wall of the south aisle is to James Fenn (d.1773) and his wife, the two figures facing each other across a table piled untidily with books. Both monuments are old-fashioned for their dates.

KEW, St Anne

St. Anne's started as a chapel in 1522, used by courtiers in Tudor and Stuart times. The present building, following a petition to Queen Anne, Lady of the Manor, dates from 1710-14, when it consisted only of a nave measuring 64 feet by 27 feet. The north aisle was added and the church lengthened in 1770, mainly at the expense of George III after he had bought Kew Palace. In 1805, the Royal Gallery supported on cast-iron columns was inserted. Two hundred free seats were provided in the church by William IV in 1836; the portico and bell-turret date from the same year. In 1884, the chancel, south aisle and side chapel were added, plus the vestry on the north side and the organ chamber, giving St. Anne's its present form. The mausoleum with lead-covered half-dome, originally erected in 1851 by Benjamin Ferrey for the Duke and Duchess of Cambridge, was moved to the east end beyond the chancel at the time of these additions. There was a restoration in 1968 and a fine Georgian-style hall added on the north side in 1977-80 to mark the Queen's Jubilee. Effectively sited on the side of a beautiful green with many Georgian houses, St. Anne's is a conspicuous building of yellow brick with arched red-brick window surrounds, having been built up piece-by-piece over a considerable period. It is long and low, extending from the portico and polygonal timber bell-turret at the west end to the octagon with curious cupola and the mausoleum at the east end. There are no transepts.

159.   The interior of Kew Church, looking east.

The pleasing interior consists of a nave with arcades in the form of five Tuscan columns of timber, supporting lintels and a vaulted ceiling. The crossing has pink scagliola columns, the apse white and gold columns. The dome is decorated with gold stars on a blue ground.

This unusual and internally beautiful church is chiefly noted for its intimate royal connections. Many members of the Royal Family at varying times worshipped in it. The Duke and Duchess of Teck, Queen Mary's parents, were married in St Anne's and the Duke of Cambridge (son of George III) and his Duchess were originally interred in the mausoleum, although moved to Windsor in 1930.

Furnishings
The stained glass of the east window of 1893 is by Kempe. In the centre of the west gallery (of 1805) are the Royal Arms of Queen Anne. None of the monuments is outstanding. The major ones are to Lady Capel (d.1721), who owned Kew House before it was leased to Frederick, Prince of Wales, to Francis Bauer, botanical draughtsman, (d.1840) by Westmacott Junior, and to Sir William and his son, Sir Joseph Hooker, Directors of the Botanic Gardens, who both made important contributions to botanical science. The memorial to Sir William (d.1865) is by Woolner & Palgrave, with a Wedgwood medallion and panels of ferns; the one to Sir Joseph (d.1911) also has ceramic panels of plants. In the churchyard are the graves of Thomas Gainsborough, the famous landscape and portrait painter who died in 1788 (middle south side), and of Johann Zoffany, painter of portraits, conversation pieces and theatrical scenes, who died in 1810 (east side).

KINGSTON UPON THAMES, All Saints

The presence of the Coronation Stone by the Guildhall (moved from the Saxon chapel of St Mary when it collapsed in 1730) and the mention of the church in Domesday underlines the age and importance of this large town place of worship, but, throughout the ages, it has been subjected to a series of alterations and restorations which have largely deprived it of its medieval, let alone Saxon, character. The site of the Saxon church of St Mary (there may have been an earlier one) is marked by stones outside the south door. This was probably incorporated into a Norman building erected in the early twelfth century, which itself made way for a wider fourteenth-century building, to which the piers of the nave and south transept belong. The living of the Norman church of the early twelfth century, built under the supervision of Gilbert the Norman, Sheriff of the County, was presented by him to the Priory of Merton under whom it remained until the Dissolution in 1538.

The lower parts of the tower, dating from the thirteenth century, are the oldest parts of the present fabric, but the rest of the tower has suffered a chequered career since then. Two spires – the first a lofty wooden one destroyed during a storm in 1445 and the second, faced with lead and rebuilt c.1505, which met a similar fate – have come and gone, and the present attractive brick top dates from 1708 (see fig. 81).

The nave interior is spacious, with slender late fourteenth-century four-bay nave arcades, but the main architectural interest resides in the tower and eastern parts. The chapels on each side of the chancel were constructed between the years 1340 and 1460, the north chapel (Holy Trinity) and the baptistry beyond the south chapel retaining their original roofs.

The seventeenth and eighteenth centuries saw the addition of galleries on the west, north and south sides, which must have imposed a severe strain on the structure, but these together with the box pews were swept away in wholesale restorations in the nineteenth century, first by R. Brandon in the 1860s and later by J.L. Pearson in the early 1880s. Stained glass was inserted, the nave ceiling removed, the floor lowered and the east and west arches of the tower heightened to provide a better view of the chancel. Other work included the renewal of the clerestory windows. The exterior has been completely refaced in flint with stone dressings, but its open aspect to the town on the north side and pleasing tower adds lustre to the townscape. All Saints is nearly 150 feet long.

More recently, Comper installed a new altar (1951) and had the chancel barrel roof painted in a pattern of blue and gold stars. The present century has seen the fitting out of the Holy Trinity Chapel as a memorial chapel to the East Surrey Regiment. The removal of the sanctuary in recent years to its present position under the tower has left the chancel open, with attractive vistas from the fourteenth-century arches of the south transept to its fifteenth-century clustered piers.

Furnishings
The font dates from 1669, but the pillar it stands on is not original; the font was brought back from the Vicarage garden to replace a nineteenth-century successor. Fragments of a Saxon churchyard cross, with elaborate interlacing pattern on its two sides, remain in the baptistry. Between the arches on the east side of the south transept is a wall painting of St. Blaise, much restored. The richly-coloured and striking stained glass in the window at the west end dates from c.1865. The baptistry was formerly St James's Chapel, founded in the fifteenth century by William Skerne as a chantry. North of the font is a stone slab with good memorial brasses from the tomb of Robert Skerne (d.1437) and his wife Joanna, who was a daughter of King Edward III and Alice Perrers. On the south side there is an interesting table-tomb to Sir Anthony Benn (d.1618) (*Colour Plate XV*), Recorder of

Kingston and later of London; the recumbent effigy is coloured. In the south transept are brasses to John Hertcombe (d.1488) and his wife in a kneeling posture. A fifteenth-century niche in the south chapel with quatrefoil chest front may have been an Easter Sepulchre. The most notable memorial is in the north aisle to Louisa Theodosia, Countess of Liverpool (d.1821) by Francis Chantrey, showing her seated. In the same aisle is a memorial to John Heyton (d.1584), Sergeant of the Larder to Queen Mary and Queen Elizabeth. There are also memorials to Lady Frances Meadows by John Flaxman (1795) with an almost detached cherub on a cloud below an urn, well carved: to Henry Davidson (d.1781) by Regnart, showing a standing female figure by an urn, and to another of the same name (d.1827) by Termouth, with a seated figure in a Grecian chair. Both the Davidson memorials are in the south transept. Finally, worthy of mention is the memorial to George Bate (d.1668), Physician to Charles I, Oliver Cromwell and Charles II.

KINGSTON UPON THAMES, Lovekyn Chapel (St Mary Magdalene)

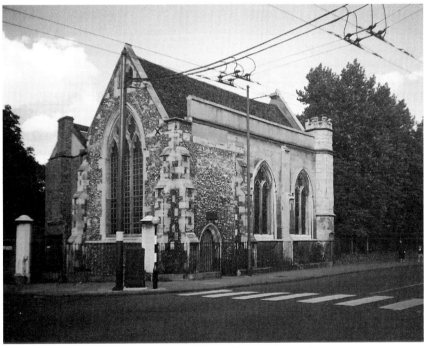

160.   Lovekyn Chapel, Kingston upon Thames from the north west.

This chapel, situated on the main road to London, is a rare example of a chantry chapel separate from a church. It was founded in 1309 by Edward Lovekyn and partly rebuilt by his son John in 1352. In 1561 Queen Elizabeth established her Grammar School and the chapel survived because it was used as the school room. It has recently been restored as a centre for music and the arts.

KINGSWOOD, St Andrew

This is one of Benjamin Ferrey's seven Surrey churches built in the early years of Queen Victoria's reign between 1844 and 1852. It is almost an exact copy of the fourteenth-century collegiate church at Shottesbrooke in Berkshire and set in leafy suburban surroundings. The lofty spire on a relatively elevated site is a landmark for miles around.

KINGSWOOD, The Church of the Wisdom of God, Lower Kingswood

This church was the offspring of Dr. Edwin Hanson Freshfield and Sir Henry Cosmo Orme Bonsor, both local residents. Dr. Freshfield had travelled much abroad and had married the daughter of an Englishman living in Smyrna, Turkey. He was imbued therefore with classical Roman and Byzantine influences, which are reflected throughout this unusual place of worship. The architect was Sidney Barnsley and it was built in brick and Ham stone in 1891-92, being dedicated on 17th July 1892. The style is Roman basilican with a bar separating the chancel from the nave, derived from the Roman court of justice, where prisoners were brought to trial. The church is notable more for its contents than its architecture and consists of a single nave and chancel, separated by the bar, and apse, with a lean-to roof stretching the full length of the west end. The nave has only two bays, and there are narrow aisles.

The exterior has a number of features. The outer west door is made of oak, bound with iron framing, but the iron studs were a gift from Mohammedan priests to Dr. Freshfield in return for a donation he had made for the care of a former Christian church in Salonica. The bell-tower was copied from a sketch made by the doctor in a Bulgarian village. Near the tower is a Roman corn-grinding stone found in the Roman wall of London. The exterior, however, leaves one unprepared for the rich decoration of marbles and mosaics within or for the unusual display of ancient Byzantine capitals and original furnishings in uncommon woods designed by the architect. The collection of marbles is probably unique in England in its variety and the fact that most of it was actually quarried by the Romans.

161. The bell steeple at Lower Kingswood.

The east end and the baptistry (panelled in 1935) are marble-lined, whilst the walls and roof above the central apse are completely covered with mosaic (*Colour Plate XXXVIII*). The marbles range from rare and genuine *verde antico* and grey north African in the apse, two small pieces of red porphyry on the steps of the apse, rare buff-coloured streaked marble in the baptistry to the more common white Carrara (also in the apse) and the pink marble on the floor of the chancel and central nave aisle. This exotic import from the ancient classical world – the work of two Byzantine enthusiasts – is a strange phenomenon in commuter Surrey, adding spice to the ecclesiastical heritage of the county.

Furnishings
There are nine capitals from fourth- to sixth-century Byzantine buildings brought here by Dr. Freshfield. The two largest in the body of the church came from the fourth-century church of St John at Ephesus. Smaller fourth- and sixth-century capitals are affixed to the west wall and there are later eleventh-century capitals. The

font is of Egyptian alabaster (onyx) with an
ebony cover. A curious link with Greek or
Coptic tradition is the presentation to their
churches of an egg to commemorate a
christening and a porcelain one is hanging
near the south door in memory of
Dr. Freshfield's sister, Zoë, and a real
ostrich egg in the baptistry commemorates
the christening of their brother, John. Two
other ostrich eggs hang in the chancel. The
wooden furnishings, including pulpit and
lectern with ebony and holly inlay, priests'
seats with canopies and inlay including
mother of pearl, the prayer desks and stalls
are by Barnsley, who also painted the
pretty wagon roof with a design of spring
flowers.

Administration is outside normal
diocesan control, being in charge of the
incumbent and the two churchwardens.

162.   A fourth-century capital at Lower Kingswood.

LEATHERHEAD, St Mary and St Nicholas

The church of St Mary and St Nicholas goes back to pre-Conquest times and originally was
almost certainly built by Edward the Confessor,
who held the advowson. In medieval times, the
living was in the gift of royal and monastic
patrons, being tossed to and fro, first from the
Royal Manor of Ewell to Colchester Abbey
*c.*1100, reclaimed by Edward I in 1279, granted
by Edward III in 1341 to the Priory of St Mary
and St Nicholas at Leeds in Kent, whence the
unusual dedication is derived, and where it
remained until 1541. It then passed to the Dean
and Chapter of Rochester Cathedral with whom
it still rests.

The present nave and chancel are basically
twelfth- and thirteenth-century in date, but the
walls above the nave arcades may be Saxon. The
transepts, first used as manorial chapels, also date
from this time, but the north transept is now
mainly nineteenth-century after Sir Arthur
Blomfield restored and extended it in 1873. The
north and south aisles date from *c.*1190 but,
whilst the south arcade consists of four bays, the
north initially was only three bays long, although
now extended to the west by a nineteenth-century
arch. In *c.*1320, the chancel was extended
eastwards by 14 feet; in 1874 it was restored by

163.   The north-east nave capital at Leatherhead.

Ewan Christian. In addition to his work on the north transept, Blomfield renewed the roofs in 1891 and restored the tower in 1894.

The exterior is all renewed, with dormer windows inserted in the nave, but the flint-faced tower with angle buttresses, dating from *c*.1480, is a prominent feature. Set markedly askew, it cuts into the south arcade; this was to provide space for processions between the church and the boundary wall along an ancient right of way. An agreeable offset to the general renewal is the use of Horsham slates on the north transept and lych-gate roofs and some chequerboard flint and stone masonry from the old Perpendicular north transept.

The interior is more pleasing. Although nineteenth-century restoration is all too apparent (north transept, chancel and roofs), the general impression is early thirteenth-century and the nave roof is of crown-post design. The height suggests Saxon origin. The slightly later chancel arch, inserted in a wall of chalkstone, which stops well short of the roof, is large and sophisticated work. The carved shell stops at the top of the chamfers are believed to be unique. A rare double hagioscope cut through the south-east corner of the north transept had to be re-aligned to give a view of the high altar in its new position, when the chancel was extended eastwards by about 14 feet in the fourteenth century. The nave arcades are supported on alternate circular and octagonal piers, the north-easternmost capital of which is reminiscent of those at Reigate of *c*.1200, having single upright trefoiled stiff leaves. The insertion of a nineteenth-century arch in the north arcade must have been due to the demolition and rebuilding of the west wall. The four-centred tower arch of three orders is a good foil to the chancel arch. A Tudor doorway leads to the tower staircase and, high up to the left of the doorway, is a gallery which was used by seven boys from a local school who sang the anthem 'All glory, laud and honour' when the Palm Sunday procession entered the west door.

Furnishings
The font is of fifteenth-century octagonal quatrefoil type. Medieval fragments of stained glass of various dates are skilfully assembled in the north-west aisle window. A chest of 1663 in the south aisle, bound in leather with stud patterns, came from Slyfield House and was a muniment chest. There is another of thirteenth-century date in the north aisle. The furnishings also include a triple sedilia and piscina and a double squint of unusual form from the north transept.

On the west side of the entrance to the south transept is a memorial to Robert Gardiner, Chief Sergeant of the Cellar to Queen Elizabeth I, with his funeral helmet behind. On the north-east wall of the chancel, a monument commemorates Richard Dalton (d.1723), a mediocre tablet completely enclosed in militaria, with a relief of a man-of-war below. A ledger-stone of 1410 in the baptistry has fragments of brass insets remaining; it commemorates Matild Hamdun, ux (wife) of Thomas at Hull. A ledger stone in the porch is in memory of a lady who would not go to church. The novelist, Anthony Hope Hawkins, son of a headmaster of St John's School and creator of 'Ruritania', is buried in the north-west corner of the churchyard; he died in 1933.

LEIGH, St Bartholomew

This small unaisled Perpendicular church built of Reigate stone was the victim of two Victorian restorations which have taken away much of its village character, the first by H. Woodyer in 1855 and the second by F.C. Lees in 1890, when the lean-to porch was added and much of the interest of the interior removed. The church is attractively situated on a green with views through trees to the North Downs. The original west bellcote with a pyramid roof was replaced by a stone tower and then, when St Bartholomew's was extended westwards, by a nineteenth-century bellcote. The windows have two and three lights, some square-headed and some segmental. This has produced a picturesque, but somewhat affected exterior.

Furnishings
The font is fifteenth-century in date and the east window by Kempe of 1890 is a fair example of his work. However, the most interesting of the internal features is the brass to John Arderne (d.1449) and his wife, with their daughters below. They are shown full face in civilian dress and the main effigies are three feet high. They lived nearby at Leigh Place.

LIMPSFIELD, St Peter

A Domesday church, this was given by William the Conqueror to the Abbey of Battle as a thank-offering for victory at Hastings, although the Abbey did not appropriate the living but merely appointed the rector. The present church appears thirteenth-century in date, when the chancel was rebuilt and lengthened, but the tower and west wall are of the late twelfth century (*c*.1180). The nave retains its original proportions, but all four walls are pierced by later work, so that its character is entirely changed. The east-end lancets have also been reconstructed. A doorway and two-bay arcade opening from the north side of the chancel into the Gresham Chapel and the south arcade of the nave are of the thirteenth century. The north arcade dates from 1851 when the chancel arch was raised and, possibly slightly earlier, a new west window inserted, replacing a fifteenth-century window of five lights. At the same time the extension of the west gallery along the north wall may have been removed. J.L. Pearson carried out further work in 1871/2, when the nineteenth-century triple lancets of the chancel and the Gresham Chapel were filled with new glass and the whole of the upper part of the east wall was rebuilt.

The approach through a restored fourteenth-century lych-gate roofed with Horsham slates is picturesque. This rugged southern aspect of the exterior, with Horsham slate and tiled roof sweeping down to low walls without clerestory, and the Norman tower with pyramidal roof in an unusual position east of the south aisle (*see fig. 11*), and set in a beautifully tended churchyard, is the most attractive view. The stone is ironstone, sandstone rubble and Wealden sandstone. The interior is less agreeable as the medieval character is largely obscured by nineteenth-century alterations. The roofs, however, retain much of their original timber, although the north aisle was added in 1851.

There is a most unusual feature in the east wall behind the Communion table in the form of a cupboard, rebated to take a door and perhaps intended for a sacred relic. South of this, there is a second recess with a 6-inch diameter flue built into the top. The latter was an oven for baking the Communion bread, a comparatively rare survival. It was lit by a small window at the east end of the south chancel wall. There is evidence in the tower that this was also used for the administration of Communion.

Furnishings
The thirteenth-century font with a plain, square bowl has been recut. The pulpit dating from 1764 was once much taller and had a sounding board, but has been cut down and now stands on a stone base. The nineteenth-century lancets in the chancel and chancel chapel have Clayton & Bell stained glass, no doubt commissioned by Pearson as at nearby Titsey, and inserted in 1871. The monuments include memorials to Marmaduke Hilton (d.1768), in a Palladian frame (in the south aisle) and to Lord Elphinstone (d.1860), a well-executed effigy showing him in the robes of the Order of the Bath. Frederick Delius, the composer,

164.   Limpsfield Chart.

was brought from France to Limpsfield for re-burial in the churchyard in 1935 and his wife is interred in the same grave. Sir Thomas Beecham gave a funeral oration by torchlight as a tribute to the composer whose works he had helped to make widely known.

LIMPSFIELD, St Andrew, Limpsfield Chart

Many private residences were erected in this parish at the end of the nineteenth century and, to serve those in the Chart area, St Andrew's Church was built in 1895 to the plans of Sir Reginald Blomfield. The architect seems to have got his styles somewhat mixed, but there is an Arts-and-Crafts reredos by H. Wilson.

LINGFIELD, St Peter and St Paul

Although not mentioned in Domesday, it seems probable that a church existed here at the time of the Conquest. The lower parts of the west wall indicate an early medieval place of worship but whatever there was probably underwent rebuilding in the fourteenth century and this included the tower which is earlier than the rest of the existing fabric. This reflects the influence of a branch of the Kentish Cobham family, who lived at Sterborough Castle (demolished in 1648), two miles east of the church. Sir Reginald, Third Baron Cobham – who fought at Agincourt – received in 1431 the perpetual advowson and licence to convert St Peter's (St Paul had not then been added to the dedication) into a collegiate church, the college to consist of six chaplains, four clerks and thirteen poor persons. He was the driving force behind the complete rebuilding of the church (except the tower and spire) and so furnishing Surrey with its only late medieval place of worship, if one excepts St John the Baptist at Croydon (largely rebuilt after a fire in 1870). The material used for the walls was mainly Tunbridge Wells sandstone but subsequent restoration has been in Sussex sandstone from West Hoathly. Attractive Horsham slates cover the roof except for part of the internal slopes for which clay tiles have had to be used. A restoration in 1846/7 was not well carried out. Many of the original medieval furnishings were destroyed. The flooring at the east end of the chancel and of the north chapel was lowered.

The church is sited at the north end of a small square of attractive buildings – one of the most picturesque churchscapes in Surrey. The view from the entrance gate shows the south aisle with three-light windows, bare of tracery under a two-centred hood-mould, and the fourteenth-century south-west tower (*see fig. 35*), with projecting parapet enriched with blind quatrefoils under the coping. There are no pinnacles and the spire is a simple splay-footed example. Clerestories are conspicuous by their absence, making this building externally a modest example of the Perpendicular style. On the north wall, where the north aisle and north chapel meet, a half-octagonal rood stair-turret rises, topped much later with a stone chimney linked with the heating furnace installed in 1858. With the exception of the window over the west door, the windows are typical of the Perpendicular style, but the one

165 & 166.   Two misericords at Lingfield.

over the west end of the north aisle is of special interest, in that it has carved hood-mould stops of grotesques and another carved head on the apex stone. These may have come from the earlier church.

The interior is spacious with a north aisle and chapel extending the whole length of the church, giving a two-nave effect, one of which may have been collegiate and the other parochial – a rare combination (compare with St Helen's, Bishopsgate in London). The south aisle between tower and vestry is much shorter. A transverse arcade with chancel arch in the middle runs across from north to south – another unusual effect. The nave arcades and chancel arch have standard slender piers consisting of four attached shafts and four hollows between them. The respond against the west wall of the north arcade is noteworthy. At the east end is an undercroft with vaults and external access from the north side. The oak roof is of arched brace construction with panels.

Furnishings
The church has a fine set of late medieval fittings. Of especial interest are the stalls, probably provided when the church was made collegiate in 1431. There were sixteen but five on the north side have disappeared – probably during the 1846/7 restoration – and have been replaced by a bench with Renaissance panels of medallion heads of Philip of Spain and possibly Queen Mary – and the Royal Arms; one should particularly note the warrior, with goatee beard, in sixteenth-century armour. The remaining eleven stalls retain their tip-up seats with projecting ledges (or misericords) underneath and eight of these are carved (angels bearing shields but also, and more interesting, a bishop and two other heads). The parclose screens separating the chancel from the north and south chapels are, in contrast to the stalls, of indifferent workmanship. The fifteenth-century octagonal font has an ogee-shaped wooden cover, with crocketed ribs, which may be contemporary with the font. The double-sided wooden lectern is of uncertain date and has a chained bible dating from 1688 on one desk. Other fittings to note are the eighteenth-century brass chandelier, suspended by a wrought-iron pendant like a sword rest and the Royal Arms of Queen Anne on the north wall of the nave. Fragments of medieval stained glass remain in the south window of the chancel, but all the rest is nineteenth-century, the best being in the main east window.

The monuments are the *pièces de resistance* of the church and are mainly to members of the Cobham family: four table tombs (three in the Lady Chapel), the earliest being to Sir Reginald, first Baron Cobham (*see fig. 68*), and the latest to Sir Reginald, third Baron Cobham. These two have effigies; the others have, in the case of the second Baron, a simple slab of Purbeck marble with an inlaid brass figure and, in the fourth, nothing to indicate with certainty who it commemorates. It is said to be the tomb of Sir Thomas Cobham, who died in 1471 and his wife Anne, great grand-daughter of Edward III. The first Baron's tomb is situated on the south side of the Lady Chapel and is constructed of Caen stone with the effigy in firestone (Reigate stone). Sir Reginald's face is uncovered and he is dressed in full plate armour, but the most appealing features are the Moor's head helm, on which his head rests, supported by two boyish angels, and the knavish-looking Saracen's head (*see fig. 69*) under his feet. The tomb-chest is battlemented. He died of the plague in 1361. His wife is buried in Southwark. The sides and ends of the tomb are decorated with shields. The tomb of the second Baron is situated on the north side of the Lady Chapel and is made of firestone with, on the top, a slab of Purbeck marble, which encloses his brass, showing him in full armour. He died in 1403. His wife was buried in Lewes Priory. The tomb of Sir Reginald, the third Lord Cobham, also of firestone but embattled like the tomb of the first Lord Cobham, occupies the most important situation in the middle of the chancel. The effigies are of alabaster and well carved. At the head is another Moor's head-helm with angels, but at the foot a sea wolf with a wicked expression. As with the tomb of the first Lord, the sides are panelled with shields and, in this case, also heraldic emblems; the vignettes at head and feet are a detail to note. Unlike the other two, Sir Reginald is accompanied by his second wife, Anne Bardolph (d.1453): she has a knavish-looking wyvern at her feet. It was this Sir Reginald who founded the college and rebuilt the church. Sir Reginald, who died in 1446, is dressed in plate armour except the head and hands. Other memorials include two good Baroque cartouches on the south wall of the chancel, to Francis, Lord Howard (d.1694) and Lady Mary Howard (d.1718); they are enclosed in exuberant high relief foliage and cherub heads.

The brasses are the best set in Surrey, although not the equal of the Kentish Cobham set, which are generally regarded as the best in the country. At Lingfield, there are five in the Lady Chapel, three to members of the Cobham family, all good, especially the one without inscription – probably to Elizabeth, second wife of the second Baron, a full-sized figure with her head on a tasselled pillow and a pet dog at her feet. The second Baron, like the other Barons, is shown in armour. There are two others in the Lady Chapel, one, a small demi-figure brass, to Katerina Stoket of *c*.1420, one of the first Lady Cobham's 'damsels', and the other to John Hadresham in military costume. In the chancel, there are five other brasses, all, except for one small female figure, of priests connected with the college and who died between 1445 and 1503.

LITTLE BOOKHAM (dedication unknown)

167. The blocked arcade at Little Bookham.

The building was begun *c*.1080 to which *c*.1150 a south aisle was added; this latter date was contemporary with the building of the nave of St Nicholas, Great Bookham. The aisle was removed, however, at an unknown date and the arcades blocked up, making the church a single-celled building – an unusual example of a church being reduced in size, when in most cases the growth of population in the county necessitated enlargement. Restored in 1864, situated in a secluded site and still quite rural in appearance, the exterior shows a simple single-roofed country church, with a small wooden west bellcote capped by a low, pyramidal shingled spire. One original window remains at the west end and another at the north-west end of the nave. The interior has been stripped of most of its interest.

Furnishings
A large tub font, probably twelfth-century, is bound with a complicated arrangement of iron straps which may date from the seventeenth century. There is a good Grecian tablet, with a boldly carved urn, to George Pollen (d.1812) on the north side of the chancel.

LONGCROSS, Christ Church.

About two miles from Chertsey on the north side of the B386 road stands a small chapel-like structure – Christ Church, Longcross – with numerous graves to the Tringham family, who have been closely connected with the history of the building. The area is one of attractive woodland and common with scattered houses amongst the trees.

The church was built by Willoughby in 1846/7. In 1878 it was extended by one bay and a chancel added to the designs of Ralph Nevill of Godalming. One enters the churchyard through a gabled lych-gate of *c*.1920 and a long, narrow path leads to the church. When one enters by a richly decorated door (with scrolling ironwork on the outer face and carved tracery, including the shield of the Tringham arms, on the inner) one is charmed by the small interior. The aisleless nave measures 47 feet by 23 feet and the chancel 22 feet by 15 feet, with a north organ chamber and vestry. There is much stained glass. The country atmosphere about it all is very appealing and this is an endearing little building.

LONG DITTON, St Mary,

St. Mary's has a long history going back to Domesday Book, when a church at 'Ditune' is mentioned. The adjacent Manor was held in the twelfth century by Geoffrey de Mandeville's heir, William, who gave it to the Priory of St Mary without Bishopsgate, who assumed that they, therefore, had the right to appoint rectors. This, however, was challenged by the Priory of Merton who had been confirmed by the Bishop of Winchester in the grant of the advowson. Merton won the ensuing legal battle and retained the right until the Dissolution. The first recorded rector is Robert Picot, appointed in 1166. The present church was one of the last to be designed by G.E. Street, architect of the Law Courts, and was built between 1878 and 1880. It succeeded a brick building of 1776 in the form of a Greek cross, with the curious feature of only four windows, one at the end of each limb of the cross. Apart from the Saxon church mentioned in Domesday, there is a pen-and-ink sketch, dating from *c*.1720, of a late medieval building, but no firm evidence of any other church.

Built of buff-coloured stone, the most prominent exterior feature is a double bell-cote between the nave and chancel. The interior presents a Gothic Revival place of worship with aisles and transepts dominated by the east window, richly coloured and based on the Gospel of St John, XII. 32, and which replaced a war-damaged predecessor. The high four-bay nave arcade walls are pierced with three triple-lancet clerestory windows on each side. On the south side, Street has varied the cross-sections of the piers (circular, clustered and medieval church, although some capitals and bases at the west end came from an earlier church. The north transept serves as a Lady Chapel with altar, aumbry and sanctuary lamp, the south as a children's chapel.

Furnishings
In a baptistry formed at the west end by two projecting walls is the most enjoyable furnishing – the font of green marble dedicated in 1891. The pulpit is of carved stone and there is a wrought-iron chancel screen. The reredos, dating from 1930, has three alabaster figures of Christ, St Matthew and St Luke. The precise date of the eighteenth-century Hanoverian Royal Arms in the baptistry is not known. Many windows were destroyed during the 1939-45 War and have been replaced either with modern stained or white glass.

Above the door to the vestry at the end of the north aisle are brass effigies to Richard Hatton (d.1616, aged 81) and his wife Mary (d.1612). The Hattons rose to high office in the county. Above the altar in the Lady Chapel is a brass to Sir Robert Castleton (d.1527) and Elizabeth his wife with their six daughters, but the portion commemorating their five sons is lost. Sir Robert was Clerk of the Pleas to the Exchequer of Henry VIII. On the south wall of the chancel, an early sixteenth-century brass commemorates John Haymer, instituted Rector in 1492. This brass originally formed part of a stone memorial.

LOWFIELD HEATH, St Michael

This charming 1867 building, designed by William Burges, one of the most original and characteristic of High Victorian architects, is tucked away under the shadow of Gatwick Airport (which it has now followed into the Diocese of Chichester) and is little known to the hundreds of tourists who pass through this area. It is small and aisleless with an attached south-west tower and pyramid spire. Above the lean-to west porch is an outstanding rose window described by Ian Nairn [39] as 'being a first-rate bit of picturesque composition'; it has eight shafts connecting round-headed openings and there are four carvings at the cardinal points, with a seated figure of God the Father at the top. Another notable feature is the rose window above two lancets at the other extremity of the building; the stained glass is dramatically coloured with an Art-Nouveau type of design. The pulpit and the west door enriched with radial ironwork add further to the attractions of this distinctive little church.

168.   The rose window at Lowfield Heath.

LYNE, Holy Trinity

At a meeting held in Chertsey on 14th October 1846, it was proposed to build and endow a new church to minister to a community of about six hundred people dwelling in the Botleys and Lyne area, most of whom lived two miles or more from the existing churches Chertsey

and Lyne area, most of whom lived two miles or more from the existing churches Chertsey and Addlestone. Holy Trinity Church (originally consecrated Trinity) was built by F. Francis between May 1848 and July 1849 and is cruciform in shape.

169.   *Lyne Church from the south west.*

Furnishings
The east window was erected in 1864 in memory of Thomas Musgrave who was Archbishop of York from 1848 to 1860. His local connection was that he married Catherine Cavendish, daughter of Lord Waterpark of Lyne Grove. The artist who designed and made the window was O'Connor of London, who worked with Pugin (*Colour Plate XXXV*). At its apex is a triangular shape, referring to the ancient symbol of the Holy Trinity. The south transept has been enlivened by a window commissioned by Sir John Borthwick, whose family has long-standing connections with the church. It was designed and made in 1983 by Patrick Reyntiens, one of the country's foremost stained-glass artists. Its subject is the Tree of Jesse, which has long been popular and appeared as early as the twelfth century at the west end of Chartres Cathedral. The Lyne window is notable for its use of colour, which the artist has heightened by painting over it. In 1990 a second window by the same artist was installed in the south transept; it shows angels holding the arms of Borthwick. In the north transept is a window by Clayton and Bell.

The organ was built by Lewis in 1878 and was entrusted to Robin Rust of Fleet in Hampshire for repair, completed to a very high standard in October 1985.

MALDEN, St John the Baptist

Old Malden, like Ockham, is a village associated with a famous medieval figure, in this case a clerk named Walter who came from Basingstoke, but who from an early age lived at

Merton Priory, which was closely linked with the Royal Court. He entered the Royal Chancery, taking the name of de Merton and rising to become Chancellor of all England in 1261 under King Henry III. It was de Merton who founded Merton College at Oxford in 1264, which has good reason to claim to be the oldest college of the University.

170.   Malden Church from the south east, showing the Jacobean brick nave and tower.

A church at Malden is recorded in Domesday Book, but Saxon traces are hard to find, although they may exist in the lower part of the stone chancel, which is the oldest part of the building, but now part of the Lady Chapel. The church fell into a dilapidated state during Queen Elizabeth's reign and had to be rebuilt between 1609 and 1611, mainly due to the efforts of the Bishop of London (although not in his diocese) and John Goode, Lord of the Manor, whose monument is inside the church. Red brick was used although the lower part of the chancel was patched up and retained. The eastern gable-end was rebuilt in brick and the whole building re-roofed. The place of worship was again in a sorry state in the mid-nineteenth century and a new nave and chancel was built in 1875 by T.G. Jackson, the old church being reduced to an aisle and chapel. Major restoration was carried out in 1975. The link with Merton College survives since they retain the right of presentation, which they received when the college was founded.

Although Perpendicular windows remain, this is basically a Victorian church, but preserving the very plain Jacobean brick tower, in English bond and with parapet, and the old nave and chancel in the form of an aisle and chapel. Entrance is now through a west door moved from the south side during the Jacobean reconstruction. There is a typical interior of the 1870s with Victorian painted decoration on the chancel rafters. One of the most interesting features is the inscription over the old altar which reads: 'here stood the Lord's Table on Maeldune, for well-nigh a thousand years, until the consecration of the new church, December 7th. 1875'.

Furnishings
The pulpit, made of Caen stone, dates from 1883 and has high-relief alabaster panels. There are two coats of arms of historic interest in the south-east window of the Lady Chapel chancel. One in the contemporary stained glass of 1611 in a Victorian surround shows the arms of Thomas Ravis, impaled with those of the Diocese of London which, although not responsible for Malden, became linked because Thomas Ravis, who rose to become Bishop of London, was born in Malden about 1560. The other shows the de Merton arms, impaled with those of the Diocese of Rochester, under which Malden came between 1877 and 1905.

MERROW, St John the Evangelist

St. John's dates from the twelfth century, but the church we see today, including the tower, is a rebuilding in 1842/3 to the original plans by R.C. Hussey, plus the addition of a north aisle by Sir Arthur Blomfield in 1881. The medieval parts that remain are the much renewed north door of *c*.1150 with chevron decoration, moved forward when the north aisle was built, and the arcade to the south aisle, probably late twelfth-century in date. It has round arches supported on large cylindrical columns and plain circular capitals; low down on two of the columns are pilgrims' crosses. In addition, the arch at the east end of the south aisle leading into the Onslow Chapel and that between the chancel and the chapel, possibly a re-sited chancel arch, may be of the early thirteenth century. The north porch has a Horsham slate roof and attractive medieval barge-board. The rebuilt west tower has a shingled splay-footed spire rising forty feet above it. All walls (except the south) are constructed of knapped but not squared flints. The south aisle tie-beam roof has scissor-braces: all other roofs, except that of the north aisle, are fourteenth-century and were once ceiled. At the east end of the south aisle is the Onslow Chapel, formerly a chantry chapel and later during the seventeenth and eighteenth centuries a burial place for the family; Victorian memorial brasses record deaths back to 1622. In the north-east corner is a Memorial Chapel furnished in 1921, the altar of which was designed by the Wareham Guild and which has a carved wooden reredos brightly coloured with figures of the four patron Saints of Great Britain and Ireland. The sanctuary floor is of black Irish and white Sicilian marble laid in 1910.

Furnishings
The font dates from 1845, but the canopy came from the old font and is equipped with lock and key to protect the holy water from theft and desecration. The lectern, of uncertain date and origin, was given to the church in 1886. Behind the altar table is the old stone altar, probably of the fourteenth century, with original ball-flower decoration. The chest is thought to be Jacobean. There are two brick-built mounds under the south aisle pews marking the burial places of Mary Harward (d.1625) and W. Luck and his wife (d.1777). Beside the porch is a gravestone to Sarah Battey (d. 6th June 1799 at the age of 103): the quaint inscription, largely worn away, ends with the words 'But at one hundred years and three The Graves the Bed that best suits me'.

MERSTHAM, St Katharine

Reference to the parish of Merstham goes back as far as A.D. 675, and it would seem that there must have been a pre-Conquest place of worship. Domesday records that the Manor belonged to the Prior and Convent of Christ Church, Canterbury, with whom it remained until the Dissolution. The right of presentation, however, to the church of Merstham has always belonged and still belongs to the Archbishop of Canterbury, although the parish is now in the diocese of Southwark.

St. Katharine's is perched on a hillock of Merstham firestone, better known as Reigate stone. Material from the Merstham quarries was used in the Middle Ages for Windsor Castle, Henry VII's Chapel at Westminster Abbey and, in 1445, for work on Eton College; it was also employed at old London Bridge and at St Mary Overie Priory, Southwark. It was natural, therefore, for this material to be used at Merstham itself, although there is some admixture of chalkstone. Horsham slates are used for the roof on the south side. The present building is mainly of the first half of the thirteenth century, with later additions: south porch of the fourteenth century, with original

171. Merstham Church from the south.

stone benches, north and south chantry chapels, flanking the choir, of the fifteenth century and early sixteenth century respectively, and nineteenth-century vestries. The heavy, sturdy tower dates from *c.*1220 and the splay-footed, octagonal spire – still with much of its original timber – from the fourteenth century, but the tower buttresses are nineteenth-century. The most interesting face is on the west side where a large three-light window was inserted in the late fourteenth century; below is an early thirteenth-century doorway with cusped head and angle shafts carrying dog-tooth ornament, one of the most noteworthy features of the church (*see fig. 26*). The shafts have well-preserved capitals whilst the outer label, with much decayed heads as label stops, is probably Perpendicular. The door itself also dates from the thirteenth century, including much of the ornamental ironwork.

The church was insensitively restored in 1861. The north aisle and the clerestories are renewed, although a fragment of one thirteenth-century lancet window remains at the west end. The south aisle, including the windows, was rebuilt in 1874/5 in the same style. The east wall with a five-light window (inserted in 1877) was reconstructed in the fifteenth century. One is immediately struck by the fact that the interior is still plastered. The nave arcades are thirteenth-century with octagonal piers and capitals on the north side and circular ones on the south side. The chancel arch is contemporary with these but the acanthus leaf decoration on the capitals suggests a slightly earlier date and possibly French origin. The main roof of the nave once extended over the aisles but this was cut back in the thirteenth century when the south aisle was rebuilt. Inserted into the apex of the tower arch is a carved stone, with heraldic device, which is said to have come from old London Bridge. On both sides of the choir are chapels, once chantry chapels, that on the north called the Albury Chapel and the other on the south the Alderstead Chapel, the east window of which has some fragments of fifteenth-century stained glass. The mosaic floor of the north chapel was the work of Constance Kent, a child of 11, while in prison for the alleged murder of her stepbrother. The chancel ceiling is seventeenth- or eighteenth-century work and the nave windows are all modern or fifteenth-century windows re-used. There is also preserved in fragmentary condition giant blank arcading of the thirteenth century in the chancel (as at Merton).

Furnishings

These include two piscinas of interest, a double one on the south side of the altar with beautiful stiff-leaf carving below the bowls, and a small triangular example in the south chapel. Double piscinas had a limited life in the thirteenth century before celebrants were ordered to consume the rinsings from the chalice. The Sussex marble font dating from *c*.1150 has rough ornamentation on three sides and the four corners are decorated with trefoil leaf carving. Other items are a Jacobean table in the south chapel and two old sanctuary chairs with fifteenth-century carved backs. There are several brasses, the best of which are those to the two wives of John Elingbridge (d.1473) on a table tomb in the north chapel. A small brass of 1585 in the south aisle depicts Peter Best as a child in a long gown with a handkerchief tied to his girdle (*see fig. 66*). An effigy in the north aisle was found face downwards in the north chapel, where it was being used as a paving stone; it now rests upon part of its original tomb. Severely mutilated, the effigy with angels and a vine-trail represents a merchant in fifteenth-century dress with his purse hanging at his side: it is thought to be that of Nicholas Jamys, whose daughter was married to John Elingbridge. A nice tablet commemorates Lt. George Joliffe, R.N., who died on the *Bellerophon* at the battle of the Nile; under the inscription is a lively naval relief. The lych-gate, erected in 1897, was made of oak from the old parish windmill.

MERTON, St Mary the Virgin

There is no trace of the Saxon church mentioned in Domesday Book and most of what one sees today dates from Victorian additions (1856 south aisle and 1866 north aisle) to cope with the growth of population from 813 in 1801 to 35,000 in 1851. The church lies a mile to the west of the site of the important Augustinian Priory of Merton, famous for having educated both Thomas à Becket and Walter de Merton who founded Merton College at Oxford. The Statute of Merton, by which the earls and barons declined to introduce certain rules of Canon Law into English law, was passed at the Priory. Both priory and church were built by Gilbert the Norman, the church dating from 1115, two years before the Priory was founded. From the Norman period, the small window near the west end of the nave and the north doorway survive. The latter has been badly rebuilt, but the door itself is fine Norman work with interesting rough ironwork. The nave, too, is basically Norman, although the arcades date from the addition of the aisles in the mid-nineteenth century. A new and larger chancel was built, with unusual blind arcading, between 1200 and 1230, replacing the earlier apsidal chancel of the Norman church. There are also four thirteenth-century lancet windows recessed into the Early English wall arcades. Other medieval structural work includes the western arch of the fourteenth century, the nave and chancel roofs, the fine fifteenth-century north porch and the east window of 1400, by which date the church was established substantially as it remained until the Victorian rebuildings of the mid-nineteenth century. A recent addition in 1965 is St Augustine's Chapel, designed on simple, even austere, lines.

Nearly all of the exterior is renewed as a result of adding the aisles, which necessitated the north porch and doorway being resited. The structure is humble in size, of low elevation with an attractive splay-footed shingled timber spirelet of 1547, resting directly on the roof, but rebuilt in the eighteenth century. The interior shows fine roofs, both in the nave and especially in the chancel (*see fig. 45*). The latter is of chestnut, dating from 1400 and is of hammerbeam construction, with the coving boarded. Most of the nave roof is even earlier (perhaps thirteenth-century) and was ceiled until 1929, when new dormer windows were added to improve the light of the church; the tie beams may date from even earlier and a date of 1125 has been suggested. A priest's door, dated as thirteenth-century, now inside has good ironwork; it gives access to the vestries.

Furnishings
The south aisle has a series of historical stained-glass windows by Burne-Jones made at the nearby former Morris Works at Merton Abbey. The historical theme is continued in the north aisle by other glass-makers; the east window, a modern replacement of one blown out by a flying bomb in the 1939-45 War, contains the registration number of the car of a churchwarden in 1950 when the new window was dedicated by the Bishop of Southwark.

The only old glass is in a rose window in the north aisle and dates from the fourteenth century; it includes the arms of Merton Priory and those of Edward III. The Royal Arms near the west door are those of Charles I, dating from 1625 when he ascended the throne. The hatchments include that of Admiral Lord Nelson who lived in Merton from 1801 to 1805, whence he left for victory and death at Trafalgar. The most notable memorial is that to Sir Gregory Lovell (d.1597) on the south wall of the chancel, a hanging wall-monument of alabaster, showing – on one side – Sir Gregory with son and three daughters by his first wife beneath and – on the other – his two wives and the five sons of his second marriage: the figures are all kneeling. He was 'cofferer' or treasurer to Elizabeth I's household.

172.   Nelson's hatchment at Merton.

There are also fine memorials to Henry Meriton, Gentleman of the Privy Chamber to George II and two well-executed carved memorials on the chancel floor to Sir Henry Stapleton of Yorkshire (d.1679) and his daughter Grace who died at the age of 25 in 1676. At the east end of the north aisle, a finely carved marble tablet to the Smith family, erected by Captain Cook's widow, was made in Rome in 1832 by the sculptor, R.J. Wyatt.

The most exciting feature of the churchyard is the splendid Norman archway from the old Priory, rebuilt here in 1935, leading to the vicarage; it may have been the entrance to the guest house of the Priory. Although not of artistic merit, the memorials include one near the archway, which is the oldest inscribed tombstone in the churchyard, to Thomas Sawyer (d.1675) and, just outside the north doorway, another to the oldest local inhabitant who died in the 106th. year of his age. On the north side is a solid stone tomb, surrounded by iron railings, to William Rutlish (d.1687), 'imbroiderer' to Charles II.

MICKLEHAM, St Michael

Although basically Norman, St Michael's was drastically restored and enlarged in 1871 and 1891, the latter carried out by Ewan Christian, who gave the church a new east end and largely replaced Norman by Neo-Norman. An external circuit will reveal little original work except the early sixteenth-century Norbury Chapel (enclosed by later work) on the north side – a rare example in the county of flushwork with a chequerboard of flint and firestone walling – and the stubby Norman west tower with later stepped buttresses rising to the top, capped by a widely-splayed shingled spire. The fifteenth-century porch and Norman doorway, with shafts terminated by scallop capitals, however, make a simple and

173. The west tower at Mickleham, showing a 'bed board' in the churchyard.

satisfying entrance. Within the porch are two thirteenth-century Purbeck marble coffin slabs the one on the right retaining fragmentary Lombardic lettering. Ewan Christian, when building the new east end, added what Bruce Watkin [40] describes as 'a chubby round tower on the south side'. The interior is mainly neo-Norman, but part of the original chancel arch survives with diamond fret and dog-tooth decoration and also good-looking shafted windows with billet moulding.

Furnishings
The standard twelfth-century Petworth marble font is overshadowed by the Belgian pulpit of *c.*1600 which, although altered, is elaborately decorated with richly carved panels and even figures mounting the staircase (*Colour Plate XXVIII*). Stained glass in Flemish style effectively fills the three windows and the rose of the east end: there is more glass, which may be Flemish dating from the early sixteenth century, in the west window. The oblong panel set in the woodwork of the west gallery seems of the same provenance. A tomb-chest decorated with quatrefoils and a canopy recessed into the wall commemorates William Widdowson (d.1515) and his wife Joan. Inside the recessed arch are brass effigies of them about 12 inches high at a prayer desk with scrolls issuing from their mouths; between them are the arms of the Mercers' Company of which Widdowson was a member. In the churchyard there are several graveboards (sometimes familiarly called 'bed-boards'). These are long narrow wooden boards, supported on short posts, with name and dates either carved on a slightly angled upper edge or, as here, recorded in black lettering on a white painted background.

Fanny Burney, while staying at Norbury Park, met there General D'Arblay, one of a group of distinguished French émigrés, which included Mme de Staal and Talleyrand, living at Juniper Hall. They were married in Mickleham Church in 1793; so too was George Meredith to his second wife, Marie Vulliamy. The Merediths' home on Box Hill became a magnet for leading literary figures of the time, including Stevenson, Kipling and Barrie.

MILFORD, St John

St. John's Church dates from 1844. After restoration in 1859, a north aisle was added. The main features of interest are two Burne-Jones stained-glass windows of 1897 and 1907 in the aisle and a small Lawrence Lee window in an alcove at the west end. The last window will have to be moved as a consequence of certain extensions planned for that area. There is a large mausoleum in the churchyard to the Webbs of Milford House.

MITCHAM, St Peter and St Paul

The church, which lies west of the Green, on which cricket is still played, together with the annual fair, helps to preserve the air of a country town amidst the bricks and mortar of a London suburb. It is a church of Commissioners' type in simplified Perpendicular style, built by George Smith in 1819-21. It has a medieval north-west tower and is stuccoed outside. The interior is tall, with attractive tierceron and lierne vaults, and was restored by S. Dykes-Bower in 1951.

Furnishings
The church is fortunate in having a large monument, with two medallion portraits of his usual high standard by Rysbrack, commemorating Ambrose Crowley (d.1713) and Lady Crowley (d.1727). Other memorials include a Westmacott tablet of 1821 to Mrs. Tate, in the form of a woman holding a chalice.

MORDEN, St Lawrence

The extension of the Underground Railway to Morden in 1926 led to a wave of house building that threatened to engulf the rural character of the district. However, the parish church still retains much of its old world charm. A church has existed here since at least 1200. The present place of worship dates largely from the rebuilding of 1636, a period when few churches were built. The brick exterior, mainly in English bond with stone quoins, encloses the walls of an earlier structure. St Lawrence's has an embattled west tower (*see fig. 55*). A vestry was added in 1805 and a large extension to the north in 1985 contains a hall and parish office.

   The interior is an aisleless nave and chancel in one, separated only by a step. It has a barrel vault supported by king posts and tie beams between which on either side is a splendid series of thirteen hatchments. These, together with the stained glass windows, provide a blaze of colour against the pink plaster of the walls. The windows are Perpendicular, although probably of 1636 rather than re-used, the east window containing some seventeenth-century and some 1828 glass.

Furnishings
The pulpit of 1720 retains its original stair and sounding-board, whilst the three-sided altar rails with spiral balusters and wainscotting are contemporary with the pulpit. The gallery dates from 1792 and the font by Legrew from *c.*1843. There are a large number of monuments to the Garth family, lords of the manor, together with monuments to members of the Leheup, Hoare, Roland and other families. The Leheup monuments date from the 1770s – Peter in the form of a bust before a blank triangle and Mrs. Leheup a 'good, large, simple' (Pevsner [41]) tablet. Such brasses that exist contain inscriptions only, with some coats of arms.

MORTLAKE, St Mary the Virgin

The first recorded place of worship in the village of Mortlake was erected in 1348 under licence of Edward III as a chapel to the Manor House. It was near the house which belonged to Canterbury until 1536, when Archbishop Cranmer transferred it to Henry VIII in exchange for other lands and was on the site of the brewery. During Henry's occupation the chapel was replaced by St Mary's church on the present site. From the Tudor building survives the brick-built tower with stone dressings and octagonal stair-turret on the north side, erected on Henry's orders. To this was added, probably in 1694, the top stage and, later, the cupola. The next addition was the attractive brick vestry house of *c*.1660-70 on the north side, which effectively created a north aisle, although this was extended to the west in 1816. St Mary's was enlarged in 1725 and almost entirely rebuilt by Sir Arthur Blomfield in Victorian times, the chancel in 1885 and the nave and south aisle in 1905. In 1979/80 there was extensive reordering, with a nave altar to create greater flexibility, and the installation of light oak pews. Selected memorials were reset, a new window replaced the original coloured glass one in the east wall of the south aisle and the north aisle was redeveloped to provide meeting rooms, parish offices, etc. In 1983-86, the churchyard was restored through collaboration between the church, the Borough of Richmond upon Thames and various local amenity societies to provide the attractive open space and garden we see today.

   Dr. John Dee, whom Elizabeth I used to consult on many occasions, lived on the riverside facing the church. He was one of the most learned scholars of the age, noted for his interest in alchemy and astrology. He lived from 1527 to 1608. Built on the site of Dr. Dee's house in 1619 were the famous Mortlake Tapestry Works, which flourished until 1703, reaching their heyday in the reign of Charles I; the building was restored in 1877 but demolished in 1951.

   The Perpendicular west tower with its attractive open cupola and the mid-seventeenth-century vestry are the main features of the exterior. The inscription on the west face of the tower 'VIVAT RH8 1543' is a replacement in concrete of the original inscription. The north wall, constructed of brick with plain round-arched windows, dates from 1815. Very light and airy, the interior has benefited from a refurbishing recently carried out. The nave consists of five bays with arches dying into the piers, but the conversion of the north side into meeting rooms, parish office and vestry has unbalanced the overall effect and one of the more interesting monuments is tucked away at the east end of it. The new low pews, however, are of pleasing and comfortable design. The Tudor tower arch is no longer visible; instead there is a Perpendicular west doorway, probably re-used.

Furnishings
There remains from medieval times the fifteenth-century octagonal font, which originally was in the chapel. It was given by Cardinal Bourchier, Archbishop of Canterbury in 1486. The panels are decorated with rare heraldic devices. Below the memorials at the west end of the north aisle stands a large fifteenth-century chest of German or Italian workmanship; there are two others, one of iron with a complex lock, which is German, and the other said to be early sixteenth-century and of English workmanship in the chancel. Two black armchairs in the chancel are of the James II period. Four hatchments on the north wall, at the east end of the nave and on the south wall of the chancel, commemorate various local notables. Three memorials are of note. The first is the monument to Francis Coventry (d.1699) at the east end of the south aisle. This is in the form of a hanging wall-monument with an inscription plate flanked by two young standing figures, carrying the entablature and open pediment, with an urn in the middle. The second is the memorial to Nicholas Godschall (d.1748), with a group of three cherubs' heads in the predella at the east end of the north aisle. Thirdly is the one to Viscountess Sidmouth (d.1811) by Westmacott, in the form of a relief with the dying young woman on a couch held by an allegorical figure and Faith standing on the left; this is at the west end of the north aisle. She was the wife of Henry Addington who was Prime Minister from 1801 to 1804 during the Napoleonic Wars and who is buried in the churchyard. Nearby there are three small brasses, one of which

commemorates Edward Myles, servant to Prince Henry and Prince Charles, the sons of James I.

In the churchyard is an arch, created out of the materials of the south aisle doorway, erected about 1865. South of the church is a Roman Catholic cemetery where there is a monument to Sir Richard Burton (d.1890), explorer of Arabia and the Nile and translator of the Arabian Nights, and his wife Isabella. The monument is in the strange form of a life-size stone tent decorated with crescents and stars with a crucifix above and inscriptions on the west side.

NEWDIGATE, St Peter

Not mentioned in Domesday Book, the earliest reference is in a charter (probable date 1163) confirming the grant of the living to the Priory of St Mary Overie, Southwark of the 'Cappella de Neudegat'. For a time in private hands – William de Newdigate held it in 1357 – the living reverted to St Mary's until the Dissolution. The earliest rector traced is Ranulf de Brok (*c*.1271 to *c*.1285). Newdigate was a scattered wealden parish with isolated homesteads carved out of the forest. The earliest part is the thirteenth-century chancel with lancets and a two-light window of *c*.1260. The south-west window and the priest's door date from *c*.1250. The south arcade and aisle are fourteenth-century, the central pier being incised with crosses – probably by pilgrims. The aisle was extended to form the chantry chapel of the de la Poyle family of Cudworth and, although subsequently disused as a chapel, has now been restored. The medieval nave roof is of collar-and-rafter design with tie-beams, one of which supports a post under the collar.

174.   Newdigate Church from the south west.

The church's most striking feature – the tower – was added in the fifteenth century when there was already a west wall and, as at Burstow and Great Bookham, is built up from ground level. This is the dominant feature of the exterior. Consisting of three stages (the top and lowest weatherboarded and the middle shingled) with a splay-footed spire, it has been much restored and lacks the charm of the Burstow tower although of the same type. But inside the timber framing of the tower, mainly supported by four great oak posts 16 to 17 inches square and 11 feet apart, is striking. An aisle which runs outside the posts, forming a sort of skirt, helps to buttress the tower, which is further strengthened by elaborate cross-bracing. At the same time that the tower was built, the south arcade was renewed.

As often happened, St Peter's fell into a state of disrepair in the eighteenth century and the growth of population in the nineteenth century led to a major restoration in 1876-77, when the north aisle was added, with arcades corresponding with those on the south side. Alterations were made to the chancel arch and included the renewal of the east window. A new chancel roof of collars and rafters, of similar design to the previous one, was constructed and the nave roof has been left exposed. The variety of material used owing to the lack of building stone in the Weald is of interest. One will find Sussex marble, Tilgate sandstone, Bargate stone, Reigate stone – all obtainable within a range of six miles. One of the gains from the restoration was the re-roofing of the church with Horsham slates. In recent times, the tower and spire have been re-shingled with oak instead of the cedar normally used today.

Furnishings
The oldest furnishing is a chest hollowed out of a single log, called a 'dug-out' but difficult to date, kept in the belfry of the tower. Fragments of armorial glass, mainly in the form of ogee canopies, are to be seen in the north-east window of the north aisle. A grave slab of Sussex marble – once in the nave – is now in the tower. It is thought to commemorate William de Newdigate, Sheriff of Surrey and Sussex in 1372, who died in 1377; the shield represents the Newdigate arms of three lions' paws. On the chancel wall is a small brass plate with the inscription under a skull and crossbones – 'Here lieth ye body of Joane daughter of Thomas Smallpiece, and late ye wife of George Steere Parson of this parish. Shee died Dec 7 An. Dom. 1634 and expecteth a blessed resurrection'.

NUTFIELD, St Peter and St Paul

The church is situated on a hillside at the bend of a road off the A25 and overlooks Holmesdale to the North Downs. It is mentioned in Domesday Book and there was probably a Saxon place of worship on the site. Whatever was there was rebuilt in c.1200 in Early English style, consisting of nave, chancel and possibly north side chapel. This was followed by a north aisle in c.1230 and an enlargement of the chancel in c.1300 when it was made ten feet longer and the roof five feet higher. The battlemented Perpendicular tower dates from 1450 and has a patched brick top of 1786 capped with a short splay-footed shingled spire. The interior is a mixture of styles, including two Perpendicular windows as well as lancets, with a blocked arch to the north chapel. The fifteenth-century tower arch with continuous mouldings is quite impressive. There was a vigorous renewal in 1884 when a south aisle was added to cope with the needs of the large houses that had been built in the area. Rough-cast facing to the exterior does not add to the appeal, but this is relieved by the Horsham slates used on the chancel roof. Severe damage in the 1939-45 War was made good afterwards.

Furnishings

There are late medieval parts of the font, the pulpit and the screen, and also in the north aisle window a few fragments of old glass, which have been gathered together into a design featuring the Archangel Michael slaying the dragon. But the outstanding glass is that of 1890 and 1891 designed by Burne-Jones and made by Morris & Co. in the east window and the south aisle window; the former depicts the 'Angels of Paradise' and the latter 'Mary and Elizabeth'. The space formerly occupied by the rood loft is now filled with large panels inscribed with the Ten Commandments and the Lord's Prayer, installed in the nineteenth century. The font has a fifteenth-century octagonal bowl supported on a stem of 1665. The hexagonal pulpit contains a number of good sixteenth-century parchemin panels in two tiers and the screen, although originally sixteenth-century, is heavily restored. On the south side of the chancel is a table tomb to 'Sire Thomas de Fulham' who was rector of Nutfield from 1305 to 1328, with an inscription in Lombardic characters. A brass just inside the altar rail commemorates William Grafton (d.1465), his wife and John their son. William may have been rector in the period 1412-1447 but, although described as a priest, he is wearing lay clothes, is not tonsured and is shown with his wife. On the south wall of the south aisle is a small seventeenth-century brass with a Latin inscription to Edmund Molyneux, a Papish recusant. To the right of the door on entering there is a memorial to Richard Jewel whose death is recorded twice, because of a change in the calendar, in 1745 and in 1746. On the south side of the chancel is a modern window which includes the arms of Winchester Diocese and of Jesus College, Oxford – patrons of the living since 1685. The top panel contains a squirrel eating a nut (for Nutfield !).

OCKHAM, All Saints

All Saints lies isolated amidst trees at the end of a rough track away from the former estate houses with gardens, which form the pleasant village of Ockham. The track leads to the east end of the church, where one is immediately confronted with a medieval seven-light east window (*see fig. 24*), unique in the country except for one other at Blakeney, Norfolk (although there is a Victorian copy of the Ockham window at Holy Trinity, Millbrook, Southampton and an eight-light example in the Lady Chapel of Ottery St Mary, Devon). Marks in the wall indicate the position of an earlier three-light lancet predecessor.

In Domesday Book reference is made to a church at *Bocheam* in Woking Hundred which is probably a 'scribal error' for Ockham, perhaps due to confusion with Bookham. After the Conquest the Manor passed to Richard de Tonbridge of the powerful Clare family to whom were granted no fewer than 38 manors in Surrey and it remained in this family for many centuries. Eventually, in the eighteenth century, the Manor was obtained by Peter King, first Baron King of Ockham, the son of an Exeter grocer who rose to

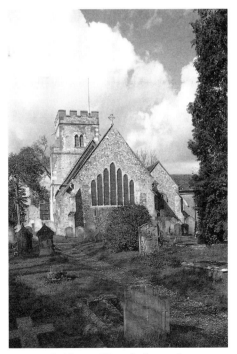

175.   Ockham Church from the east.

become Lord Chancellor and whose monument is one of the major features of the church. The fabric, except for the lower parts of the west wall which probably belonged to a Norman church and possibly the round-headed tower arch, goes back to the early part of the thirteenth century, when a chancel was added together with a north aisle, separated from the nave by a slender pier between two arches. In the fourteenth century the aisle was extended to form the chapel of St Margaret. Apart from the east window, the chief external feature is the curvilinear tracery of the fourteenth-century windows on the south side where there is also a blocked priest's door. A window in the chancel with wooden lintel is early fifteenth-century. The tower – plain and crenellated – bears a family resemblance to that of St Mary's at Send and, like it, may be late medieval or early post-Reformation. Later additions were the King Chapel, housing the King memorial, on the north side in 1735 and the north porch and organ chamber/vestry in 1875. The church is built of flint and pudding-stone with freestone and chalk dressings; thin red bricks are incorporated in the tower and buttresses, and the King Chapel is of brick (all headers, i.e. laid end-wise rather than lengthwise).

Upon entering one is immediately struck by the satisfying proportions of the nave arcade and the wide chancel arch, which draws the eye to the chief treasure of All Saints, the seven-light east window. This is a sophisticated work for a village church and one is led to ask from whence it came. The obvious answer of neighbouring Newark Priory is now to some extent discounted but the question remains unanswered. There are signs that the window had to be altered at the sides to fit but the work was expertly done and, with its Sussex marble shafts, dog-tooth mouldings and capitals of leaf design – all different – together with the elegant stepping up of the lancets, this is a notable example of Early English work. The slate blue of the Victorian glass and the two tiers of figures are well suited to their framework but the figures are weakly drawn. The wagon roof in the nave, and a cambered roof in the aisle are both boarded and panelled with zig-zag pattern decoration. The ceilings are early-sixteenth century and are enlivened with bosses, including in the nave a bird, fish-trap and a grinning face. The bosses mentioned are difficult to discern but there are photographs nearby.

Furnishings

There is much to enjoy, apart from the monuments. The medieval stained glass consists of fragments in the upper part of the chancel and south-east nave windows. The chancel south-east window has a choir of angels with musical instruments in the tracery lights whilst below is a most intriguing small pane with a mushroom shown sideways; both these are of early fifteenth-century date. In the chancel south-west window is a fourteenth-century piece with a lion's face and border of Stafford knots. Just under the lion's face is a pane on which has been scratched 'W. Peters new leaded this in 1775 and never was paid for same'. Opposite in the north-east window there is another lion's face together with a vine pattern. Post-medieval glass is seventeenth-century and eighteenth-century Dutch glass, not of particularly good quality. The fourteenth-century girl's head which is exquisitely carved is below an elaborate canopied image niche to the left of the chancel and close to the organ. Two pairs of stall-arms of late fourteenth-century or early fifteenth-century date have been worked into the clergy seats on either side of the chancel. Later woodwork includes the eighteenth-century hexagonal pulpit and, of the present century, the credence-table and sanctuary chair, designed by a former churchwarden and made of Ockham oak. One other item not to be overlooked is the double piscina, with trefoil head in the chancel. Double piscinas are not common, as towards the end of the thirteenth century a papal edict ruled that the rinsings of the chalice after administration must be consumed.

176.   The base of an image niche in the east wall at Ockham.

Among the monuments, pride of place artistically must go to the large King monument by the great Flemish sculptor, J.M. Rysbrack (*see fig. 88*). The faces are melancholy but beautifully modelled especially that of Lord King (d.1734). He and his wife are seated disconsolately leaning on an urn with pyramidal background. In the same King Chapel is a fine bust by Richard Westmacott the Younger to Peter, seventh Lord King (d. 1833). There is also a stone casket on a pedestal containing the ashes of Ralph, second Earl of Lovelace, (d.1906) and of his wife, in front of which are two excellent heraldic enamel plaques. There are two brasses on either side of the altar, the one on the north being the earliest in the county to a priest. It is to Walter Frilende (d.1376), the former rector who built the St Margaret Chapel; the brass is only 15 inches high, showing him as a demi-figure (*see fig. 59*). The other, on the south side, is to John Weston who died in 1483 and his wife; it is 20 inches high and shows him in armour and his wife wearing a butterfly head-dress. There are also brass inscriptions to Robert Kellett, rector from 1485 to 1525, and to John Wexcombe dating from about 1390.

William of Ockham is thought to have been born about 1285 in Ockham. He studied at the famous Franciscan house at Oxford. His gift for argument caused him to be known as the Invincible Doctor. He challenged two popes, charging them with error and heresy and was kept in confinement in Avignon until he escaped to Munich, where from 1330 until his death in 1348 he lived in the Franciscan convent under excommunication, but protected by Louis of Bavaria. In 1985 a window was placed in Ockham Church to commemorate the seventh centenary of his birth. Another Franciscan monk and notable medieval theologian, Nicholas Occam, may also have come from Ockham.

177.   The west tower at Ockley.

OCKLEY, St Margaret

St. Margaret's lies in a raised circular churchyard half a mile north east of the village which runs along the old Roman Stane Street. It is largely a rebuilding of 1873, when a north aisle was added and the brick chancel enlarged in stone. Previously the church was a simple unaisled sandstone building, an indication of which can be seen in the Decorated tracery of the easternmost nave window. The tower, rebuilt in 1700 in Perpendicular style, and the fifteenth-century timber south porch create an agreeable impression. The lower stage of the tower has strongly battered angle buttresses, but the upper stage is unbuttressed. The windows, doorway and walling of the south side are of the first half of the fourteenth century. Inside, under the tower there is a small thirteenth- or fourteenth-century archway into the nave and the three other sides of the basement show similar arches but filled in; they are all 7 feet high and 43 inches wide. The suggestion is that there was once a cruciform church, but this is unlikely and is possibly a later deception.

OKEWOOD (or OAKWOOD), St John the Baptist

Described as the most isolated in the county, the church stands on a grassy knoll amid trees. Built about 1220 as a chapel of ease to Wotton, it was first recorded in 1290, when it was stated that Sir Walter de Fancourt presented a priest to the chantry. In 1431, Edward de la Hale – in gratitude for a seemingly miraculous intervention when the shooting of an arrow saved his son from being killed by a wounded boar – granted lands to the chapel to the value of £ 200; he also restored and enlarged the building. In the mid-fifteenth century, buttresses were added to prop up the east and north walls. This involved blocking up the existing window space at the east end and all that could be provided instead at that end was a small window (with triangular head), which does not provide much light. In 1547 during Edward VI's reign the chapel was closed because, mistakenly, it was thought to be a forbidden chantry chapel, but it was re-opened in 1553 following the protestations of local yeomen. By 1701 the building was in a very dilapidated state but, with the aid of gifts of money, was gradually restored. A hundred or more years later repairs were again needed and in 1879 the north wall was pulled down and a north aisle added by Basil Champneys. This greatly altered the character of the church, turning it into a rather featureless rectangle. The eighteenth-century gallery was refronted. Patronage has always been in private hands and was vested in the Evelyn family in 1853, when the building virtually became a parish church. The sweeping Horsham slate roof and the graveyard make the exterior more attractive than the interior. A small spirelet was erected in 1879 in place of a turret, and a larger west porch added. The addition of the north aisle, creating two equal and unco-ordinated halves to the interior, has taken away the village character and the small east

window makes it dark. The most pleasing feature
is the original nave roof which was ceiled during
the 1879 restoration. New furnishings were also
provided.

Furnishings
The oldest is the cut-down eighteenth-century
pulpit with tester but most are modern. Altar,
reredos and choir-stalls date from 1879. The font
is also Victorian in black marble but handsome
and restrained (*Colour Plate XXXIII*). The only
old stained glass consists of fragments of
thirteenth-century and fifteenth-century glass in
the heads of the two lancets on the south side of
the chancel of flowers, fruit and leaves. In the
lower parts there is Powell glass of 1905 on the
subject of the Annunciation, the right-hand light
of which depicts the Virgin and the Archangel
Gabriel. A brass of Edward de la Hale, who died
in 1431, lies in its original position on the north
side of the chancel floor, which is some six inches
below the present one; it is protected by a sheet
of plate glass. The figure is in armour and 18
inches high.

*178.   Brass of Edward de la Hale at
Okewood.*

OXTED, St Mary

St. Mary's stands in attractive isolation nearly a mile north-east of the old village, named in
the Domesday Survey as *Ac-Stede* (the Place of the Oaks). Although mentioned in
Domesday Book, there is no trace of a pre-Conquest church. However, St Mary's has a
circular churchyard, surrounded by a low stone wall. This often indicates a pre-Conquest
burial site. The present building goes back to the mid-twelfth century, from which period
the tower dates. The sturdy, brick-battlemented, low tower of Bargate stone, with walls
five-feet thick below ground, was made to appear even more squat by the heightening of the
aisle walls in the fourteenth century with clunch stone. (Previously they were lean-to.) Other
building materials are ironstone and sandstone. Of slow growth the church retains
thirteenth- and fourteenth-century details in the chancel whilst the nave arcade and south
porch are of the fifteenth century. There is fourteenth-century Decorated tracery in the east
window but this was planed down in 1637. The west doorway is fifteenth-century. Damage
by lightning in 1637 and 1719 – all the bells were melted in the later fire – plus a severe
restoration in 1877 have altered the character of this place of worship but it well repays a
visit.
    One enters through a fifteenth-century south porch of Bargate stone which has a well
detailed arch and hood-mould with arms of the Cobhams of Lingfield in the spandrels and a
small statue in a niche above. The door is original of *c.*1475 with applied tracery. The nave
arcade is also of the fifteenth century and is of similar type to that at Lingfield, with piers
consisting of four shafts and four hollows – a routine style of the period – but the east
responds with graceful shafting, together with the east arch on the north side, remain from
the earlier thirteenth-century arcade. As well as the east window, the side windows of the
chancel and the chancel arch (raised after 1828) are early fourteenth-century. Stairs to the

former rood-loft survive at the east end of the north aisle, from which a curious curved passage leads into the chancel. The overall proportions of nave and chancel are satisfying. The chancel, 37 feet long, has a thirteenth-century priest's doorway on the south side, as well as an arched niche on the north side for a thirteenth-century Easter sepulchre. The north transept formed part of the 1877 restoration.

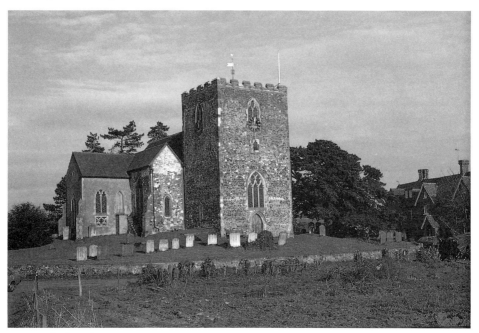

179.   Oxted Church in its circular churchyard.

Furnishings

The altar was enlarged in 1931 and improved by the addition of riddel posts, surmounted by angels and lights. The pavement is tiled as far as the brass altar rail. A side chapel off the north aisle has a carved reredos and a two-light east window, depicting St Martin and St Gregory. The pulpit is Victorian but the font is fifteenth-century, octagonal, and decorated with quatrefoils enclosing shields and flowers alternately. Two screens are set respectively at the entrances to the chancel and the tower. They are good modern work. In the north transept there is an iron Armada chest, probably fifteenth-century in date and of Flemish craftsmanship. Its locking mechanism covers the whole of the inside of the lid and consists of twelve bolts all operated by one turn of the key. Four Burne-Jones windows, made by Morris & Co., in the aisles illuminate the nave and there are Kempe windows in the chancel, but the most interesting is the fourteenth-century glass in the east window tracery, representing the four Evangelistic symbols with scrolls (*Colour Plate IX*). In the north-west angle of the tower there is an attractive small oak staircase with rail and slender balusters, possibly early eighteenth-century.

Brasses include one of the fourteenth century and two others cut in the sixteenth century and seventeenth century. On the south wall of the chancel is a brass to Thomas, son of Sir Thomas Hoskins, whose family were patrons of the church. The brass records that 'aboute a quarter of an houre before his departure at the age of 5 in 1611, Thomas did of himselfe 'without any instructions speake these wordes . . . and leade us not into temptation but deliver us from all evile . . . being ye last wordes he spoke'. On the same wall is another brass to John Hoskins, fourth son of Sir Thomas, who also died at the age of five, two years later in 1613; he is shown in trunk-hose, doublet and cloak, like an adult. An earlier brass on the wall commemorates Johanne Haselden, who died in 1480. More substantial memorials include an attractively carved typical Jacobean monument, dated 1616, to John Aldersley with his wife and seventeen children, all in an attitude of prayer. He was a haberdasher and merchant adventurer of London. A well carved Palladian tablet on the chancel south wall commemorates William Finch (d.1728) and his wife who is rather curiously described as a spinster.

OXTED, St John, Hurst Green

St. John's, Hurst Green, Oxted is a neo-Decorated building by J. Oldrid Scott of 1912, enlarged by J. Douglas Matthews in 1962 with a west rose window.

PEPER HAROW, St Nicholas

Peper Harow is one of several villages in the neighbourhood with names said to be derived from Norse for a holy place or for a god, Harow possibly from 'heag' or temple; compare with Thursley from 'Thor or Thuner's field'. Heavily screened by trees, the church lies under the shadow of the large Park House, in grounds of over 350 acres laid out by 'Capability Brown', the home of the Midletons who became lords of the manor in 1719. They exercised benevolent control and kept the hamlet rural. St Nicholas has been a parish church since before 1301, being originally served by monks at Oxenford before they moved to Waverley Abbey. Michael Haydock remained Rector throughout the Commonwealth despite having held this position when Charles I was executed. The church suffered a heavy restoration in 1844, when Augustus Pugin, contrary to his 'True Principles' that the Middle Pointed style should be used, built a north aisle in Early English style, a chancel uncompromisingly Decorated and a neo-Norman chancel arch. As Ian Nairn comments,[42] he must have been trying to imitate a slow-growth medieval church. Pugin's work at Peper Harow and his slightly earlier alterations at Albury Park Church heralded the introduction of Victorian Gothic into the county and this made itself felt even more severely at Peper Harow with the 1877 restoration when the west gallery was removed.

The lych-gate dates from 1893 and the west tower, in an unassuming Gothick style, from 1826. Most is renewed but the south wall of the nave is old and may be twelfth-century; there is one Decorated ogee-headed window in this wall. The neo-Norman of the chancel arch may be due to traces of the original Norman arch remaining; it is enriched with modern mouldings. The flanking recesses for altars are original. The single north aisle added by Pugin has clustered shafts of Irish marble which came from the Midleton quarries in Co. Cork. Although the interior is Victorian, he has given it character and the varying styles provide interest, including the stained glass which has been described as 'exciting'.

Furnishings
The monuments are the most notable feature, especially that to Sir Thomas Broderick (d.1641) and his wife (d.1678); a large black marble tablet behind with an inscription supports two splendid busts on its base (see fig. 73). Ian Nairn [43] draws attention to the treatment of Sir Thomas's hair and clothes and rates the memorial as 'the best thing of its date in the county'. It came from All Saints', Wandsworth in 1900. There is a mural tablet

to another Thomas Brodrick (d.1769), who was Vice-Admiral of the Red in the days when the Royal Navy was divided into three squadrons, Red, White and Blue. He was a member of the court-martial which sentenced Admiral Byng to death for failure to capture Minorca, in the Seven Years' War, which was not his fault. The full-length recumbent marble effigy of the fourth Viscount Midleton (d.1836) lies in the nave. A brass to Joan Brocas, widow of William Brocas, Lord of Peper Harow, her second husband (the first being John Adderley, Lord Mayor of London) dates from 1487 and shows her kneeling in widow's veil and mantle under an ogee niche. About 14 inches high, it is placed on the north side of the chancel. A brass cross with inscription also commemorates her on the chancel floor. A memorial to Elizabeth Wood of 1621 shows her in a peaked bodice and high collar. Sir Henry Dalrymple White, who led the charge of the Heavy Brigade at Balaclava, is buried in the churchyard.

PETERSHAM, St Peter

180.   The west tower at Petersham   *181.   The font at Petersham.*

The name 'Petersham' is derived from 'Piterichesham', thought to mean a 'ham' or enclosure of Patricius or Patrick. Lands in the vicinity were endowed to Chertsey Abbey and St Peter's remained a chaplaincy of the Abbey until the Dissolution. Thereafter it came under Richmond until a separate parish was formed in 1769. A church at Petersham is mentioned in Domesday Book but no trace of a Saxon building remains and the only early feature is the thirteenth-century chancel, with a blocked lancet window visible from outside. St Peter's history as we see it today starts in the early sixteenth century when, apart from the chancel of 1266, it was rebuilt and the base of the tower constructed. About 1600, small transepts and the upper part of the tower in red brick at the west of the church were built.

The gallery in the north transept was added shortly afterwards. The transepts were extended in the late eighteenth century or early nineteenth. At about this time, the west porch was added and the upper half of the tower rebuilt. In 1840, extensive enlargements were introduced including the lengthening and addition of galleries in the south transept. In 1874 the chancel was completely refurbished under John Gilbert Scott, son of the famous Sir Gilbert. The chancel screen was erected in 1899. Some damage was sustained in the 1939-45 War, to the repair of which the city of Vancouver made a substantial contribution.

This charming ensemble lies along a path west of the main road away from the worst roar of traffic, and is made of brick with a pretty cupola and octagonal lantern over a battlemented west tower. The long, south transept, enlarged on the south side in 1840, has arched windows and the general effect is of a short west-to-east axis, with long, extending transepts; the length north-to-south is 62 feet, but west-to-east only about 38 feet. The interior is essentially Georgian, with box-pews, a two-decker pulpit (*Colour Plate XX*) and a raised reading desk, which may correspond in date with the pulpit, and galleries to the transepts. This forms an unusual and appealing rarity in Surrey.

Furnishings
There is a font of 1797 with a Jacobean cover and baluster stem, a pulpit of 1796 with an iron handrail to the steps and an elaborate Royal Arms of George III, dated 1810, well placed above the entrance to the chancel. Against the north wall of the chancel, lie the stiffly reclining recumbent effigies in Elizabethan dress of George Cole (a barrister), his wife and grandson, also George Cole, erected in 1624. The recess is flanked by columns and the shallow arch coffered. The grandson is placed in the predella (horizontal strip below the main structure). On the corners at the top of the gaily coloured monument are two symbolic figures representing on the right Death and on the left an angel sounding a trumpet signifying the Resurrection. An imposing tablet on the south wall of the chancel commemorates Sir Thomas Jenner who was made Recorder in 1683 and died in 1707. Petersham's most celebrated son, Captain George Vancouver, R.N., who circumnavigated the world and discovered Vancouver Island, is remembered in a memorial on the west side of the north transept, but his grave in the churchyard, which is perfectly plain, is better known and is the scene of an annual commemorative service in May. He died in 1798 at the early age of 40.

St. Peter's is associated with three marriages, one of which is not certain. First is that in 1664 between Prince Rupert of the Rhine, cousin of Charles II, and Lady Francesca Bard. This is the marriage which is not proved. The second is that in 1672 between the Countess of Dysart and the Duke of Lauderdale, a member of the notorious Cabal ministry of Charles II – an unscrupulous pair. The third took place in 1881 between the future Earl of Strathmore and Nina Cavendish-Bentinck; their youngest daughter became Elizabeth, the Queen Mother.

PETERSHAM, All Saints, Bute Avenue

This is a striking very red church in Waterhouse vein, built in 1907-08 by John Kelly, using brick and red terracotta. It is large with a tall campanile on the south side in early Italian Lombardesque style. The interior is faced and decorated with various marbles. There is an octagonal baptistry with ambulatory.

PIRBRIGHT, St Michael

The Chapelry of Pyrefrith, which was dependent on the Rectory of Woking, was appropriated to the Priory of Newark in 1262, where it remained until the Dissolution of the Monasteries in 1536-39, although it appears that Chertsey Abbey also enjoyed a portion of the tithes. The earliest record is contained in the grant of land by a parson named Jordan during the years 1210-14. In 1368, the 'Chapel of Pyrbright' had to be solemnly purged after being polluted with blood during a brawl in which Simon Serle of Horsehull was killed. For reasons unknown, Newark Priory leased the chapelry to Sir Edward Newbe in 1527. By 1783 the church was in a bad state of repair and it was decided to rebuild (*see fig. 82*). The present church, apart from the chancel, dates mainly from this period. The chancel was rebuilt in 1807 and embattled like the tower, part being used as a mortuary chapel for the Halsey family, Lords of the Manor; later the south chapel was added and the battlements removed. There were extensive alterations in 1872.

This attractive Georgian place of worship – one of the few in Surrey – has an unbuttressed tower of coursed sarsens obtained locally, a nave of red and grey brick with a stone base and rubbed heads to the windows, and a chancel mainly of sarsens. The stone is galleted (small pebbles inserted in the mortar providing a decorative effect and possibly additional structural strength). The tower is completed with a lead-sheathed spike surmounted by a gilt ball and a gilded vane in the form of a flying dragon. One enters the churchyard through an attractive lych-gate and the church by the south porch, substituted for the old one in 1911. The interior is bright and open, with an unusual post-and-lintel arcade separating the nave from the north aisle. The arcade was supported at first by Doric and then by three wooden Tuscan columns on high plinths, substituted probably in 1848. There is a west gallery which was extended down the north side, but later the extension was removed. Nave and aisle have flat ceilings. The opening into the chancel is through a moulded Gothic arch of chalkstone, to which the central figure from a former rood-beam (erected in 1924) has been separately affixed: two other figures are alongside the arch. The open chancel (originally apsidal) has a very pretty ceiling, consisting of 36 panels painted in pale blue relieved by mouldings, 'Nativity' stars appearing in a darker shade of blue. The twelve panels over the sanctuary are more richly adorned, being gilded and decorated in the corners with a flaming sword (emblem of St Michael); in the centre of each panel the sacred monogram IHS is surmounted by a crown.

182.   Stanley's grave at Pirbright.

Furnishings

There is a churchwardens' chest of *c*.1625-49 in the north-east corner of the nave. The octagonal font is modern. The lectern was made in Japan in 1922 to a Dorking architect's design. There are many memorial tablets in the chancel to the Halsey and allied families, but the most famous are those in the north aisle to Henry Morton Stanley, and Ross Lowis Mangles, V.C., J.P. of the Bengal Civil Service, the first civilian to receive the V.C. That to Stanley, who died in 1924, states that 'He discovered Livingstone, and revealed the Sources of the Nile and Congo; and was the Means, through Providence, of Crushing Slavery; introducing Civilisation into Central Africa, and the First Christian Missionaries into Uganda'. A granite monolith weighing six tons was transported from Dartmoor with difficulty to place above Stanley's grave in the churchyard. Roughly hewn, it bears only the inscription:

' HENRY MORTON STANLEY '

1841-1904

'BULA MATARI'

(his African name meaning breaker of the rocks) and, for epitaph, the one word 'AFRICA', a fitting memorial to this intrepid explorer.

PIXHAM, St Martin

This attractive village church (*Colour Plate XXXIX*), close to the town of Dorking, lies in the angle formed by the A24 and A25 main roads running north and south and west and east respectively. Built by the eminent architect, Sir Edwin Lutyens, it is his only excursion into ecclesiastical architecture in Surrey, perhaps partly due to the nave having been built for secular purposes with a screen to separate it from the sanctuary. As a result, each part is treated differently, the nave having a large plain tunnel-vault and the sanctuary a graciously proportioned dome on a square base, patterned with chalk, tiles and sandstone. There are many Lutyensesque features such as the use of tiles in voussoirs and the twin gables on the north side.

PUTTENHAM, St John the Baptist

There is no evidence of a pre-Conquest church and none is mentioned in Domesday Book. The nave, however, is probably of early twelfth-century date, to which were added a north aisle (mid-twelfth century), chancel and north chapel (end twelfth century) and a chapel on the south side of the nave (first half of the fourteenth century). The west tower, which once carried a timber spire – lost in a fire in 1735 – dates from c.1400. The north or Lady Chapel was converted in the fifteenth century, to a chantry chapel for saying masses for the souls of Richard Lugher and his family. Later in the eighteenth century Thomas Parker, who had bought the Priory farm house and changed it into a country mansion, agreed with the rector to repair the Lady Chapel if he might keep it as a Priory manorial chapel for himself. It has finally become the vestry. History since the 1735 fire has been one of repairs and restoration, especially by Woodyer in 1861 when most of the windows were replaced by others in Bath stone and most of the walls refaced in Bargate stone. Little of the medieval church remained untouched. In medieval times, the gift of the living lay with the Augustinian Priory of St Mary-without-Bishopsgate, London from 1307 until 1533; the manor, however, went to Newark Priory.

The west tower stands guard at the end of the attractive 'Street' but much changed. After losing its spire in 1735, a brick parapet was built, but this has been replaced with a modern stone parapet. The grey sandstone walls have been repaired with red brick and tiles and the south-east stair turret refaced internally in brick. There are diagonal buttresses at the western corners. On the north side, the upper part of the former Lady Chapel was rebuilt in brick in c.1770 when Thomas Parker converted it into a family mausoleum and Woodyer

183.   The west tower at Puttenham.

inserted a new north doorway and dormer windows into the north aisle when he restored it in 1861. In the interior, although the handsome four-bay Norman nave arcade and the two-bay chancel arcade separating the chancel from the north chapel remain, Woodyer's restoration is all pervasive. Despite this, the interior with its plastered walls still preserves a village atmosphere. The Norman nave arcade shows the local Surrey feature of crimped plasterwork in the surrounds (compare with Compton and Worplesdon), but is unusual in that the moulded bases are on plinths of varying heights, indicating an incline upwards from west to east without a chancel step. The south doorway has a moulded semicircular arch of *c.*1200 but with modern capitals on the jamb-shafts. A small Norman window west of the porch has been completely renewed, but still preserves its round-headed form. The rebuilt chancel retains its south-west window of three main lights, with six tracery lights in a square head, the western main light of which comes down lower than the others and has a heavy iron grille. The south chapel which now houses the organ has an original fourteenth-century window in the east wall and a small medieval window in the west wall with a single cinquefoiled light. The roofs, apart from that over the north chapel which has been reconstructed, are all of late medieval collar-and-rafter construction, with tie-beams but no crown-posts.

Furnishings
Apart from three chests, one inscribed M I N 1705 with panelled front and drawer below, and a stone altar slab set in the floor under the communion table, all the furnishings including the stained glass are modern. There have been five pulpits, the last dating from 1936. The vestry (former north chapel) has two floor-slabs with small brass inscription plates, one to Richard Lusher and Ethelreda his wife, undated with indents for two figures, and the other to Dorothy (d.1604), daughter of John Hunt and wife of Nicholas Lusher. As Dorothy Lusher's body was laid in lime, it is probable that she died of plague which was raging at the time. On the north wall is a brass plate to Francis Wyatt (d.1634) and Timothie his wife. The outstanding monument is the twenty-inch-long brass reset in the chancel floor, of Edward Cranford in eucharistic vestments with an inscription. He was rector from 1400 to 1431, but length of incumbency is more strikingly represented by the brass on the sill of the south-west window of the chancel to two Henry Bedells (father and son), who between them were responsible for the spiritual life of the village for nearly 100 years (1598 to 1692) and who, together with their successor, Thomas Swift (rector for 59 years) spanned the reigns from Elizabeth to George II.

PYRFORD, St Nicholas

184. St. Nicholas' Church, Pyrford from the south east.

Set on a bluff overlooking the low-lying meadows where lie the ruins of Newark Priory, St. Nicholas is the most authentic of the three Surrey Norman village churches (the others being Farleigh and Wisley), which stand as a complete building of one period. Changes have, of course, been made during the ages, but its Norman proportions remain as they were, unaltered by the usual additions of aisles, chapels or tower – though a bell-turret was later built over the west end, a Tudor porch outside the north door and a Victorian vestry outside the south. This church fits admirably into its elevated site, surrounded by a circular churchyard, which is evidence of a pre-Christian burial-ground (as at Oxted) so it is probable that this site has had religious significance for over 2,000 years. A prehistoric standing-stone (the Pyrford Stone) on the grass verge at the top of the hill may well have been linked with a sacred place where the primitive settlers came up from the river bank to worship their ancient gods. The entrance – probably because of the lie of the land – is on the north rather than the more usual south or west side. Constructed of flinty conglomerate or pudding-stone covered with a rough daubing of mortar and dressed with iron-stone and chalk-stone or clunch, the building is without foundations and has had to be buttressed comprehensively since early times. The present buttress at the west end (likely to have replaced an earlier one) and those at the corners were erected in the fifteenth century: all three of these are built of sarsen stone, a very hard siliceous sandstone consisting of natural geological formation of rock or boulders found, amongst other places, in the Bagshot sands. Other buttresses had to be provided in the nineteenth century. St Nicholas, like the church at Wisley, – both now in the same parish – dates from the mid-twelfth century and has the rare distinction of keeping three of its internal consecration crosses: on the north and south walls of the chancel and the west wall of the nave. The window on the north side of the chancel, the small west windows and both the existing doorways are Norman, the north door – slightly later than the south – enriched with chevron ornament and provided with a stoup for holy water, inserted into the west jamb. Later work includes the insertion of a fourteenth-century east window with medieval glass in the tracery. In the fifteenth century, the roofs were probably renewed and possibly raised, but the most notable addition of this date was the beautiful north porch with an oak framework with plastered panels (now partly repaired in brickwork), and with the original pierced barge-boards.

Newark Priory purchased the right of presentation to the living from Westminster Abbey in 1258 and held it until the Dissolution. In 1869, an excellent restoration was carried out by Sir Thomas G. Jackson, who not only restored the pulpit to its former state and gave it a new base, but brought the church generally into good condition without prejudicing its medieval appeal.

The interior is delightfully unspoiled, largely thanks to Sir Thomas Jackson, and is long and low, only seating 110 people. The roofs are of collar-and-rafter construction and the undersides of the timbers were once ceiled. The 'celure' or canopy of honour over the rood at the east end of the nave remains, although no longer 'painted with yellow flowers and rosettes on a red ground', as recorded by Jackson. The chancel arch is genuine village Norman work of chalkstone without moulding, chamfers or decoration of any kind, impressive by its simplicity. On the north side there still remains a niche which held a statue and this would probably have been balanced by the image bracket, now on the south wall where, unfortunately, it breaks into the wall paintings. Alterations were made to the south window in the chancel but, as stated earlier, the north is original. The small 'dot-and-line' crosses carved beside these windows are votive crosses made by travellers praying for a safe journey.

Furnishings
An exciting discovery was made in 1967 when Mrs. Eve Baker's team was repairing a wall-painting, the remains of a Flagellation and dated from *c*.1200. This was in outline but underneath they found a fresco in solid red ochre dating from *c*.1140, when the church was built. This remarkable find, fragmentary as it is, has been described by experts as unparalleled in the sense of superimposing a second painting so soon over a Norman original. Mounted horsemen fight with spears, and men with staves appear to be moving towards a boat containing others. The fourteenth-century stained glass in the tracery of the east window depicts the Trinity with the Holy Spirit shown as a dove over the Cross. The Jacobean pulpit (*see fig. 56*) to the south of the chancel arch retains its sounding board and, until they were stolen in 1980, was furnished with its original fine brass candlesticks; Jackson equipped it with a new base. It bears the date 1628 and the initials N.B. These suggest that it was presented by Nicholas Burley, who lived in the Old House in Pyrford in the early part of the seventeenth century. Some of the pews at the back near the south door are from the fifteenth century.

Modern additions include the font and an altar frontal, dedicated in 1968, designed by Miss Joan Edwards, a specialist in medieval embroidery, and worked by Captain Gerald Colpoys, R.N., a former submarine captain who was a local resident. The figures in the design, which depicts the Pilgrims' Way, echo figures in the wall paintings. There is thus a link between the newest and the oldest decoration of the church. There are no monuments of artistic note, but a rectangular brass commemorates Arthur Joseph Munby, M.A., F.S.A. (d.1910). Coming from a privileged background, Munby was on intimate terms with many of the leading intellectuals, authors and artists of his time, and is also known for his sociological studies of working women. He lived at Wheeler's Farm, close to St Nicholas Church, in the latter part of his life. In July 1992, in removing decayed floor boards on the north side of the nave, the cylindrical top of a tomb was revealed under the front pews. It was believed to be that of Richard Owen Cambridge (d.1804). Also a memorial stone was found beneath an old Victorian boiler when it was removed from a pit below the chancel floor. It commemorated Eliza Langston (d.1685).

A branch from the ancient yew-tree in the churchyard has been carved into the shape of a cross for the Church of the Good Shepherd, designed by David Nye and consecrated in 1964 to cope with increased population, thus linking the old with the new. The font in the new church was made with chisel and hammer by the sculptor, Penelope Staniforth, from a 24-cwt. block of Ancaster limestone brought from Lincolnshire.

RANMORE COMMON, St Bartholomew

This is one of Surrey's finest Victorian churches, built in 1859 by Sir George Gilbert Scott. Cruciform in shape, it has an octagonal central tower with tall spire, the tower being entirely faced with cobbles and the spire enriched with elegant dormers above the tower belfry stage (*see fig. 97*). The interior is less impressive than St Martin's, Dorking but has fine furnishings of the period. It does not have the good proportions of Woodyer's church but the multiple marble shafts and naturalistic capitals under the vaulted crossing catch the eye.

Furnishings
The furnishings include a striking font in maroon and black marble, a pulpit of variegated alabaster on fluted white marble columns (*Colour Plate XXXIV*), a luxurious reredos and plenty of Clayton and Bell stained glass. On a commanding site near the top of the hill leading off the Downs to Dorking in the valley below, St Bartholomew's is an impressive sight and it is interesting to compare it with Dorking's St Martin's, another of Surrey's notable nineteenth-century churches built by Woodyer a little later.

REDHILL, St John

Ease of communication with Brighton led to the growth of this companion town to Reigate. First came the turnpike road of 1807 and later the London and Brighton Railway of 1841. Rail links with Tonbridge followed in 1842 and with Guildford in 1849.

St. John's Church is situated south west of the town on Redhill Common. It was built in 1843 but largely rebuilt by J.L. Pearson who added the prominent south-west tower and spire in 1895. Inside, the chancel is vaulted and has a large iron screen in front, also by Pearson. Nairn [44] writes 'The Nave is formidable with a giant order embracing the earlier arcade and the added

185.   St. John's Redhill.

clerestory, roofed with transverse bows combined with a kingpost roof.' Redhill's other main church is St Matthew's in Station Road dating from 1866. It has a firestone body with gabled dormers and a free-standing Bargate stone tower with broach spire.

REIGATE, St Mary Magdalene

186.   Reigate parish church from the east.

Although no church is mentioned in Domesday Book, there probably was one. A fragment of interlaced carved stonework in the old vestry, likely to have been part of the shaft of a standing cross, may be a relic of a pre-Conquest place of worship. The first mention of a church is in the late twelfth century, when it was presented by Hamelin, Earl of Warenne, and Isabella, his wife, to the Augustinian canons of the Priory of St Mary Overie, Southwark, with whom it remained until the Dissolution, after which the living passed into private hands. The list of vicars starts with Edward de Dorking, instituted on 10th July 1311. The clerestory-less nave, except for the easternmost parts, is late twelfth-century in date, its aisles thirteenth-century, the chancel chapels early fourteenth-century and the west window of the north aisle about 1280. In the early part of the fifteenth century, the church of St Mary Magdalene was greatly altered and enlarged. Both nave and chancel were extended, the chancel being rebuilt: a chancel arch was erected as well as arches to both chapels, whilst a west tower and south porch were added. This basically is the church as it has come down to us today, plus a north transept added in 1908, except for the two vestries. The old vestry, which was erected in 1513 due to the generosity of a local man, John Skynner, has two storeys, the upper of which houses an interesting collection of general and theological books and a few manuscripts, in a library (*Colour Plate XXIV*) founded in 1701 by Andrew Cranston, the vicar of the time. Since lending was allowed from the beginning, this is the oldest public library in Britain and is zealously maintained by the Trustees.

Although structurally so little has been added since medieval times, harsh nineteenth-century restoration has laid its all too apparent mark on what we see today, particularly the restoration carried out in 1845 by Henry Woodyer: he not only replaced the Perpendicular east window with a poor substitute filled with tasteless highly coloured glass, but also mutilated the chancel and chapel monuments so that there is little left to enjoy. The later work, however, by George Gilbert Scott, junior, of 1877-81 is worthy of much praise; he restored some of the features destroyed in previous restorations and rebuilt the nave arcades, stone for stone, and the west tower in their original form and it is to him that we owe the opportunity of seeing the nave arcade in its late twelfth-century style. The tower, however, he felt compelled to reface and to substitute Bath for Reigate stone.

The interior is notable for its nave arcade, so well restored by Scott. The westernmost arcades date from 1180 to 1200, shortly after William of Sens was working on the choir of Canterbury Cathedral and, therefore, possibly influenced by him or his successors. As such, the arcades represent one of the earliest examples of Gothic work in the country. The piers vary from round to octagonal and, in one case, quatrefoil, whilst the capitals show every variety of foliage, not yet stiff-leaf, but well carved. These capitals and the palm-branch carving which fringes the inner arches of the south arcade were probably executed by the same masons who carved the similar features seen on the choir arcades of New Shoreham Church, Sussex. The piers are out of alignment with those opposite and the width of the nave increases from 18 feet at the west to 20 feet at the east end. The south aisle is also four feet wider than the north one. The early fourteenth-century chancel chapels have suffered from restoration, although the Decorated window in the north wall of the north chapel retains its reticulated tracery (only visible from outside). The Perpendicular fifteenth-century chancel has a fourteenth-century stone reredos in two stages (restored beyond recognition in 1845), and a piscina and sedilia of the same century with ogee canopies, much spoilt by gilding. The chancel arch and chancel chapel arches were contemporary with the chancel.

Furnishings
The large font is modern, encircled round the rim with small human heads. The fifteenth-century screens to the chancel and chancel chapels have been sadly mistreated. The Royal Arms of Queen Anne, as assumed after Union with Scotland, are well executed but, being set high in the tower, are difficult to see. The fine brass chandelier at the east end of the nave was given by Sir John Parsons in 1704, the year he was Lord Mayor of London.

Dismembered and mutilated remains of two Jacobean altar tombs are to be seen in the north chancel chapel – that nearest the chancel contains recumbent alabaster figures of Richard Elyot (d.1608) and his son Richard (d.1612), a servant of Henry, Prince of Wales. The other tomb bears effigies of Sir Thomas Bludder and his wife (both

187.   *The chandelier at Reigate.*

d.1619). Female figures on the ledge above are parts of the Elyot tomb, whilst the small figure under a pleasing ogee arch in the south chapel is Kathleen Elyot (d.1623); this originally lay at the feet of her parents in the Bludder monument. There was some shifting of the monuments under Woodyer and some suffered in the process, although admittedly they were poorly carved in the first place. One of the best monuments is that to Richard Ladbroke (d.1730) in the north transept, by Joseph Rose the Elder (only one other monument by him is recorded). This is a lofty, three-part composition of polychrome marble in eighteenth-century classical style, with the reclining figure in Roman dress flanked by figures of Justice and Truth. The centre is a huge broken and split Corinthian pediment. A far more famous man than Ladbroke – Charles, Lord Howard of Effingham, who led the English fleet to victory over the Spanish Armada in 1588 – is only commemorated by a modern brass tablet on the south wall of the sanctuary, recording the inscription on his coffin in the family vault beneath. He lived to the age of 87.

A small brass plaque (undated) to Adam Lambard and his wife Agnes may be the oldest memorial in the church but the earliest dated ones are the small mural tablets to Anthony Gilmyn (d.1575) and his wife (d.1580) in the north aisle. Below the east window of the south chancel chapel is a block of white marble with a classical frieze, commemorating William Elliot, M.P. (d.1818). The lack of any inscription is ascribed to differences which arose over the most suitable eulogy. Next to the Lambards lies Peter Hughes 'who dyed at the bath, the 28th. of May, 1693'. A murder is recorded on the wall of the north transept: 'William Burt, surgeon in the army who was murdered at Godstone in Surrey on 13th. April 1786'. A murderer lies buried in the chancel, although this fact is not recorded about Edward Bird, who shares a grave with his virtuous wife Catherine. He was hanged in 1718 for killing a waiter in a tavern brawl.

Although some of the stained glass remained untouched at the Reformation, it was destined to suffer at the hands of a madman. 'Thomas Glynn, late of Reigate, glazier, forcibly and unlawfully smashed and tore out the windows of the parish church.' He was fined 12d.

In the churchyard two tombs show striking contrasts of nineteenth-century sentiment. A ten-foot high obelisk commemorating Baron Masseres of 1825 has dull Grecian scenes around the base and what Nairn [45] describes as 'sickly carving', whilst the tomb to Rebecca Waterlow (d.1869), south of the Masseres obelisk, depicts more demonstrative grief. Two angels guard a sarcophagus on an enormous Egyptian base.

Other Churches in Reigate
St. Mark's and St Luke's are ecclesiastical parishes, formed respectively in 1860 and 1871 out of Reigate parish. St Peter's, Dover's Green was built in 1955 on a council estate south of the town and there is a pleasant small church (the Heath Church), which was opened for worship in 1907 on the eastern side of Reigate Heath. The most interesting – and also one of the quaintest churches, also on the Heath – is St Cross Chapel or the Mill Chapel (generally known as the Mill Church). Erected in 1765 as a post-mill, the brick round-house, seating some 50 or 60 worshippers, has been used as a chapel since 1880. It has a tarred weather-boarded top. There was once a chapel, used by pilgrims and linked with Reigate Priory, called 'The Chapel of the Holy Cross', from which the Mill Church derived its dedication.

RICHMOND, St Mary Magdalene

Although the building is centrally sited it makes little impact on the townscape because of its low elevation and the uninspiring surroundings. The only part of the old fabric of the church that remains is the west tower in Perpendicular style dating from *c*.1530, but largely rebuilt in 1624. It is of flint and stone, with a stair-turret on the south-east angle. The north aisle was reconstructed in brick in 1699, whilst the nave and south aisle were built in 1750, forming a typical Georgian brick rectangle with arched windows, incorporating both yellow and red bricks. On the south side, the three central windows are surmounted by a pediment, creating a cross-accent, likened by Bruce Watkin [46] to an orangery.

There was redecoration in 1823 and restorations in 1866 and *c*.1912. The nave arcade is of five bays with slender Tuscan columns and a straight entablature. The open timber roof by A.W. Blomfield rests uncomfortably on the main body of the church, but the tower arch is authentic work of *c*.1500. The higher chancel of flint and stone was designed by G.F. Bodley in 1904; he also provided the chapels.

188.   The pulpit at Richmond.   *189.   The font at Richmond.*

Furnishings
These include a pleasing eighteenth-century font, with a fluted bowl on a new stem, and a suitable modern cover, and a most attractive eighteenth-century pulpit with nicely turned slender spiral legs and balusters of similar design on the staircase. Of modern additions, the stained glass in the windows of the eastern part is by Bodley. The monuments form the most interesting feature of the church. There are a number of seventeenth-, eighteenth- and nineteenth-century examples. Earlier than these, a brass plate with kneeling figures commemorates Robert Cotton (d.1591), an 'officer of the Wardroppe' to Mary Tudor and Elizabeth. The seventeenth-century memorials include a curious one to John Bentley (d.1660) with three busts in a thin architectural frame and an achievement on top. The eighteenth century is represented by an excellent hanging monument to Randolph Greenway (d.1754) with rococo decoration; others are to James Thomson (d.1748), poet

author of 'The Seasons' and to William Rowan (d.1767) in the form of a bust before an obelisk. From the first half of the nineteenth century, there are memorials to Major Bean (d.1815) by John Bacon Jr. 'with a kneeling desperate woman by an urn on a pedestal' (Pevsner [47]), to Barbara Lowther (d.1806) by Flaxman and, at the west end of the north aisle, to Edmund Kean, the actor (d.1833), with draperies enclosing a profile medallion. In the churchyard there is a memorial to Viscount Fitzwilliam (d.1816), founder of the museum bearing his name at Cambridge and a sarcophagus and obelisk by Scheemakers to Sir Matthew Decker (d.1759).

RICHMOND, St Matthias

Scott's impressive Church of St Matthias dates from 1858 and has a north-west tower and spire and a rose window at the west end (*see fig. 96*). It is situated on high ground to the south-east in Friars Stile Road.

RIPLEY, St Mary

St. Mary's is a combination of Norman chancel, made of pudding-stone (*see fig. 3*), and a Victorian flint nave, built by Benjamin Ferrey in 1846. The south aisle by Sir Thomas Jackson was added in 1869. The chief architectural attraction of St Mary's is the enriched string course of Caen stone in the chancel and the corner shafts and attached mid-wall piers (*see fig. 8*) which seem to have been designed to carry a rib-vault. The east end has three thirteenth-century lancets; two more on the south side face two Norman windows with nook-shafts on the north side. The Norman work looks as though it dates from the twelfth century.

Mention is made of a church in a document of 1549 in which it was called a chantry chapel 'builded long time past for a hospital and often altered, into which the parishioners dwelling here have used for their own ease to resort to hear Divine Service . . .'. St Mary's did not become a separate parish until 1878; before then it was a chapel of ease to Send. It is situated at the south-west end of the High Street, once the old Portsmouth Road along which Lord Nelson travelled in 1805 from his house at Merton to Trafalgar.

In the early days of enthusiasm for cycling, Ripley was the goal of London cycling clubs. Not only was it a convenient 'run' but the Dibble family at the Anchor Inn gave the cyclists a warm welcome, when they were barred from many 'respectable' hotels. Charles Harper [48] wrote '. . . cycles were stacked by the hundred in the village street on Saturdays and Sundays in the 1870s'. The cyclists subscribed for a memorial window (*Colour Plate XXXVII*) in Ripley Church to Annie and Harriet Dibble, with the following brass inscription below:-

'To the Glory of God and as a token of respect to Annie Dibble who died July 24th. 1895 and Harriet Dibble who died October 20th. 1896, this window was erected by their cyclist friends'.

SANDERSTEAD, All Saints

All Saints enjoys a dominating position at the cross-roads, commanding fine prospects from its cemetery on the opposite side of the road. Although now surrounded by suburban

190.   Sanderstead Church from the south west.

development and only three miles from Croydon, the church has retained its village proportions and atmosphere. The Manor of Sanderstead (spelled 'Sanderstede' in Domesday Book) was granted by the mother of King Edward the Martyr in about 964 to the Benedictine Abbey of Hyde, near Winchester, with whom it rested until the Dissolution. There is no mention of any church in Domesday Book. The present church goes back to 1230, although there are indications of an earlier place of worship. The low nave arcade with octagonal piers is thirteenth-century in date, followed by the chancel arch and tower in 1310 and the chancel later in the fourteenth century. The dedication of the church did not become 'All Saints' until after 1485. Previously it was known as the Church of Alhalon. There was little alteration to the fabric after that until the nineteenth century, in the first half of which there was a crop of restorations (1828, 1832 and 1846). In the 1832 restoration all the windows were replaced. Immediately prior to the 1939-45 War in 1937/8 the north aisle was widened and, during the war, bomb damage was suffered. In 1980, as part of the commemorations of the church's 750th Anniversary, an extension to the Lady Chapel, called St Catherine's Aisle, was built. The main building material is flint. The west tower is surmounted by a shingled spire; it is unusual in being oblong below and square above. The sturdy west wall is strengthened by two large buttresses and the roof catslides over both nave and aisles. Despite restoration, the interior retains its village atmosphere. There are good corbel heads. The nave arcade includes some of the oldest parts of the church. The chancel unfortunately has been excessively restored, although it possesses a pleasing arched-brace roof with bosses.

Furnishings
The east window is flanked by two early fourteenth-century elongated wall-paintings believed to depict St Edmund, King and Martyr and St Edmund, Archbishop of

Canterbury when the church was built. The Royal Arms are those of Charles I; very large, they are painted on the chancel arch. Other furnishings, including a pulpit of 1962 designed by J.S. Comper, are modern. Comper also designed the organ-case. The brown marble font with octagonal stem dates from the nineteenth century. One of the two oak settles is thought to date from the seventeenth century. The other is modern. The settles were known as a dog-whipper's bench, for servants in charge of dogs.

There are many monuments of interest. At the end of the south aisle, a black-and-white marble monument, with the effigy wrapped in a shroud lying on a sarcophagus, commemorates Mrs. Mary Audley (d.1655), wife of Lewes Audley, J.P., a Parliamentary military officer. This rather macabre type of monument was fashionable at the time and should be compared with those of Dr. John Donne in St Paul's Cathedral and Sir John Denham at Egham. The finest monument is a small hanging memorial to John Ownstead (d.1600) which has been recoloured and regilded (*Colour Plate XVI*). It is on the chancel south wall and represents Ownstead, who was sergeant of the carriages to Queen Elizabeth for 40 years, in armour and ruff, beneath an arch with flowers, and a lion's head as keystone. Arabesque decoration and the family crest on a background of scroll work enclose the kneeling figure. Other memorials commemorate George Mellish (d.1693 at the age of 23) near the north-west corner of the north aisle, in the form of a bust with wig, under an arch and with fulsome verses below, sometimes traditionally ascribed to Dryden; it is in marble. The earliest memorial is in the chancel, a brass to John Atwood (d.1525) and his wife; another brass depicts ten children. Trooper Beeson is commemorated by a headstone near the south porch. He survived the charge of the Light Brigade at Balaclava. After leaving the Army, he joined the police and for many years was Sanderstead's village policeman, riding the roads on a white horse.

The parish records include a reference to a legacy for the Parson in Sanderstead to preach a sermon on 1st November 'in thankful remembrance of God's great mercy in delivering Church and State from the horrid treason of the Gunpowder Plot'. Rectors have kept up the custom of mentioning the subject in early November.

SEALE, St Laurence

Although there is evidence of earlier churches, St Laurence's church rebuilt by J. Croft in 1861-73 is almost all new, constructed in a Picturesque style with large central tower and pyramidal spire. The church lies on a geological meeting ground, the main fabric being in clunch and the tower green Bargate stone. There are a few medieval fragments incorporated as, for instance, the fourteenth- or fifteenth-century wooden south porch and the late twelfth-century font.

SEND, St Mary the Virgin

Although there is no trace of pre-Conquest work in the present church, there is reference to a place of worship in Domesday Book. In 1210, Beatrice de Sandes who, with Ruald de Calna, had granted an earlier charter to Newark Priory, confirmed that this included the construction of a church at Send. The living remained in the hands of Newark Priory until the Dissolution, the list of incumbents going back to John de Crandall in 1289. The first part to be built was the chancel in the early thirteenth century and presumably a nave was added in the same Early English style soon after but, apart from the re-use of thirteenth-century stone dressings on two small windows, the present nave was built in the late fifteenth century (*c*.1475) and this is the date of the west tower. Prior to the Reformation, there were two small side chapels but these have disappeared. The south porch also dates from the fifteenth century. In 1600 St Mary's became a parish church embracing Ripley, which did not become a separate parish until nearly 300 years later.

Framed in a well-kept churchyard, St Mary's presents an unassuming exterior with flint and pudding-stone walls rendered in lime plaster and chalk or sandstone dressing, and a plain crenellated tower. On either side of the present east window dating from 1819 can be seen the stone dressings of an earlier east window; below, on the ground, is a small upright stone reputedly marking the entrance to a vault beneath the communion table where a priest, a refugee from the French Revolution, was interred. On the south side of the chancel there are two Early English lancet windows (one of reconstituted stone) and, of the same period, a priest's door and low-side window. The nave has two Perpendicular windows on each side, the heads of the lights trefoiled and protected on the exterior by square hood mouldings; on the south-west corner of the window immediately to the right of the south porch is a fine example of a mass dial. There are two smaller windows on either side of the east end of the nave, set lower than the others, which were angled to admit light to the former side chapels. The lower courses of the roof are covered with Horsham slabs, the most northerly use of these in the county apart from Chobham and Esher. Some putlog holes, in which scaffolding was erected, are to be seen in the tower and on the north side of the church. The tower widens by two feet towards the top and has diagonal buttresses.

Entrance is through the south door inserted into a clunch doorway. The door, which is heavily studded, dates from the fifteenth century and retains its original wooden lock case, closing ring and escutcheon plate. The nave, rectangular in shape without aisles, is exceptionally wide. The lack of aisle was probably due to scarcity of building stone for arcades. Originally, nave and chancel were on one level but in 1901 the floor was excavated to a depth of eight inches and filled with concrete, the present wood-block floor being laid in the nave and Spanish marble in the chancel. There is no chancel arch but two open-sided squints cut into the stone quoins of the chancel opening gives further evidence of the existence of side chapels. A gallery and a vestry partition at the west end obscures the tower arch. At one time there was access from outside to the gallery, but is now by a steep stair passing through the tower arch. The chancel is lit by four Early English lancets, splayed internally at 45^0 on all sides, heads and cills. To the east of the north wall, about four feet from the floor, is a plain stone corbel, which may have supported an image of the Virgin Mary, to whom the church is dedicated.

Furnishings
The octagonal fifteenth-century font at the west end of the nave is mounted upon sandstone slabs; there is evidence of provision for a clasp and staples for a padlock to lock the font cover. Incised roughly on the side of the bowl is the date 1660, but this presumably refers to later work; the present cover dates from 1935. A chancel screen in the Perpendicular style, erected soon after the nave was built, is sadly mutilated, having lost its mullions, and has new battlemented cresting; it was extended on the north and south sides to form parclose screens for the side chapels, but these have been removed and the saw marks left can still be seen. Although roods were swept away at the Reformation, the rood beam with mounting sockets is still in position, with simple balustrading dating from *c*.1670. The Royal Arms, originally placed in the tympanum above the chancel screen and now hanging over the south door, are those of George III. The chest was probably made about 1325 and is of the early dug-out type, formed by roughly squaring a large log with a slice sawn off to act as a lid and then bound with iron straps. An order issued by the Synod of Exeter in 1287 decreed that each church should have a chest for books and vestments. A plain Early

191. The Royal Arms at Send.

English piscina is situated in the south-west corner of the chancel wall near the altar. The only medieval stained glass consists of thirteenth-century fragments in the centre light of the south-west nave window.

There are no major monuments inside the church. A small but appealing feature is a brass with rough engraving to Laurence Slyffeld (d.1521) and his wife Alys on the north wall of the chancel; the effigies are only 13 inches high and below is a charming little group of three sons. Above is a brass inscription to Thomas Marteyn, vicar from 1501 to 1533. Amongst good examples of monumental sculpture in the churchyard is the tomb of Lieutenant General William Evelyn, situated north-west of the church; he was a great grandson of John Evelyn, the diarist. It is by Robert Chambers, who made a practice of signing his work in Hebrew. Near a wall west of the church is a memorial to William Hargreaves, descendant of the inventor of the Spinning Jenny. The inscription includes the words 'in principle a Republican'. (He died in 1874 when the monarchy had lost popularity because of Queen Victoria's widowhood 'seclusion and the extra-marital adventures of the Prince of Wales.)

SHALFORD, St Mary the Virgin,

Prior to the present church there had been a fine old cruciform place of worship with a central tower and spire but, 'being greatly decayed', it was pulled down in 1788. This was followed by a second church, a poor building in pseudo-classical style, which lasted only fifty years. St Mary's is one of Benjamin Ferrey's seven Surrey churches built in the early part of Queen Victoria's reign. The style is thirteenth-century with lancets, but the proportions suffer from the building being too high for its length, although externally the tower and graceful shingled spire, ascribed to Woodyer, at the west end of the north aisle, add dignity to the church. The doors, especially the yellow south door, are of fine quality and the churchyard immaculate.

Internally, there are interesting memorials from the old church, including a Tudor brass on the south wall of the sanctuary to the children of Roger and Margaret Elyot and several eighteenth-century tablets to the memory of the Austen family. Later memorials include one to Colonel Haversham Godwen Austen who discovered K2 mountain in the Himalayas and another to Colonel Frederick George Sewell who managed to save a remnant of his men from the Charge of the Light Brigade at the battle of Balaclava in the Crimean war of 1854-55. The east windows of the Lady Chapel contain some old Flemish glass.

One of the vicars of Shalford was the Rev. David Railton, who, after serving as chaplain in the 1914-18 War, conceived the idea for the tomb of the Unknown Warrior which was taken up by the Dean of Westminster.

SHERE, St James

This goes back to pre-Conquest times; a church at 'Essira' (Shere) was recorded in Domesday Book. The building we see today is basically a Transitional Norman structure of the late twelfth century, the nave, base of tower, south aisle and chancel dating from this period. Particularly enjoyable is the south doorway with zig-zag chevron decoration, Petworth marble shafts and leaf capitals, and the arch which separates the south aisle from the south chapel. In the mid-thirteenth century, the tower was heightened, possibly influenced by contact with Netley Abbey near Southampton, the Abbot being Lord of the Manor of Gomshall Netley. The splay-footed shingled spire dates from the late fourteenth century. The west doorway, also embellished with Petworth marble shafts, was inserted c.1200. Around 1300, the south chapel

192. *Shere Church from the west.*

was lengthened to provide for the Bray Chancel. (The Bray family were lords of the manor from 1487 and a descendant, William Bray (d.1832) was joint author with Owen Manning, who was vicar of Godalming, of *The History and Antiquities of Surrey*.) In 1329, permission was given to an anchoress to enclose herself in a cell, which was added outside the chancel and to re-enclose herself in 1332, after she had left her cell 'inconstantly and returned to the world'. The signs of where she was incarcerated are still evident in the quatrefoil and squint cut into the north wall of the chancel. In the mid-fourteenth century, the chancel was extended (*see fig. 33*) and, at the end of the century, the St Nicholas Chapel was added north of the crossing. This may have been the time when the east and west round arches of the tower were replaced by pointed arches. Post-Reformation additions included the installation of a west gallery in 1748 and a musicians' gallery on the north wall (removed in 1861). A fairly gentle restoration was carried out in 1895/6 by S. Weatherley, concentrating mainly on the chancel in order to provide seating for a robed choir so much favoured by the High Victorians but the fittings are the much later modern work of Louis Osman. The present east window dates from 1902.

The general effect of the exterior is heavy with large roofs, but relieved by its splendid siting at the end of a village street, which funnels up to it, and by the powerful tower, with fine single bell-openings towards the west and its splay-footed spire. The shortage of good building stone in Surrey is illustrated by the macedoine of different materials used in the church's construction – Bargate stone and rubble, ironstone, flints, Caen stone, re-used Roman tiles, clunch (chalkstone), Horsham slabs and Tudor brick. Although the tower is central, the shortening of the north transept and the extension of the south aisle has changed the original cruciform shape and the Cracklow drawing of the 1820s, made from the north

193.   The font at Shere.

west, gives a lop-sided appearance which is still evident. The churchyard is entered through a Horsham-slab-roofed lych-gate of 1901, designed by Sir Edwin Lutyens, and the church itself through the noteworthy early thirteenth-century west doorway, the door dating from 1626. The windows are of varying periods from Norman to Perpendicular. The interior is wide and spacious with an uncluttered chancel reminiscent of East Anglia. The oaken roofs, mostly of the scissors-truss type are old and the plaster ceilings were removed in 1937 in the nave and 1956-8 in the chancel.

Furnishings
There is an Early English font of *c.*1200 in Purbeck marble, with a central stem and four corner shafts, completed with stiff-leaf capitals, and a large early thirteenth-century chest, probably one of those put into churches by order of Pope Innocent III to collect money for the Crusades. There are many fragments of medieval stained glass, including thirteenth-century grisaille glass in the angle lights of the east window, tracery quatrefoils and a richly coloured eagle – perhaps the best – in the Bray Chancel east window, also three red roses and one white in St Nicholas Chapel. On a respond north-west of the Bray Chancel is a tiny thirteenth-century Madonna and Child, only two inches high, discovered in 1880. On the east side of the south-west respond of the crossing is a carving of St James. The set of chancel fittings in metal designed by Louis Osman in 1956 include an altar cross and candlesticks in iron, plated copper and gilt, a fine silver ciborium, an aumbry cast in bronze and a stainless steel altar rail. There is a memorial to William Bray in the Bray Chancel. There are brasses to John, Lord Audley (d.1491), a 20-inch figure in armour, finely executed, on the floor of the chancel; to Robert Scarclif, rector (d. 1412), a 12-inch figure; to John Redford and to Oliver Sandys (d.1512) in the south aisle.

STOKE D'ABERNON, St Mary

The name 'Stoke D'Abernon' is derived from a Saxon word 'Stoc' meaning a palisaded manor to which was added the name d'Aubernoun of the family to whom the manor passed after the Conquest. St Mary's has a most interesting history and is believed to be the oldest church still standing in the county, going back to the early eighth or even seventh century. Three approximate main dates govern the church's subsequent medieval history: 1190 when the north wall of the nave was pierced to provide for a low north aisle: 1240 when the old Saxon apse was squared off to form the noble two-bay vaulted chancel and 1490 when the Norbury Chantry Chapel was added on the north east. A significant but much later date for St Mary's was 1866 when it underwent an extensive Victorian restoration, which included stripping the exterior rendering (thus exposing the flints from the nearby fields and the Roman tiles used in its construction), adding a small turret tower in the north-west corner, extending the nave by 15 feet and erecting a transept on the north side. The church was almost completely re-roofed at that time.

The unpromising northern exterior as seen from the lych-gate leaves one quite unprepared for the wealth of attractive features within. High up on the south wall (*see fig. 5*) can be seen the jambs and stone lintel of a door (blocked by the Normans) which led to a western upper storey for the thegn and his family, where they did not have to mingle with the ordinary worshippers. It would have been approached by a wooden external staircase. This type of structure is typical of early rather than late Saxon work and there is Roman material in the walling. St Mary's is next door to the manor house – a rare example in these parts of the lord's private church or *eigenkirche*, adjacent to, and in this case, almost embraced by the big house. The two nave bays have circular columns with pointed arches in the Transitional style (between Norman and Early English). The nave is separated from the chancel by an arch of the 1866 restoration replacing one of a few years earlier which in its turn had been substituted for a narrow Saxon entrance with abaci made of slabs of Roman building. The Norbury Chantry Chapel north of the chancel is entered by wrought-iron seventeenth-century gates of Italian origin and is in the Perpendicular style of Henry VII's time. It was built by Sir John Norbury shortly after the battle of Bosworth Field (1485), which set the Tudor line on the English throne, and may have been built as a thankoffering for the outcome of the battle. There is a fireplace in the chapel. Structurally the chancel is the chief attraction of St Mary's and it houses a fine set of seventeenth-century furnishings. It is a notable example of vaulted thirteenth-century work (*see fig. 19*), with the well moulded ribs carried on shafts rising from stone benches encircling the chancel – an early form of church seating. The lancet windows on the south side are contemporary.

Furnishings

These are many and varied. In front of the chancel are two of considerable interest – a lavishly adorned seven-sided pulpit of walnut, given by Sir Francis Vincent in 1620 and a lectern dating from the seventeenth century. Below the pulpit are strange caryatid figures, part animal part human. Its tester is held up by wrought-iron stays of very fine workmanship and, on one of the sides, the words 'Fides ex auditu' (faith comes from what is heard) are inscribed. Next to the pulpit is an hour-glass stand. The lectern is of unusual type supported on a stem with a barley-sugar-stick twist. The large quantity of stained glass is of varying origins – English, French, German and Dutch dating from the end of the fifteenth century or the beginning of the sixteenth and Flemish from about 1610. The most notable are the Trier (Germany) panels of the Virgin and of St Anne, the group of three connected panels of Rhenish glass in the east window and the two French roundels of the Virgin (*Colour Plate XXV*) in the south of the nave. The centre-light panels of the east window depict Christ before Caiaphas, the Nailing to the Cross and the Resurrection, a colourful group well preserved. (These are the so-called Costessey panels, see also Great Bookham.) The roundels of the Virgin show her both smiling (the Queen of Heaven) and weeping. The glass is spread round the church with many varied motifs including Susanna and the elders, the desecration of the Temple by Antiochus Epiphanes, various saints and heraldry. The glass has been fully discussed by the Rev. John Waterson [49] who was rector of St Mary's for close on 35 years.

The chancel furnishings include a Laudian altar-table with movable top, credence table, a stool with carved figures, and Laudian altar rails with twisted balusters. These are all of the seventeenth century as is the brass candelabrum. On the east wall, there are fragments of a thirteenth-century mural painting depicting the Adoration of the Lamb which was cut into early in the fourteenth century, when it was felt necessary to provide more light with a window at the east end. To the left of the chancel arch is a striking Renaissance statue of the Madonna and Child, dating from *c*.1500. It was made in northern Italy of limestone and retains traces of its original colouring. The organ is an outstanding instrument and was voiced expressively for the church by Frobenius of Copenhagen in 1975. Before the pulpit is an interesting chest with the stiles prolonged to raise it off the ground and with chip-carved roundels on the front; it dates from the early thirteenth century and was probably placed in the church to conform with an edict of 1199 requiring churches to collect for the Crusades. There are two other chests of later date.

194.   The fireplace in the Norbury Chapel at Stoke D'Abernon.

The Vincent monuments in the Norbury Chapel (*Colour Plate XIX*) are typical and rather routine early seventeenth-century examples. They include memorials to Sir Thomas (d.1613) and Lady Jane Vincent (d.1619) on the north wall and to Lady Sarah Vincent (d.1608), under a crested semi-circular canopy, on the east wall. Sir Thomas and Lady Sarah lean on their elbows whilst Lady Jane lies recumbent on her back. The lost tomb to Sir John Norbury may have been designed as an Easter Sepulchre and as such incurred the displeasure of the Elizabethan reformers 'being by injury of time demolisht'. Above the seventeenth-century memorial to him, showing him in Carolean armour, is a funerary helm. The oldest and newest features among the monuments are combined in the memorial to Viscount d'Abernon, who died in 1941 at the age of 84; this includes a small Roman funerary casket from the catacombs of the second century. In the north wall is a rare pre-Reformation fireplace to enable the family to worship in comfort; this would also have warmed the chapel when it was used later as a schoolroom. On the opposite wall is the entrance to the rood loft.

Perhaps the best known features of St Mary's are the large D'Abernon brasses on the floor of the chancel. Recent research[50] has shown that the dates offered for these were too early and it is now known that the older one relates to Sir John D'Abernon II, who died in *c.*1327. This is one of the finest in the country (*see fig. 32*). Measuring 6½ feet in height, it shows him full-faced and with outstretched feet resting on a spirited lion who grasps his lance, a far more effective animal than his rather insipid companion under the feet of Sir John's son next to him. This is Sir John III of *c.*1340-5, who is depicted in plate armour rather than chain mail. There are five other brasses, one only an inscription (from the lost tomb of Sir John Norbury) below the engaging Caroline monument to him in kneeling posture which replaces his destroyed tomb. A late rectangular brass of 1592 in an alabaster memorial depicts Thomas and Frances Lyfelde kneeling with their daughter Jane. The other three are quite small but of much interest, the first being Sir John Norbury's mother, who died in 1464 and showing the figures of eight children within the folds of her robe – an unusual design. Another is of a child, Ellen Bray, swathed in her chrisom robe to signify that she died (1516) within a month of her baptism. The seventh is a copy of a priest's brass, of which the original, apart from the inscription, has been lost, to John Prowd, Rector (d.1497).

   The d'Aubernouns were succeeded by the Norburys, the Brays and the Vincents, all of whom have left their mark on the church. After the departure of the last member of the Vincent family, the manor house has become an educational establishment, but the church is still permeated with memories of the great families who lived next door and it is largely due to them that we have here one of the most interesting of Surrey's churches. Among the many fascinating associations of St Mary's is the record of the earliest English honeymoon (spent at the manor). This was described in Norman-French in the contemporary poem of 1189, *L'Histoire de Guillaume le Maréchal*, on the occasion of the marriage of the Earl of Pembroke's heiress to the future regent of England and guardian of Henry III.

STOKE-NEXT-GUILDFORD, St John the Evangelist

There was a church at Stoke mentioned in Domesday Book but its site is not certain. The oldest part of the present building and the most prominent feature is the handsome flint-and-stone-chequered, fifteenth-century west tower, enlarged in 1851, with its south-east stair turret and square-headed belfry windows. Inside, the south chancel arcade with round abaci and multi-moulded arches is probably of the fourteenth century and the nave arcades are of the same date but difficult to identify today. The north chapel (the Stoughton Chapel) is probably sixteenth-century in date, but its windows have simple seventeenth-century mullions and transoms. The large east window, with mullions running up into the head of the arch and deep concave splays both inside and out, is a fine feature. A Victorian restoration was carried out in 1858 and, in recent years, the church has been re-ordered with wall-to-wall carpeting. This spacious interior with its wide arcades, the arches of which die into the piers without capitals, create what is probably one of the most comfortable churches in the diocese. Also a fine centre was built on the south side in 1981 and named after Sir James Stirling, who developed the Swan River Colony in Australia, separate and distinct from the convict colony of New South Wales, and became the first Governor of Western Australia, founding the City of Perth in 1829.

Furnishings
These include an attractive eighteenth-century font with a black marble bowl and base with a swelling white marble stem, and pulpit understood to date from James I's reign and therefore Jacobean. The communion rail was installed in 1732. There are fragments of largely armorial fifteenth- and sixteenth-century English glass in the east window of the Stoughton Chapel, where there is a north window by F.J. Shields, to designs by his friend

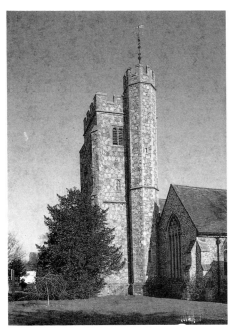

195. Stoke-next-Guildford – the west tower.

Dante Gabriel Rossetti and in memory of R.S. Budgett (d.1888), with two sets of four lights in fairly weak colouring except for the greens. The fine east window has glass of 1877 donated by the brother officers of the regiment of Sir George Pomeroy Colley, whom the window commemorates.

Of the memorials, several are worthy of mention. The tablet to William Aldersey (d.1800) in the north aisle is by Flaxman, with a typical motif of a woman mourning over an urn. There is a similar one, attractively carved by Bacon Jun, to John and Elizabeth Creuze. She died in 1804 and a painting of her by Gainsborough is to be seen in the Paris Louvre. Just inside the door on the north wall of the Stoughton Chapel are three memorials to members of the Stoughton family – Sir Lawrence Stoughton, who entertained James I at Stoughton Place (d.1615), his heir Thomas who pre-deceased him in 1610 and his third son, George (d.1623). These monuments have fine alabaster frames and are surmounted by the Stoughton family crest of a robin redbreast perched. On the north wall of the chancel is a memorial to Charlotte Smith, who married at the age of 15 in 1764, but whose husband left her with ten children to support; this she did for 22 years by writing novels and poems that were much appreciated by Wordsworth, Coleridge and Sir Walter Scott. In the north-east corner of the north aisle are two tablets with a marble surround to the inscriptions and cherub-heads above and below, to bachelor brothers Henry and William (d.1799) Parson, who established the Stoke Hospital Almshouses in 1796 for 'six poor widows of the Parish'. Another of unusual interest is found above the south-west door to Dr. James Price who died aged 25 in 1783. He became notorious as one of the last alchemists, claiming to be able to turn mercury into gold. When required to repeat his experiments in front of witnesses, he committed suicide with prussic acid while they were examining his apparatus. His epitaph reads: 'Heu! Qualis erat' (Oh! What a mistake).

Other Churches in Stoke

The northern part of Guildford has greatly increased in numbers and out of Stoke have grown the parishes of St Saviour (1899), Stoughton (1902) and Christ Church (1936 – *q.v.*). St Saviours has a sizeable north-west tower with spire and a large wagon-roofed space inside.

STOKE-NEXT-GUILDFORD, Christ Church

Christ Church was built as a daughter church of St John the Evangelist, Stoke, to serve the needs of Guildford's growing population and was largely inspired and financed by members of the Paynter family, two of whom were rectors of Stoke and a third who had acquired the right to nominate the rector. Ewan Christian (as at St Nicolas, Guildford) was engaged as architect and the nave was built and consecrated in 1868. Chancel, north aisle, north-west porch and lowest stage of the tower followed in 1873 and the place of worship was completed at the turn of the century with the addition of the south aisle and the completion of the tower. In 1936, Christ Church became a separate parish. Redecoration to the plans of Sir Edward Maufe, to provide a brighter interior, following the example of what he had done at the Cathedral, took place in 1962.

Christ Church has a plain, honest exterior benefiting from the good stone used in the construction – Bargate (also used for the low surrounding wall) and Bath stone dressings; particularly fine small bricks are used for in-filling. The south-west pinnacled tower has large and well-proportioned belfry lights with plate tracery. The east end is apsed, as at St. Nicolas. The interior is inoffensive but uninspired, consisting of nave, aisles, chancel with apsed sanctuary. There is a slight incline from west to east. The nave is enhanced by the robust columns of Devonshire marble supporting the arcades, each completed with an individually carved capital. There are small decorative columns of red granite on either side of the north-west porch.

SUTTON, St Nicholas

The village of Sutton, which lay between the Green at the north end of the High Street and the parish church further south, was transformed during the period when the main Brighton Road passed along the High Street (1775-1809). It then grew into a town after the railway came in 1847, although the population in 1881 was only 10,334. The church was rebuilt by Edwin Nash in 1862-4 of flint with a broach spire. In the south-west corner of the churchyard is the mausoleum of 1777 of the Gibson family of London, with a pyramidal roof and rusticated quoins and doorway. In 1793 Elizabeth Gibson left money for the vicar and churchwardens to open the door and inspect the coffins annually. This is still done on 12th August.

Other Churches in Sutton
All Saints, Benhilton was built by S.S. Teulon in 1863-1866. It is a large church with a broad west tower, very prominently sited. The stained glass, consisting of an east window by J. & W. Kettlewell and south aisle windows by John Hayward, receives high marks from Alec Clifton-Taylor,[51] the eminent architectural historian. Christ Church was erected by Newman & Jacques in 1888 of red brick. It has a polygonal apse, but no tower, with an interior enhanced by a striking rood screen supported on an openwork crown. One other church that deserves mention is the red brick St Barnabas dating from 1884 to 1891 and designed by Carpenter & Ingelow. The outstanding feature is the glass of the east window by Morris & Co., the subject being the Sermon on the Mount, a pictorial design spread across five lights.

TANDRIDGE, St Peter

Set apart from the village in the midst of large trees, one of which is famous (see below), it is appropriate that St Peter's should be noted for its woodwork including a tower, dating from about 1300, which – as at Horley – rises straight up from the ground being supported on massive posts inside the church. It is surmounted by a shingled spire. There is nothing left of the pre-Conquest church, but it is said that when it was built the foundations were arched over the roots of the famous tree to avoid cutting them. The earliest part of the existing

196.   *Tandridge Church from the south.*

church dates from *c.*1100. In Norman times, it consisted of chancel and nave and had no aisles, but all that is left of this is the priest's door on the north side of the chancel and the slit window beside it (*Colour Plate III*). The body of the present church is twelfth- and thirteenth-century in date. A fourteenth-century south door was rebuilt into the modern porch and there is a date of 1616 above the west window, but clearly this is restored. Otherwise, the fabric is largely nineteenth-century, the aisles being built by Sir G.G. Scott (who lived nearby at Rooksnest) in 1844 (south) and 1874 (north).

The view from the main approach on the south composes well with the tall western tower and spire, attractive south porch and long sweeping roof over the nave with two dormers. The building stone is of a pleasant buff colour. Inside the most notable features are the four corner oak posts supporting the steeple, measuring about 14½ inches square, with irregular cross-bracing. The collar-and-rafter roofs of the nave and chancel have been given a date of *c.*1300; a tie-beam east of the timbers supports the turret.

St. Peter's was linked with a small Priory of three Augustinian Canons and seven poor brethren, founded in 1226 and known as St James' Hospice; it was a daughter house of the Priory of St Mary Overie at Southwark. As Maxwell Fraser points out in his book on Surrey,[52] the Priory's record 'seems to have been a tarnished one'. Never wealthy, the Bishop of Winchester had occasion to reprimand its Prior for slackness and the Cellarer was dismissed for falsifying the books. This seemed to have had little effect as, 27 years later in 1335, the Archbishop of Canterbury demanded the Prior's resignation. In 1426, a later Prior got into trouble for claiming the revenues from the Annual Fair held at Tandridge on 25th July; the king's officers, in retaliation, sold the right to hold the Fair to three London citizens for two shillings. All that remains of this Priory, separated from the church by nearly a mile, are the fish-ponds north of the A25 road. After passing through various private hands following the Dissolution, the patronage of St Peter's now rests with Oxford University.

Furnishings
The reredos is by Scott. There are no memorials of note within the church, but Lady Scott (d.1872) is buried in the churchyard and is commemorated by a richly sculptured, marble tomb-chest. Also interred at Tandridge are several members of the Pepys family, including Sir Charles Pepys, first Earl of Cottenham, who was twice Lord Chancellor.

Churchyard
The Tandridge yew-tree to the west of the church is reputed to be one of the largest in the country. Although hollow inside, it is still vigorous and about three feet from the ground has a girth of 32½ feet. The largest girth of a yew tree in the country is over 35 feet at

Ulcombe in Kent, but the Tandridge umbrage (the shaded area below) of about 85 feet may well be unrivalled.

TATSFIELD, St Mary

Lying as it does, isolated on the crest of the Downs south of the green, 788 feet above sea-level with a splendid view over the Weald, St Mary's has the most elevated situation of any church in Surrey. Basically Norman, the church dates back to *c*.1075, but the chancel is mainly from the thirteenth century. The nave walls are Norman and of dark sandstone with light sandstone quoins. There are two very small Norman windows on the north side, and one of *c*.1300 and a Perpendicular one on the south. The chancel of firestone, including the east window with trefoil lights, was rebuilt in 1330. It has two Early English moulded windows and a fourteenth-century low-side window. The chancel arch, segmental-headed and without capitals, is flanked on each side by two lancets, the north one of which in chalkstone is enriched with impressive mouldings. In 1838, the roofs were restored but some old tie-beams remain in the chancel. At the same time the tower, rising from inside the nave, was erected. There was further work in 1882 and a more comprehensive restoration in 1966/7 when the floors were restored to their original levels. A new porch was added then and the central entrance opened up, but the original fourteenth-century one to the east of the porch remains blocked.

Furnishings
The font is carved out of a plain stone and is supported by a fifteenth-century pier. The pulpit, clergy stalls and the altar are modern works of local craftsmen. A fragment of medieval stained glass representing an angel is to be seen in the upper light of the east window. An unusual piscina and credence shelf with an ogee head, and a large and deep double aumbry, with square heads, all on the east wall of the chancel, are other furnishings of interest. On the north wall there is a copy of a painting in Antwerp, of the Crucifixion, reputed to be by one of Rubens' students. The Royal Arms in the narthex are those of George III, probably after 1801, because they do not include the lilies of France. There is a hatchment over the chancel arch. On the south side of the nave a monument carved in painted wood commemorates John Corbett (d.1711) 'Carpinder' and his wife, Alice (d.1710). The inscription is placed between Doric columns, supporting a pediment surmounted by an urn.

THAMES DITTON, St Nicholas

There is evidence of the existence of a church at Thames Ditton in the twelfth century, but the oldest parts of the present building are the early thirteenth-century west tower (*see fig. 25*) and the chancel. The early thirteenth-century chancel lancet window on the north side has a round-headed rere-arch, but a lancet-shaped opening. These were followed by the Lady Chapel, north of the chancel, in the fourteenth century and the original narrow north aisle of the fifteenth century. The north nave arcade, with octagonal piers and depressed rounded arches, is late Perpendicular and a low, four-centred brick arch (under the thirteenth-century lancet in the chancel), which opens into the north chapel, may be early sixteenth-century in date. A dormitorium or burial place for the Hatton family was built next to the Lady Chapel in 1676 and was converted into the vicar's vestry in 1781. The

197. The Judgment Day panels at Thames Ditton.

north aisle was widened in 1826 and a gallery added and this was partly removed in 1937. The south nave arcade, aisle and chapel were added by Benjamin Ferrey in 1864.

The eastern view from the High Street of the four gable ends and the low, broad thirteenth-century tower, with attractive weatherboarded belfry and lead-sheathed spike, make a pleasant picture and the combination of materials (flint and stone for the fabric, tiles for the roof, wood for the belfry and lead for the spike) is a typical Surrey mix. The building is low, and broad rather than long. Inside the older parts are hard to detect under later alterations and most of the window details have been renewed. Formerly a chapel of Kingston, St Nicholas did not become parochial until 1769.

Furnishings
The font and the Easter Sepulchre are the highlights. The font is Norman (*see fig. 13*) and is in the shape of a block capital, with crude symbolic carvings in medallions including the Lamb and the Cross and an ibex falling on its horns; there are small heads at the corners. The Easter sepulchre is a most unusual structure, Perpendicular in style, in the form of a six-poster bed; the top is crenellated. The Judgment Day painted panels above the chancel arch date from *c*.1520; the remaining panels – on the beam above the arch – are said to be the only examples of their kind near London.

The monuments consist of the canopied tomb on the north side of the chancel to Erasmus Forde (d.1533) and his wife (d.1559) with their children: a hanging wall-monument with bust above an inscription plate to Sidney Godolphin (d.1732) and brasses of the first half of the sixteenth century to Robert Smythe (d.1539) and his wife (d.1549), kneeling with their children, and John Cheke (d.1590).

THORPE, St Mary

Although the earliest evidence of a church or chapel on the site is mid-twelfth century, there may well have been an older place of worship for, as long ago as 675, Chertsey Abbey were given '5 manses in loco qui dicitur Thorpe'. There is no mention, however, in Domesday Book of any church. St Mary's came under the Abbey until the Dissolution although the history of their relationship is not very edifying. There were frequent arguments, involving the Bishop of Winchester, about providing sufficient resources for a vicar to live on and, because of the lack of means, Thorpe was deprived of the services of a chaplain for a long time. In 1428/9, the parish secured from the Abbey the right of burial for which they had to provide the ground (as at Chobham). The oldest part of the church is the twelfth-century chancel arch. Decorated windows survive on the north side of the chancel, probably inserted by Abbey masons in the fourteenth century when considerable work was undertaken. This included the building of the original nave arcades. A little Decorated detail also remains on the south side. It would appear that St Mary's was of cruciform shape, but this has been obscured by the extension of the aisles when they were rebuilt in 1848, at which time the nave arcades were also reconstructed. There was a further comprehensive restoration in 1893. The walls of the church are of flint and rubble, with clunch and sandstone dressings, but the west tower is a good example of seventeenth-century brickwork. After the Dissolution, the patronage passed to the Crown until the middle of the nineteenth century, after which it went through private hands, until being presented in 1932 to Keble College, Oxford.

The church is situated in a quiet backwater at the end of a short lane with old brick cottages on the left and the large brick-built, eighteenth-century house of Spelthorne St Mary on the right. Backed by trees, the church makes an attractive picture with its fine embattled tower, approached from the house through a pleasing brick arch (*see Frontispiece*). The tower has a square-headed, three-light window with tracery in the lower stage and a round-headed, two-light window in the belfry stage; the buttresses are diagonal. Although much renewed, the interior retains a village atmosphere helped by the twelfth-century chancel arch of two orders, plain but with an interesting large squint on each side, divided into two lights with fifteenth-century tracery. The nave roof is of tie-beam-and-crown-post construction but plastered; at the east end it is panelled in two bays which once formed a celure for the rood and nave altars.

Furnishings

The most individual are two graded fourteenth-century sedilia, separated by a shaft with moulded capital and base, and flanked by identical piscinas with double basin (one a modern imitation without a drain); these are all ogee-headed and are under a hood-mould. The font is neo-Perpendicular and may be eighteenth-century in date. The altar rails with twisted balusters were formerly the front of a singing gallery at the west end of the nave. There are two eighteenth-century chandeliers in the nave, each consisting of a globe with eight sconces. Above the font is an elaborately carved, eighteenth-century Royal Arms, painted and gilded in 1958. There are many fragments of medieval stained glass, which are worth inspection, especially in the west window and one notable modern east window by Lawrence E. Lee. Smaller items of interest are the group of four fragments of medieval tiles, probably made by Chertsey Abbey, and a modern mural on the celure panels. There is only one substantial memorial; this is situated north of the altar and is to Admiral Isaac Townsend (d.1765) and his wife Elizabeth. It is in white marble and is of allegorical design with a large-headed cherub praying in a niche above the inscription. The monument was carved by Sir Robert Taylor. Of more interest are the brasses to John Bonde and to William Denham in the chancel. The Bonde brass consists of several separate parts – the Bonde arms, Bonde himself, his wife, their seven sons, seven daughters and an inscription. He was Clerk of the Household to Henry VIII and died in 1578. A particular feature is that the brasses are palimpsests. The Denham brass has the arms and crest of Denham and a separate plate with six lines of black-lettered inscription; the plate is within a frame of variegated marble and depicts the deceased with his wife, five sons and ten daughters; above are the arms of the Goldsmiths' Company and the word 'Jehovah' in Hebrew characters. On the floor of the chancel is a slab commemorating Sir John Foster of Fosters (d.1685), son of Chief Justice Foster.

THURSLEY, St Michael and All Angels

198.   Thursley Church from the south.

A Saxon structure going back to *c.*1030, but overlaid by Victorian alterations and additions so that, apart from the late fifteenth-century belfry and the internal platform to support it, which were mercifully spared, the simple village church drawn by C.T. Cracklow in the 1820s is hardly recognisable today. The Victorian 'improvers' were Benjamin Ferrey who, in 1860, removed the north gallery and added the north aisle, and, more comprehensively, J.W. Penfold who, between 1883 and 1886, removed the west gallery, inserted the present east window, removed the ceiling, added the south transept and opened up the west end with a large arch and new west window, lengthening the church by ten feet. The style used was a crude Early English which contrasts ill with what was left of the older building.

The belfry and splay-footed spire dominate the exterior, whilst inside one's eyes are immediately drawn to the unduly massive, but skilfully constructed timber cage in the middle of the nave, not integrated with the belfry above but supporting a platform on which it rests. The corner posts are moulded oak tree trunks, 2 feet 6 inches thick, joined by tie-beams. The view to the east end is carefully left unblocked. Other features are the two small Saxon double-splayed windows, still retaining the mid-wall windowboards to hold panes of thin horn or oiled linen (*Colour Plate II*). They were only discovered in 1927 on the north side of the chancel. Also pre-Conquest is the Saxon oven recess below them in the north wall of the chancel, for baking wafers used in the Mass. A Norman window remains above the north nave arcade and there are two lancets in the south wall of the chancel. The chancel arch, which has no capitals, probably dates from *c.*1270.

199.   The frame upon which the bell turret rests at Thursley.

200.   The north wall of the chancel at Thursley, showing the two saxon windows, each with its timber window frame.

Furnishings
The tub-shaped font, made of Bargate stone and decorated with a crude chevron band, is pre-1100 and possibly Saxon (*see fig. 14*). The fine chest of local design dates from 1622. Other furnishings include a twelfth-century sedile on the south side of the chancel, also uncovered in 1927. There is a well preserved George III Royal Arms of 1783 and, in the north aisle, fifteenth-century Flemish stained glass from Costessey Hall, Norfolk, depicting the Presentation of Christ in the Temple. (Other glass from this source is to be seen at Great Bookham and Stoke D'Abernon.) The carved front of the altar comes from an early sixteenth-century Flemish chest and the oak and walnut altar table is eighteenth-century, but the reredos of painted figures is nineteenth-century. The memorial in the chancel to Katharine Woods (d.1793) is of polychrome marble with an urn and sarcophagus.

The best-known of all of the monuments is the sailor's stone in the churchyard, a tall stone to the north west of the church with a long sorrowful inscription recording his murder at Hindhead on 24th. September 1786 by three men, whom he had treated to a drink and to whom he had probably disclosed a full wallet. He 'fell a Victim to three Ruffians' Rage'. The murderers were hanged on Gibbet Hill, Hindhead in chains made at Thursley forge – a reminder of the medieval iron industry which used to exist at Thursley. A headstone to Richard Court (the village blacksmith who died in 1791) is inscribed with the oft-repeated lines: 'My Sledge and Hammer lie reclin'd, My Bellows too have lost their wind'. Three table tombs of *c*.1800 lie opposite the west end of the church. There is a cross to Lutyens' mother (d.1906) and to his nephew, Derek (d.1931), with bronze reliefs. Others commemorated are John Freeman, the poet (d.1929 at the age of 49) and Alfred Bossom (d.1951), the New York skyscraper architect. The open and attractive churchyard was once famous for its impressive chestnut-tree, destroyed by storm in 1977.

TITSEY, St James

Built by J.L. Pearson in 1861 in a hard, unsympathetic style, the church of St James illustrates how uneven his work was. Surrey can show examples of his early work (St James, Weybridge 1848) and his late work (St Peter, Hersham 1887), none of which can compare with his *tours de force* at St John Evangelist, Upper Norwood and St Michael and All Angels, Croydon. The original church of St James was pulled down in 1776, being situated in the park of Titsey Place, to make way for the house built at that time. There are medieval grave-slabs at the old site. The Georgian replacement, illustrated in Cracklow, was in its turn replaced by the present edifice beside the road, with a south tower and shingled broach spire.

Furnishings
There is a good east window by Clayton & Bell (*Colour Plate XXXVI*). Among the monuments is one to Sir John Gresham (d.1643), erected in 1660, moved from the old church. There are two Victorian effigies in the north chapel to members of the Leveson-Gower family, who owned Titsey Place – Granville Leveson-Gower (d.1895) with a canopy designed by Pearson and Emily (d.1872), rather better. A moving commemorative piece is the first-war battlefield cross to Lt. R.C. Leveson-Gower, laid on top of a foliated thirteenth-century cross-slab. A brass with the main figures ten inches high remembers Wm. Gresham (d.1579), with his wife and children.

UPPER NORWOOD, St John the Evangelist

Almost by chance a young priest from Southampton heard in 1874 of the financial difficulties of a group of Upper Norwood residents who had erected a small iron church to provide a form of worship more suited to their needs than elsewhere available. The priest – Rev. W.F. Bateman (later to be known as La Trobe-Bateman) – offered his services and so began a ministry which lasted 26 years. So successful were his efforts that the money needed to pay off the cost of the iron church was soon raised and thoughts began to turn towards the endowment and building of a permanent place of worship. Sympathy for the minister in the loss of his 29-year-old wife encouraged the fund until Bateman felt able to engage the eminent John Loughborough Pearson to build a new church. Although the foundation stone was laid in May 1878, work did not begin until 1881; consecration taking place in April 1887.

From whichever direction one approaches, but especially from the south where the ground falls

201.   *St. John the Evangelist, Upper Norwood.*

away, the church rises impressively, this despite the fact that the planned spire above the tower on the south transept was never built. The interior is a fine work in Pearson's mature Early English style, full of subtleties and exciting oblique vistas, beautifully proportioned, with clean lines, vaulted throughout and restrained in decoration. Double aisles make the church more than half as wide as it is long and give an impression of size and spaciousness. In the south-east corner, separated from the choir by an aisle, is a richly decorated Lady Chapel, with an apse supported by six ribs. The church of St John the Evangelist is a distinguished example of Pearson's work in which his careful use of materials and his ability to impart interest in his interiors are well exemplified.

Furnishings
The furnishings are good Victorian work. The reredos in the Lady Chapel was designed by Pearson in the form of a carved and painted wooden triptych. There are modern brasses to the first two vicars, the more notable being that to La Trobe-Bateman in the centre of the choir floor, showing him beneath an ogee canopy of thirteenth-century style.

WALTON ON THAMES, St Mary

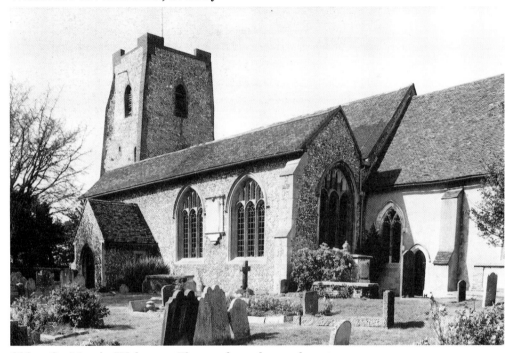

202.   St. Mary's, Walton on Thames from the south east.

Centrally situated in a pleasant town, St Mary's is its principal historic building. The original foundation was by Asher the Priest, who later became Bishop of St David's; he had been given the site by Edward the Elder, son of King Alfred. Although mentioned in Domesday Book, the oldest part – except for the core of the nave walls which may be Saxon – is the north arcade with Transitional Norman circular much-scalloped piers but with its original arches modified to a pointed design in *c*.1350, when the church was rebuilt and the south aisle and chancel added. The tower dates from *c*.1450. The building-up of the north aisle wall in Tudor times has resulted in the north arcade being out of true and gives a top-heavy appearance to the roof of *c*.1634 which, however, binds the whole together. In the nineteenth century, the set-offs of the tower buttresses were straightened and replaced by a steep slope. The battering of the west tower is more curious than beautiful. The fabric is built of flint with stone dressings. The brick parapet is an unusual feature for this part of Surrey. Entrance is through the tower at the west end. The chancel windows are nineteenth-century work, but the straight-headed Perpendicular north windows may date from the time when the brick clerestory was built. The purpose of heightening the north wall in Tudor times is revealed by the presence of a gallery on that side, the front of which is hand-carved. The chancel arch is basically of fourteenth-century date and therefore contemporary with the chancel and south aisle; the latter contains the Chapel of All Saints with a seventeenth-century altar (once the high altar) and is a link with Henry Bowett, Archbishop of York, who became patron of the living in 1407.

Furnishings

The piscina and sedilia in the chancel are fourteenth-century in date, but the finest feature is the organ casing of *c.*1700 by Schmidt which came from Windsor Castle. (The organ itself dates from 1936.) The font commemorates three children of one family, who died within a month. The interior is dominated by the monument to Richard Boyle, Viscount Shannon in the north-east corner of the north aisle (*see fig. 89*). This huge monument was made by the eminent French sculptor, Louis Francois Roubiliac, who

203. The nave roof at Walton on Thames.

executed many works in Westminster Abbey (although none larger than this one). It was erected in 1755 by Viscount Shannon's daughter, who appears seated disconsolately on the right-hand side of the base, with her right arm hanging over an urn. Viscount Shannon himself, who died a marshal, is carved in a swaggering posture in front of a draped flag and large tent. To the left and below him is a gun on a gun-carriage and to the right a tree with a drum and a flag together with the beautifully carved figure of his daughter. A more modest and much smaller monument is the brass in the north aisle to John Selwyn, Keeper of Oatlands Park, who died in 1587 (*see fig. 64*). It shows the family – workers at the Palace – and eleven children, all of whom survived childhood. John Selwyn is depicted riding a stag, commemorating his exploit in leaping on a stag, guiding it toward Queen Elizabeth and stabbing it dead at her feet. Other memorials include a hanging wall-monument with an oval relief of trees to Henry Skrine (d.1813) by J. Bacon Junior: a relief with seated lady bent over the monument of her husband to Mr. & Mrs. Christopher D'Oyly of 1821 by Chantrey; a relief to Lady Williams (d.1824); a monument to Sir James Edwards and a memorial slab on the floor to William Lilly, an astrologer who was accused of starting the Great Fire by forecasting the event fifteen years earlier. He was cleared and later became a churchwarden. On the west side of the chancel is a memorial to Dr. Matthew Kirby and his wife Elizabeth, who was a benefactor of the poor; her charities helped to found the United Walton Charities, which administer the local Almshouses. The Doctor was ejected from the living of Shepperton for some unknown reason in 1704. Another memorial commemorates the family of Admiral Lord Rodney over the south door which leads to the choir vestry. By the west door is the Anzac Memorial in memory of New Zealanders who died at their hospital in Walton during the Great War.

At the east end of the north aisle is a reproduction of a scold's bridle. The original, which was stolen in 1965, dated from 1633 and was sent to the parish around the head of a pauper in 1723 from Chester inscribed – 'Chester presents Walton with a Bridle to curb women's tongues which talk too idle'. On the column beside the pulpit is a rhyme thought out by Queen Elizabeth I during a service at the church when she was residing at Oatlands Palace:

'Christ was the worde and spake it
He took the bread and break it,
And what the worde doth make it,
That I believe and take it'.

WALTON-ON-THE-HILL, St Peter

John de Wauton has been named as the founder of St Peter's. His tomb lies in an arched recess outside the north wall of the chancel with an inscription above 'JOHANNES DE WALTUNE HUJUS ECCLESIAE FUNDATOR, A.D. 1268', placed there early in the nineteenth century. Little, however, remains to remind us of him for the church has been heavily restored and little, if any, of the original work can be traced. The only medieval part of the fabric is the chancel but, although the sedilia and piscina are good Perpendicular work, the overall impression is of the nineteenth century. The nave and vaulted base of the tower were the work of Daniel Alexander Junior and date from 1818. The north aisle was added in 1870 and in 1895 the upper part of the tower was made square instead of octagonal, removing the oversize turrets, which greatly improved its appearance. Prior to Alexander's work, there had been a wooden tower surmounted by a handsome spire in the same material.

The church, built of generally renewed flint, stands back nicely from the main road and the tower with half-octagonal/half-round stair turret on the north-east corner is an attractive feature and clearly a great improvement on its predecessor. There is a low, wide dormer window, which is tiled, in the south side. The interior is smaller than one might expect from the tower but, despite all the nineteenth-century work and Alexander's not very distinguished Gothic nave, has a pleasing atmosphere. The chancel arch is large, with attached demi-shafts and continuous moulding around and this is balanced by the impressive richly moulded tower arch. The vaulted base of the tower has largely detached ribs and a spacious circular opening for the bell ropes. The two-bay nave is separated from the chancel by a wooden screen of 1887; the high-pitched, cusped, arched-brace roof has windbraces.

Furnishings
The possession which brings visitors to St Peter's more than any other is its lead font, dated by Zarnecki [53] to c.1150-60 and probably one of the oldest surviving examples in the country (see fig. 16). These furnishings suffered severely during the Civil War when many of them were melted down for bullets and there are only about thirty left in the whole of England. They vary in date from Norman times to the end of the seventeenth century and considerably in quality, but the one at Walton is a particularly fine specimen. Only 20 inches in diameter and $13^3/4$ inches deep, it has a frieze of foliage at the top and bottom enclosing eight (possibly originally twelve) seated figures in high relief. Delicately modelled, they are placed under round arches, wearing haloes and holding books, either to their breast or on their left knee. The number 12 suggests the Apostles, but it is believed that the figures might represent the four Latin doctors of the Church (St. Ambrose, St Augustine, St Gregory and St Jerome) repeated. The sedilia and piscina are good late medieval examples; the triple sedilia mouldings are similar to those of the chancel arch, whilst the piscina has a

simple ogee arch. Fragments of mostly seventeenth-century English and Flemish stained glass, part local and part brought from Woburn Abbey, are assembled in the south-east nave window; they include three shields, one of which is the arms of the Salters' Company. The bible on the striking lectern is Victorian, but the chain which keeps it there is medieval and came from Salisbury Cathedral. Above the Lady Chapel altar is a copy by an unknown Spanish artist of the painting of the Madonna by Murillo. The light fittings are of an attractive design in the form of the keys of St Peter within a circle.

WANBOROUGH, St Bartholomew

The hamlet of Wanborough, attractively grouped on the north slope of the chalk Hog's Back, could have been settled about 10,000 years ago, situated as it is on the spring line and close to the track on the other side of the ridge leading to Stonehenge. The Saxon name 'Wenberge' (possibly meaning 'bump-barrow') confirms its antiquity. There may have been a Saxon timber church, but the earliest record of St Bartholomew's Church is *c.*1060. It was mentioned in Domesday Book, but whatever existed then was rebuilt by the Cistercian monks of Waverley Abbey early in the thirteenth century, the Manor having been sold to them for 120 silver marks. The Cistercians were skilled in sheep-rearing and the newly acquired land could have been used for this purpose, the wool being stored with the corn in the still existing estate barn. Waverley Abbey was dissolved in 1536 and the chapel passed into lay hands, but continued to be used for worship until the seventeenth century. The chapel was then utilized as a farm building until, on 14th June 1861, it again resumed its proper function as a religious building. A sensitive restoration was carried out in 1861. This was encouraged by the fact that Puttenham Church – on the south side of the Hog's Back – was closed for repairs. St Bartholomew's has remained a place of worship since that time.

A charming hamlet chapel (*see fig. 27*), it makes a compact farmyard group with the former manor house, weatherboarded barn and stable. Measuring only 44½ by 18 feet, it is one of the smallest Anglican religious buildings in Surrey. It is constructed of flint and stone rubble with a seventeenth-century west wall faced in brick, high up on which is a small open bellcote. Approaching on the south side through a well-tended churchyard, one sees mainly lancet windows with a two-light, nineteenth-century window in the south-east corner. The lancet to the west of the south door and the west window were inserted in the restoration of 1861. The interior is a single-celled space divided by a screen into sanctuary and nave with square-headed, three-light windows. Crimped plaster – a Surrey speciality – is used around the fifteenth-century east window (as at Albury, Compton and Worplesdon). A noteworthy feature is the roof with rafters, curved braces, collars and a moulded purlin joining the collars.

Furnishings
The screen separating the nave from the sanctuary is of Spanish chestnut and has fifteenth-century framing. Apart from this, the remains of an old piscina are built into the south wall of the sanctuary. The font is nineteenth-century and the oak altar rails are modern. There are two war memorials on the north wall, the lower one dedicated to the men and women of the Special Operations Executive (S.O.E.) who trained at Wanborough Manor House during the 1939-45 War. At the end of the nineteenth century the Manor House was let to Sir Algernon and Lady Mary West. Sir Algernon was Private Secretary to Gladstone and the Manor was host to many political figures including Gladstone himself and Asquith; Queen Victoria also visited the house. Asquith was a sub-tenant of the Manor and two of his children are buried in the churchyard.

WARLINGHAM, All Saints

Although not specifically mentioned, there is evidence to show that there must have been a church at Warlingham when Domesday Book was compiled. In any case, All Saints is an ancient foundation, going back to c.1250 when the church was rebuilt by the vicar – named Godfrey – and dates mainly from that period although since much altered and restored. In 1158, All Saints was presented to the Prior and Monks of Bermondsey Abbey with whom it remained until the Dissolution in 1536, after which it passed into secular hands until 1637, when it was transferred to the Archbishop of Canterbury. The patronage now rests with the Bishop of Southwark and Merton College, Oxford. Restorations were carried out in 1857 and 1887, but the main changes were made by P.M. Johnston in 1893 when the south aisle was built, the church extended westwards, the south porch moved stone-by-stone to its present position, a new porch added and the original bell turret – as shown in Cracklow's drawing of the 1820s – replaced by the present one.

All Saints is set on the north side of two small triangular greens in an area that has been developed and has lost most of its village character. Lancets (some copied from the original) and two-light Perpendicular windows are to be seen on both sides of the church and there is an east window of c.1340. The building material consists of flint with green firestone dressings. The interior is a single cell without chancel arch. The chancel floor is lower than that of the nave. Putlog holes (used for supporting scaffolding) have been left in the north wall of the nave, as well as large square recesses, which supported the rood beam, near the pulpit and opposite on the south wall. There are also piscinas and sedilia on each side, presumably to serve altars which were once placed before the rood. A third piscina and sedile remain on the south side of the chancel, as well as a blocked low-side window and priest's door. The chancel ceiling contains old timbers.

Furnishings
The octagonal font at the east end of the south aisle dates from c.1450 and is decorated with sunk quatrefoils, one of which contains a grotesque head. The two-light stained-glass window beside the pulpit contains medieval glass, consisting of yellow and white canopy work and small figures of angels. In 1865, this window was badly damaged but the opportunity was given to remove some unworthy nineteenth-century figures and to substitute plain glass. Fragments of thirteenth-century glass are to be seen in the lancet window next to the west door and the tracery of the east window contains mid-fourteenth-century glass. A large but somewhat roughly painted mural of St. Christopher carrying the Christ Child was uncovered in 1881 on the north wall, originally almost opposite the south door before it was re-sited; the painting has been attributed to the fifteenth century. St Christopher murals were placed opposite entrances to churches in a conspicuous position because it was believed that whoever looked upon such a figure would be free from sudden death that day and thus have an opportunity for repentance. A simple oak communion rail was provided in 1957.

According to legend the English Prayer Book – later to become the Book of Common Prayer – was given its first reading in All Saints in 1549 by Archbishop Cranmer himself. The nineteenth-century glass in the two-light window on the south side shows Archbishop Cranmer presenting the first book to Edward VI in the same year. Sir Joseph Swan (d.1914), the inventor of the incandescent electric lamp, photographic plates, printing paper and artificial silk, is commemorated in a tomb beyond the oldest yew-tree.

WEST BYFLEET, St John Baptist

The church of St John Baptist started life in 1872 as a chapel of ease to St Mary the Virgin, Byfleet in order to provide facilities for worship nearer the Industrial School which had moved from Wandsworth to Pyrford Road during the previous year. It was a temporary corrugated-iron building, known as 'The Tin Tabernacle'.

Prior to the turn of the century consideration was given to building a permanent church and, in 1900, a building committee meeting was chaired by the Rector of Byfleet. This resulted in the immediate purchase of a plot of about one acre of land at Byfleet Corner and the appointment the following year of W.D. Caröe as architect. Financial and other hindrances delayed the building and it was not until 15th June 1910 that the foundation stone was laid. Consecration did not follow until the place of worship was free of debt, but eventually this was achieved on 11th October 1913.

The church enjoys a prominent site where several roads meet. The building material is pebble stone which sparkles in the direct light of the sun. The steeple has a pyramidal spirelet sheathed in 5,000 Canadian red-cedar shingles (*see fig. 103*). Entering through the narthex, one is presented with a harmonious interior with many carvings and covered with a fine concave barrel roof without tie-beams.

Furnishings
The church has benefited from many gifts, many in memory of the fallen in the Great War, including a reredos of English oak by W.D. Caröe, and altar rails in thanksgiving for the safe return of 254 men of the parish. The font was designed by Nathaniel Hitch: it has a hexagonal bowl and on each side are the outlines of a cup.

WEST CLANDON, St Peter and St Paul

Although much of what one sees today is new or renewed, the history of St Peter and St. Paul goes back to Domesday Book. Since then, patronage has alternated between ecclesiastical and lay hands (the Bishop of Salisbury in the twelfth century and the de Westons of Albury from 1319 to the end of the fifteenth century) and this is underlined at the present time in the patronage alternating between the Bishop of Guildford and the Earl of Onslow. Although Clandon Park, the former home of the Onslows, lies close to the church and the latter seems almost to have been built in its grounds, the house was not erected until the eighteenth century. The church was never, therefore, the private church of the large house; in fact, the village at that time lay close to the church and its spread northwards is a later development. The list of incumbents goes back to Peter de Bovill in 1253. Both north and south doorways are Norman. The nave may have been started in *c.*1170 when the Bishop was patron, but major changes were carried out in *c.*1220 when a chancel was built to replace the apse and sedilia and piscina provided, whilst during this period all but one of the chancel windows were enlarged or replaced. An oddly-proportioned tower was erected on the north side of the nave. Also at this time a nave altar was added with a pillar piscina, the head in the form of a capital and the bowl with palm-leaf decoration. Later, when William de Weston was patron, an early fourteenth-century window was inserted on the south side and the three lancet windows on the east wall of the chancel replaced with a Decorated, reticulated window of three lights. In the nineteenth century, choir stalls were placed in the chancel and the west gallery removed. There was a major restoration in 1874. Shortly after, in 1879, the present north tower was erected but this had to be rebuilt in 1913 after a fire. The benefice is now united with that of St Thomas of Canterbury at East Clandon. Restoration has deprived West Clandon church of much of its medieval character, nor is it helped by the unsympathetic flint with ribbon pointing used in its construction. The north tower with wooden spirelet is a prominent feature from the road. A private path leads from Clandon Park to the church. The interior shows a wide nave and chancel with walls which appear to be old.

Furnishings
The handsome Onslow pews at the west end are probably Italian of seventeenth-century date; the rear pew has a tall back and there are three more in front; the arm-rests are carved with cherubs' heads. A wooden replica, of a carving, which used to be placed outside above the south door, showing a dragon and a reptile (or dog?) fighting, is preserved in the church; this is a reference to a former local legend. A recently restored, fifteenth-century painting of three figures on a board, which was probably part of the old rood screen, is affixed to the south wall of the chancel. There is a Royal Arms under the nave roof. Various Onslow coats of arms going back to 1282 are to be seen in the stained glass of the west window and there are colourful seventeenth-century medallions reset in early nineteenth-century glass elsewhere. The twelfth-century octagonal font of Petworth marble was vandalised by the Puritans during the Civil War. The pulpit on the south side dates from the Victorian restoration.

WEST HORSLEY, St Mary

This church was founded *c*.1030, probably by Thored the Danish thane who owned the manor, and the nave walls incorporate work of this date. St Mary's is mentioned in Domesday Book under the name of 'Orselei'. What one sees today is basically thirteenth-century construction, with subsequent slow-growth development. The oldest visible part is the very short west tower of *c*.1120, unbuttressed and of flint. It is capped by a dumpy shingled spire, added in *c*.1370, with louvre openings square at the base but changing to octagonal half-way up. The tower was followed by the north nave arcade and narrow aisle together with a north doorway of clunch, all of *c*.1190. The chancel (since renewed), with triple lancets at the east end plus single north and south lancets, was built soon after in *c*.1210. There was then a long gap before the south chapel was added as a chantry chapel for the Nicholas family in *c*.1470 and the south arcade in *c*.1500. There is no tower arch but the tower doorway is late Norman (*c*.1200) and above is a window which took the place of a doorway to a west gallery (which was pulled down in 1849). Restorations were carried out in 1810, 1849 and 1887, but the impressive wall-painting of St Christopher on the west wall was not discovered until 1972.

St. Mary's stands upon a knoll above the main A245 road and opposite West Horsley Place, the old manor house with its Dutch-inspired brick south front of ten bays. The timbered west porch is dated *c*.1380 and on the south side of the chancel there is a blocked priest's door. The effects of restoration have been softened by the use of whitewash over plaster, giving a pleasant texture. Despite the slow growth, the interior is nicely proportioned. A good curvilinear window was added to the north side of the chancel in *c*.1384 and the north aisle was widened in 1849, retaining the old north door which was moved to a new position. The round piers with circular abaci in the north arcade of *c*.1190 contrast with the much later rough-and-ready octagonal piers and capitals of the south, dating from 1531. High up on the east wall beside the chancel arch is a wooden door-frame from which the rood-loft was entered.

Furnishings

These are many and varied with the St. Christopher mural as the main source of interest. Placed as it is on the west wall surveying the interior and 13 feet high, it is not likely to be missed. There were other murals including a Passion Cycle on the west and south walls but little of these is to be seen now. Another main feature of interest is the stained glass (*Colour Plate VIII*), especially the thirteenth-century medallions in the centres of the north and middle east-end lancets, depicting respectively St. Catherine and the wheel upon which she was martyred, and the Anointing of the Feet of Jesus Christ. The glass in the south lancet is nineteenth-century. Other glass of interest is the portrait of the donor of the large chancel window on the north side, Sir James de Berners, a former patron who was beheaded in 1388 for misguiding the young King Richard II. The glass, perhaps made in Chiddingfold, is original and shows Sir James kneeling. On the south wall of the chancel beside the vestry door is a bas-relief of carved alabaster (probably Nottingham work) portraying the Nativity, one of five or seven which served as a reredos behind the medieval altar. This was

204. *Monument to Sir John Nicholas and his wife at West Horsley.*

broken up for floor rubble at the Reformation and found under the pulpit in 1810. The simple chancel screen is dated to the early sixteenth century and has double doors which, when closed, form twelve narrow traceried bays with straight-headed tops. The pulpit is the upper section of a three-decker erected in 1810 and lowered in 1871; the font retains its original bowl of *c*.1190, but is supported on new shafts and is much retooled. Other furnishings include a large iron-bound parish chest, dating from *c*.1220, on the north side of the screen; George I Royal Arms above the screen and a copy of Correggio's painting of the 'Virgin in Adoration' at the east end of the north aisle. Two small brass inscriptions, dated 1504 and 1506, lie below the nave carpet.

There is also much to see among the monuments, including the Nicholas memorials in the south chapel (now called the Nicholas Chapel). There is a big tomb to Sir Edward Nicholas (d.1669), Secretary of State to both Charles I and II. It is without figures and reputed to be by Grinling Gibbons, although not in the same flight as his wood carving; the monument is in an architectural frame with barley-sugar columns and open pediment above. Sir John Nicholas (d.1704), who was Sir Edward's son and Clerk to the Privy Council, is commemorated by a much better composition, described by Pevsner [54] as 'lively square-cut'; the architectural frame encloses a delicate marble urn, with cherubs and obelisks at the side. Even better is the monument in the south aisle to James Kendall, who died in 1751 at the age of 23 when travelling abroad, by Nicholas Read. The composition consists of a marble urn, drapes and a delightful relief of a rose-tree with one blossom fallen. The sculptor was a pupil of the famous French sculptor, Louis Francois Roubiliac.

Below the chancel north window is a carved stone effigy (one of the earliest of a priest in Surrey) of *c*.1377, probably Ralph de Berners, who was an assistant priest at St Mary's; his recumbent figure lies under a crocketed ogee arch with the foliation cusps carved with monkey's heads, the badge of the Berners family. On the left of the chancel as one enters is the Weston Fullerton memorial by Bacon (1819). There is good reason to believe that the head of Sir Walter Raleigh, executed in 1618, is buried with his three grandchildren in the Nicholas vault under the south chapel. The embalmed head was preserved by his widow for upwards of a quarter of a century in a red leather bag until her death and was then buried, by the side of his grandson, Carew Raleigh, whose father of the same name was Lord of the Manor at West Horsley Place.

WEST MOLESEY, St Peter

The church retains a fifteenth-century west tower of ragstone (*see fig. 50*) and an octagonal Perpendicular font. The remaining parts were rebuilt in yellow brick in 1842. It was mentioned in Domesday Book. A notable feature is the Jacobean pulpit with a back panel and sounding board. There are also three later brasses.

WESTON GREEN, All Saints

205.   *Weston Green, All Saints from the south.*

All Saints was built in 1939 to the designs of Sir Edward Maufe, architect of Guildford Cathedral and was a foretaste of this much larger work with its cool interior. It also has the very tall slender windows typical of the Cathedral. The whitewashed exterior with its north-east campanile and open site on Weston Green makes it a conspicuous feature. The interior with plain piers and arches dying into them without capitals is also whitewashed and has the Maufe 'spatial imagination' to which Ian Nairn refers.[55] The arcade arches are round in the Romanesque style. All Saints is therefore a church of some distinction as is to be expected from an architect of Sir Edward Maufe's calibre.

WEYBRIDGE, St James

This goes back to A.D. 666 when a grant of land at 'Biflete with Weybrigge' was made to Chertsey Abbey. No church is mentioned in Domesday Book and the first mention of the existence of one is in a Chertsey Abbey document dated 1175, which alludes to a 'capelle of Weybrigge'. The right of presentation to the living was sold by the Abbey to Newark Priory at the beginning of the thirteenth century and, in 1262, the Priory obtained a Licence of Appropriation. In the middle of the fifteenth century, however, the advowson was transferred to lay hands until, at the Dissolution, it passed to the Crown where it still remains. The present building dates from 1848 but there was certainly one earlier church, if not two; its immediate predecessor, which stood to the north, was a neat much older place of worship with tower and spire set back from the west end. The tomb of the Duchess of York is said to mark approximately the position of its east end. The church became too small for the rapidly growing population and John Loughborough Pearson was commissioned to erect a new church, which was consecrated in 1848. The spire was added in 1855, an outer south aisle (later to become a War Memorial Chapel) in 1864 and the chancel lengthened in 1889; the chancel arch has also been raised by

206.   Weybridge Church from the east.

some ten feet. The main feature of the exterior is the tall broach spire, especially commanding when viewed from the public car park. The main fabric is in a rather thin Decorated style. The interior is distinguished by its good proportions and the elaborate chancel decoration of polychrome marble mosaic in which twenty-two types of marble are used. The east window with seven tall lights and intricate tracery in the head is a notable feature.

Furnishings
Especially distinctive are the sedilia with red marble seats and the double credence table, all effectively combined into one composition. The octagonal stone font in the nave is surmounted by a crocketed wooden canopy with a dove on top. At the base of the tower are various brasses, of which two are above average: one to Thomas Inwood (d.1586) and his three wives in a lively composition and a fifteenth-century example (*see fig. 67*) composed of three macabre but expertly executed skeletons with texts in between; the latter does not refer to the three children represented on the plate above as dying in *c.*1600.

Among the tablets skied under the tower are several eighteenth-century and early nineteenth-century ones and – high up – a mural monument to the eccentric, but much beloved, Frederica, Duchess of York by Francis Chantrey, showing her kneeling with a crown beside her feet. Her husband was the Duke of York, son of George III, who marched his troops up the hill and then marched them down again. They lived at Oatlands which the Duke rebuilt after a fire in 1793. The tomb of the Duchess of York in the churchyard is surrounded by an iron grille decorated with coronets.

WIMBLEDON, St Mary the Virgin

From serving a village with a population of less than 100 to catering for a large commuter area with four additional parish churches, St Mary the Virgin has had to develop from a small – probably timber – church, likely to have been 'the church' mentioned in Domesday Book in the Manor of Mortlake, to the dignified church we see today. Nothing is known of any Saxon church, which there may have been, but whatever existed in Norman times was rebuilt with a south aisle at the end of the thirteenth century. Measuring about 44 feet long by 36 feet wide, it was lit by three dormer windows and had a typical Surrey wooden belfry capped with a lead-sheathed spire and a west wall pierced by many openings. This place of worship proved adequate for 500 years for what was then a rural backwater, although only seven miles from London. With the Reformation, patronage surprisingly passed to the Dean and Chapter of Worcester Cathedral as part of the price paid by the King for land which he wanted and it still remains with them today. In Elizabethan times, however, Wimbledon became attractive as a country retreat for the Court and some of its officials, including Lord Burleigh, and his eldest son, Thomas, the first Earl of Exeter, built the Elizabethan manor house north of the church. Edward, the Earl's third son, inherited the manor and it was he who built the Cecil Chapel in brick with a ribbed vault as a mortuary chapel for himself and his family (1626-36). The manor house was demolished in the early eighteenth century.

Despite this influx of people of quality from London, the parish church proved adequate for another 200 years by which time the population still did not exceed about 450. From then on, however, the number of people increased rapidly and, even with the addition of a north gallery in 1760, St Mary's was uncomfortably crowded. This, plus structural decay, led to the decision to rebuild completely, except for the chancel, and John Johnson, the surveyor, erected in 1788 a typically Georgian building in grey stock brick with the upper windows round-headed, and at the west end a semi-circular projection upon which was a square wooden tower, with Gothic pinnacles of artificial stone at the corners. It is this church which is illustrated in Cracklow's drawing of the 1820s. This building lasted only a tenth of the time of its predecessor, for within 50 years Wimbledon's population had almost doubled, and, with the London-Woking railway arriving in 1838, a further steep rise was to be expected. Accordingly, the present building was put in hand to the designs of George Gilbert Scott (his firm was Scott & Moffatt) when he was only 30. He retained the old chancel and completed the new nave in Perpendicular style with a west tower and spire rising to 196 feet, in 1843. The chancel, however, was largely rebuilt in 1860. The only remaining changes were the addition of vestries on the south side and, in 1921, the Warrior Chapel immediately west of the Cecil Chapel, designed by Sir Thomas G. Jackson in memory of Wimbledon fallen in the 1914-18 War and now including those killed in the 1939-45 War.

Set in park-like surroundings on a ridge east of the Common, St Mary's makes an attractive picture with its imposing steeple. The building material is black knapped flint with stone dressings. The interior is a good example of Scott's early work with a wide and well-proportioned chancel arch. Especially noteworthy is the hammer-beam roof of the nave, which must be one of the best examples constructed in the nineteenth century. There are three galleries. The piers are iron shafts encased in plaster.

Furnishings
All of the furnishings, with the exception of some of the stained glass, and the Royal Arms, date from the last 100 years, being gifts from parishioners; the screen on the south wall and the font cover are in memory of men killed in the two wars. The Royal Arms of Queen Victoria, made of artificial stone, were given in 1842. The stained glass includes one of the rare Surrey survivals of medieval glass (*Colour Plate XIII*) in the form of a fifteenth-century figure of St George in a two-light window (the sixteenth-century other light contains the arms of Sir Thomas Cecil) in the Cecil Chapel, where there is also seventeenth-century heraldic glass. The Chapel also contains armour, which was made *c.*1630 and is suspended from the ceiling. A low-side window was discovered in the chancel in 1920.

The outstanding memorial is that to Sir Edward Cecil (d.1638) in the Cecil Chapel. Sir Edward was one of James I's leading generals. There are no figures and the memorial is in the form of a simple black marble altar tomb. The oldest memorial is an undated tablet low down on the chancel north wall to Philip (d.1462) and Margaret Lewston; it once stood in a niche over a marble tomb but these have disappeared. In the corner of the north wall, a Renaissance tablet commemorates William and Katherine Walter. There are two stone shields on the floor of the chancel and one of the two modern brasses on the north wall commemorates William Wilberforce, the great slave liberator, who lived for some years at a house on the Common, where he was frequently visited by the younger Pitt. In the floor of the main nave aisle in front of the chancel is a memorial to Sir Richard Wynn, friend of Charles I, who, when Charles was Prince of Wales, accompanied him on the abortive visit to Spain to court the Infanta. Wynn later became Treasurer to Queen Henrietta Maria whom Charles subsequently married. Also in the nave is a memorial to Peter Shaw, physician to both George II and III. Among the nineteenth-century memorials is one to James Perry (d.1821), erected by the Fox Club, showing him seated under a bust of Charles James Fox and another to Sir Joseph Bazalgette, the designer and engineer responsible for Putney Bridge, the Victoria, Albert and Chelsea embankments and the drainage system of London. In the churchyard, Gerard de Visme (d.1797) has a memorial consisting of a pyramid of stone blocks. Thomas Cromwell, chief minister of Henry VIII from 1534 to 1540 and responsible for the break-up of so many monasteries, was a Wimbledon born and educated man, later becoming Lord of the Manor. Among his less reprehensible achievements was the institution of Parish Registers.

WINDLESHAM, St John the Baptist

The church has a long history which, however, is not much in evidence in the fabric we see today. There may have been a Saxon building but the earliest known place of worship dates back only to the reign of Henry II (1154-89), during which time the right of presentation to the living was granted by one named Hoppeschort to Sherborne Priory in Dorset. This was contested by Newark Priory in a suit of 1266 and, four years later, Newark took the living over and retained it until the mid-fifteenth century when it was transferred into private hands, being attached to the manor of Freemantle. Subsequently, it passed to the Crown and, in the year 1598, two of the rectors were appointed by Queen Elizabeth. The early church was extensively altered in 1270 and, as such, served as the parish church until it was largely destroyed by lightning during a storm on 20th June 1676. The rebuilding in

207.   Windlesham Church from the south west.

208.   The Baillieu monument in Windlesham churchyard.

1680 retained part of the walls which, however, received an outer skin of new brick and three windows, two in the Decorated style in the south aisle and one square-headed Perpendicular one in the chancel. This is the church seen in the Cracklow drawing of the 1820s. In 1838, the tower was heightened and the building enlarged by the addition of a north transept projecting at right-angles from the fabric with a gallery at the north end. A gallery was also built in the tower. This was the work of Robert Ebbels, contrasting poorly with what he did at Ewhurst. What we see today largely derives from the work of Ewan Christian in 1874, when the old church was submerged under an outsize new nave and chancel in raw polychrome brick. He did, however, remove the inappropiate north transept. The seventeenth-century nave and chancel were retained as an aisle on the south side and the medieval windows probably reset.

Furnishings
The pulpit is part of an old three-decker and Jacobean in character. The reredos and sanctuary panelling are executed in mosaic and carved

alabaster. In a case near the lectern is a chained book, 'Jewel's *Apology*'. The case is made from a yew said to have been planted in William the Conqueror's reign. The clergy stall in St John's Chapel was presented by the Queen in memory of her residence at 'Windlesham Moor' from 1948 to 1950. The stained glass is modern. There is a Palladian tablet to Lt. Col. Robert Hemington (d.1757) on the east wall of the old chancel.

In the north-west corner of the churchyard, there are two tombs to Australian millionaires by Lutyens – one to Mrs. Clark (d.1934) with a fine altar of travertine, described by Nicholas Taylor [56] as having 'exquisite abstract curves', the other to William Baillieu (d.1936), which he depicts as having 'a confused mixture of columns and a flattened vase'.

WISLEY (dedication unknown)

This is a precious survival of a Norman village church which still preserves its completely rural character, aptly called 'The Church in the Farmyard', although the farmyard has disappeared. Although a Saxon church is mentioned in Domesday Book at 'Wisselee', there is no trace of pre-Conquest work in the present structure although the foundations of the Saxon building were uncovered in 1903. Wisley came under a succession of Lords of the Manor of Wisley, which changed hands many times and involved many lawsuits. It was not until 1594 that the Manor of Wisley went with the neighbouring Manor of Pyrford. Previously, there must have been a link between the Manor of Wisley and the Manor of Byfleet since the patron in 1344/5 and also in 1370 was the Black Prince, who owned a hunting lodge in Byfleet. In 1531, by decree of Cardinal Wolsey when Bishop of Winchester, the rectory of Wisley was united with that of Byfleet and it was not until 1631, no doubt following the linking of the Manors in 1594, that the parish of Wisley was joined with that of Pyrford. It used to be assumed that the union of 1631 was definitive, because Charles I had presented Nicholas Arundel to both churches, the first Rector of Wisley for 101 years. However, it has recently been discovered that the amalgamation was not final until 1668-9 when John Oldys, already it seems at Pyrford, was instituted to Wisley.

Both Wisley and St Nicholas Pyrford date from the mid-twelfth century and their main interest is that they have come down to us from Norman times as complete buildings of one period, that is, without addition of aisles, chapels, or towers, but with later roofs, bellcotes, porches and furnishings. In 1627 at Wisley two-light lancet windows with transoms in Gothic-survival style were inserted in the north and south walls of the nave and in the east end. Wisley shows the marks of a thoroughgoing restoration in 1872 carried out by Mrs. Buxton in memory of her husband, Charles Buxton M.P. of Foxwarren. Neo-Norman west windows and a north doorway, the latter constructed of an aggressive yellow Bath stone, were inserted.

Wisley church (*see fig. 6*) is built on low-lying land: it has no buttresses, possibly due to the ground being firmer or the building having foundations. The ferruginous stone is covered with a rendering of sand mixed with lime. Cracklow's drawing of 1824 shows an octagonal bell-turret and a wicket-gate closing the entrance to the porch. It was during the 1872 restoration that the present splay-footed bellcote was substituted and the porch entrance opened up to permit the passage of coffins.

Despite the restoration, a Norman village church of considerable appeal remains. The chalkstone chancel arch is completely plain, of one order only: embedded flints and holes made by those which have been dislodged are visible. The arch and the chancel with its deeply-splayed windows (repaired in heads and sills) are typical village work of the mid-twelfth century. There is a blocked low window on the south side of the chancel; this is dated as Early English. The only other Gothic medieval work is found in the ogee-shaped niches, cut into the jambs of the chancel arch; these were almost certainly used as side altars. The western part is all 1872 work. The roof is of queen-strut construction, probably of 1627; massive beams support the bellcote which rests partly on the tie-beams and partly on the west wall.

Furnishings

The pews mainly consist of Victorian replacements but there is one dated 1630 in the south-west angle. The font is a routine Victorian replacement of a Norman one, which has disappeared. The pulpit is also Victorian (probably 1872), but the hour-glass holder of scrolled iron next to it dates from Elizabethan times. There is no medieval stained glass and only traces of wall-paintings; but three – an unusually large proportion – of the consecration crosses remain; the glass in the east window dates from 1909. Of more interest are the restored Georgian Royal Arms on the south wall (*Colour Plate XXIII*) facing the entrance and the old chest near the vestry door with iron bands serving as feet to raise it off the ground. There are no memorials inside the church, if one excepts the east window erected to Mr. & Mrs. Charles Buxton by their four daughters. In the churchyard there is a head stone on the left of the approach path which commemorates John Choat (d.1879) and his wife Hannah (d.1890), the faintly discernible inscription of which contains the words – 'Her Children and her Children's Children numbering 160, shall rise up and call her blessed'.

John Oldys was a much-loved rector (1668 to 1703),who is associated with various briefs, which were authorised charitable collections for any public or private good cause. These included one in 1678 towards the re-building of St Paul's Cathedral, one in 1680 for the redemption of captives from Algiers, and one in 1685 for the relief of French Protestants exiled after the Revocation of the Edict of Nantes.

Throughout most of the eighteenth century the Onslow family were patrons of the living. Denzil Onslow who was patron in the early years of the eighteenth century also had Send living as well as Pyrford. Until recently Wisley was a rectory and Pyrford a curacy, but the anomaly of Pyrford being by far the larger village has been corrected, and the whole parish has now become a rectory.

WITLEY, All Saints

All Saints offers one of Surrey's picturesque vignettes when viewed from the south-east, with the adjoining cottages, of which the best known is Step Cottage. All Saints is mentioned in Domesday Book and traces of a Saxon church remain in the fabric of the north and west walls, also in a double-splayed window in the south wall and a small window high up in the west gable. The Saxon church was superseded by a Norman cruciform structure dating from *c*.1180 with a crossing tower. Some time after 1282, the large Manor Chapel north of the chancel was added. The elegant east window dates from *c*.1350 whilst the shingled spire is probably late fourteenth-century work and the pinnacles of the tower were added in the seventeenth century. There were the usual alterations and additions in Victorian times, most evident in the chancel with large areas of veined marble and in the addition of the north aisle (partly 1847 and partly 1890).

The building material is Wealden stone. Although the south porch is nineteenth-century, the bargeboard which came from the adjoining cottage is fourteenth-century. The weather cock on the tower dates from 1701. The interior is noted for its elaborate and partially restored murals on the south wall of the nave. The tower is supported on four pointed arches of clunch. The roof of the north as well as the south transept is original, as are the east and west lancets of the south transept. The chancel has been Victorianized but not so drastically as elsewhere.

209.   Witley Church from the south west, showing the Saxon window in the apex of the west wall.

Furnishings
A study in 1983 revealed that the murals date from the early twelfth century, using the real fresco technique of painting while the plaster was still wet. They were uncovered in 1889 and subsequently, the consecration cross being found only in 1980. Early conservation methods caused the paintings to darken and blister but, in recent years, improved techniques whereby the plaster was kept fresh were used on the eastern half. There are three tiers of paintings which are described in detail, so far as they can be determined, in the church. Much work remains to be done. The thirteenth-century font, more circumstantial than usual in Surrey, has an octagonal bowl with stem and eight shafts merging into one capital. The thirteenth-century piscina in the chancel has a square aumbry above, an uncommon combination. There is fifteenth- and sixteenth-century heraldic stained glass in the Manor Chapel and the Lady Chapel. A brass of 1530 on the north side of the chancel commemorates Thomas Jonys and his wife; he was a 'sewer' (food taster) in the Court of Henry VIII. Other brasses commemorate Sarah Holney (d.1641), the tablet of which recalls the virtues of a model vicar's wife, and Anthony Smith (d.1670).

WOKING, St Peter

Today the village of Old Woking straggles rather haphazardly towards modern Woking, but in Tudor times it was the scene of many royal comings and goings and could boast a palace.

210.   The west tower at Old Woking.

Margaret Beaufort, the mother of Henry VII, a formidable lady described as 'a high-minded matriarch, a political manipulator and a patroness of piety and learning', lived there. Henry VII was often at the palace and there was even a treaty of alliance signed at Woking in 1490 with envoys of Maximilian, who later became Holy Roman Emperor.

St. Peter's, however, existed long before this since it was originally Norman and the excellent west doorway and the nave walls remain from the Norman fabric. The earliest written record relates to the foundation of a minster, dedicated to St. Peter, by a nobleman, Brordar, in A.D. 675. The chancel with typical lancets was added in the thirteenth century and the south aisle in the fifteenth century. The lower, buttressed part of the west tower was built in the thirteenth century of flint rubble and pudding-stone, with some admixture of tiles especially in the buttresses. The upper part, added in the fourteenth century, is of unbuttressed and coursed grey sarsen or heathstone with occasional patches of a ginger-coloured stone (carstone?) – a more refined material. Generally, however, the church is built of pudding-stone and flintstone rubble, with squared stone for quoins, weathered in some places. Sir Edward Zouche, a crony of James I, to whom the manor passed in the early seventeenth century, erected the west gallery and the brick south porch, now used as a boiler house. Substantial restoration took place in 1878 and 1888 but, with the building of newer churches in the Woking area, the major growth of which had occurred around the railway station, this was not as severe as it might have been.

As so often in England, the most attractive part of the village is next to the church and the little cul-de-sac leading to it still retains charm and some nice houses. The lych-gate is enhanced by the use of Horsham slabs (often called slates) for the roof, whilst the churchyard is well tended and contains some good eighteenth- and nineteenth-century headstones particularly one near the path with a cherub's head in the well-shaped top and the date 1761 just discernible. The main and only entrance is under the western tower, as the south porch of 1622, with crow-stepped gable, is no longer available. The exterior of the chancel has unfortunately been cement-rendered (the date 1930 is clearly marked at the top), but has a fine renewed curvilinear window. There is a low-side window in the south-west corner which may have been inserted to give light to the Lord of the Manor's seat which was on that side. On entering the church, the visitor is immediately confronted with the most notable feature of St Peter's, the Norman oak west doorway (the outside entrance before the tower was built). Dating from *c.*1020-1090, this is of good proportions with a single roll-moulding and cushion capitals, but is chiefly distinguished by retaining its original door with excellent ironwork (*see fig. 9*). It would appear that the Norman smith was not above using Saxon motifs as, in addition to decorating it with instruments of the Passion, he added large horizontal bands penetrating the necks of inverted C-straps – a motif found on Saxon brooches. It is not clear why the top part in the soffit of the arch is sliced off, because the jamb capitals prevent it opening inwards. The other door, which is modern, still retains a lock dated 1731. The aisle windows are renewed but there are thirteenth- and fourteenth-century windows in the north wall of the nave (*see fig. 34*). The south aisle arcade, probably built at the same time as the upper part of the tower, has low fat octagonal piers. The eye is drawn to the fine curvilinear east window (but with modern glass) and to the attractive probably fifteenth-century roofs; the nave roof has wind-braces. There is a low Perpendicular window beside the pulpit and it is thought probable that there was also an altar there.

Furnishings
There are a number of wall tablets and these plus an appealing pulpit and Zouche's west gallery add up to quite an attractive interior, despite restoration. The pulpit, once part of a three-decker, used to be situated in the middle of the nave north wall, with seats facing towards it so that those seated in the centre of the church faced one another. It is contemporary with the gallery (1622 except for the aisle portion which was added later). This once housed a barrel-organ erected in the late 1830s or early 1840s, which had a good tone but was rather loud. Some of the pews, of plain design with a pair of narrow buttresses at each end, are late medieval. An Edward Hassell water-colour of 1830 shows box pews on the north side that were swept away during Victorian restoration (*see fig. 59*). The font is nineteenth-century in date. In the porch will be noted a fifteenth-century chest. There are no major monuments but the following are of interest. That to Rev. Edward Emily (d.1792), on the north wall near the west gallery, is a good design by the elder Westmacott, consisting of an urn in a classical frame. On the south wall of the chancel is that to Johannes Lloyd (d.1663), a rather overloaded tablet with a broken pediment and spiral scrolls (volutes) below. That to John Merest (d.1752) in the south aisle is a more restrained monument also with coat of arms and volutes, Baroque in feeling with an inscription framed in Ionic fluted pilasters and standing figures above. These are thought to be link boys, with their torches, who provided illumination to the people they accompanied when there was no street lighting. Two brasses on the aisle wall commemorate Joan Purdan dated 1523, part of a larger family group of which only the daughters above remain, and John Shadhet (d.1527) with wife and children. They are both about 15 inches high. There is also a brass plaque to Sir Edward Zouche on the south wall of the chancel, with a fulsome inscription, although it is said that, because of his unpopularity in the village, he was buried secretly in the churchyard at night. A white ensign above the steps leading to the pulpit, a small plaque underneath the window beside the pulpit and a brass tablet on the wall near the lectern remind one of Admiral Thomas Philip Walker, D.S.O., who commanded one of His Majesty's ships during the 1914-1918 War and was a Churchwarden of the church for 24 years.

WOKING, Christ Church

By the 1870s as the London Necropolis Company sold off its excess land, the population of Woking had risen to between 6,500 and 8,500 and, as the town developed round the railway station from the late 1860s, a need was felt for a church to serve the town centre. Temporary quarters were found in 1876 but when these became 'rusty and leaking', the Church Council decided on a permanent building. Raising the finance was a problem and, although the foundation stone was laid by the Duchess of Albany on 10th November 1887, it was not consecrated until 14th June 1893. It was, however, opened for worship on 1st January 1889 before construction was finished, the copper-sheathed flèche not being built until January 1893. Ian Nairn [57] describes it as 'big in scale, honest lancet brick'

211.   Christ Church, Woking.

adding that, as with many Late Victorian architects, the cheaper the building, the better the design. At one time, a brick tower at the east end was contemplated but, to save money, the western flèche substituted. The east end consists of a large, apsed space with kingpost roof and small ambulatory-aisles.

In the 1960s the re-development of the town heralded major changes to the church, which was in need of repair. There was even a risk of the church having to move. Fortunately the plans for the town were changed and it was decided to create a new town square immediately adjacent to the church's west end and so there was every reason to leave the church where it was. But how was it to fulfil its role as the spiritual centre of the growing town? This led the P.C.C. to 'study whether the total parish needs for church and hall could not be met by a single-purpose building'. Sale of the hall and rooms nearby made it possible to embark upon a project which involved the building of a large hall in the roof space at the west end of the church, with a coffee shop beneath, bringing the Communion table forward and constructing a large baptismal pool at the east end of the building. The formal opening service was led by the Bishop of Guildford on 17th February 1991, with the Beacon Coffee Shop, bookstall and welcome desk opening the next day. Outwardly little altered, the interior of Christ Church has been transformed.

Other Churches in Woking

St. John the Baptist's Church was built in 1842 as chapel of ease to St Peter's. The community centred on the canal side at Kiln Bridge shared in the building boom provoked by the construction of the prison at Knaphill (later Inkerman Barracks) and had grown sufficiently to be given a chapel of ease. The church was a simple, aisleless building of Kentish Ragstone with Bath Stone facings. It became a separate parish in 1887 and has had several enlargements.

St. Paul's in Oriental Road was built by Rev. William Hamilton as a chapel of ease to Christ Church and consecrated on 28th November 1895. It became a separate parish in 1959. The Rev. Hamilton also paid for the construction of St Mary of Bethany, York Road, by Caröe, opened in 1908. Holy Trinity, Knaphill was built of red brick in the Romanesque style in 1907 by J.H. Ball.

WOKING, Former Chapel of St Peter's Convent (Anglican)

Although, in general, chapels are outside the scope of this book, the eminence of the architect, John Loughborough Pearson, warrants the making of an exception in this case. This notable example of his work was designed by him shortly before his death in 1898 and built by his son (Frank Loughborough) over the next ten years. The chapel is Perpendicular in style although the two arches between the nave and the choir are respectively Norman and Early English. The east end of the building rises to the full height of the chapel from the crypt with a rood on the top of the gable carved by Nathaniel Hitch. There are apsed projections on each side of the apsed choir. The building materials are basically brick and stone but many different marbles have been used inside both for the structure and the furnishings: those in the sanctuary and Lady Chapel range in colour from red to green, yellow, mauve and grey and come from many European countries. The mosaic work in the Lady Chapel was carried out by Italian craftsmen in 1908. The Chapel as a whole consists of nave, north (St. Andrew's) chapel and the Lady Chapel (*Colour Plate XXIX*), the most striking part, in the crypt; the north chapel was completed first. The convent has moved to another site and, at the time of writing, one awaits with interest the plans of the new owners Messrs. MacLeod & MacLeod.

Furnishings
The altar and baldacchino are finely carved in alabaster of oyster and pink shades but African red marble, a particularly beautiful stone of volcanic origin, is also used to good effect. The Lady Chapel altar is made of Carrara marble with pale green colonettes of Connemara marble; other attractive stones are used in decoration. The reredos is gold leaf on copper. The stained glass is mainly by Clayton & Bell to Pearson's designs. The organ was built in 1900 by Norman & Beard, whilst the nave rood was given in 1907.

WOLDINGHAM, St Paul

One's first impression is of an East Anglian church older than in fact it is. It bears the mark of opulence, having been built in 1933 by Lord Craigmyle as a memorial to his father-in-law, Lord Inchcape, chairman of the P & O Shipping Line. The architect was Sir Herbert Baker, designer of the Bank of England and, with Sir Edwin Lutyens, of New Delhi, India. Neo-Perpendicular in style, the material used for building was flint. The East Anglian aspect is most strongly emphasised in the tower with its flushwork decoration on three sides creating the words – 'Praise Him, Magnify Him, Forever'. Diagonal buttresses reach up to a point just short of the traceried parapet. St Paul's is a worthy example of twentieth-century work in the county and a credit to its founders (*see fig. 105*).

Furnishings
The font is decorated with a palindrome in Greek meaning 'Wash my sins, not only my face'. The organ is by Harrison. Opulence is further emphasised in the interior by the 300 agates, presented by the Nizam of Hyderabad, on the rounded wall of the apse where there is more flushwork. The apse roof is decorated with a chalice in gold and the early Christian Chi Rho monogram. The stained-glass windows of the nave are by H. Hendrie. They are in triple sets of three, one set depicting Biblical figures representing Goodness, Truth and Beauty, the second, Faith, Hope and Charity and the third inspired by the three virtues in the Craigmyle arms, Misericordia (pity), Fidelitas (faithfulness) and Jus (justice). The baptistry at the west end has two lines from a Latin poem in the dome and three windows with stained glass by Dr. Strachan, who also designed the five windows of the sanctuary. The latter recall the church's associations with the P & O Shipping Line and depict various scenes connected by water (Christ walking on the water in the moonlight, the Portuguese navigator, Prince Henry, etc.). It is pleasing and expressionistic in character.

WOLDINGHAM, St Agatha

Set up on the Downs and said to be the smallest church in Surrey, this little chapel was a rebuilding in 1832 of a church dating from the thirteenth century.

WONERSH, St John the Baptist

212.   Wonersh Church from the south west.

St. John the Baptist Church is reached by a path from the street across the attractive Church Green. The original humble 'capella', known as 'Wogheners Chapel', probably consisting of a nave and small sanctuary, was referred to in 1224 as dependent on the parish of Shalford, but by 1295 the description had been changed to 'ecclesia' or parish church, denoting its independent status. Evidence found during a restoration of 1901/2 points to the north wall of the nave being pre-Conquest and dating from *c*.1050. During the restoration the architect discovered traces of two round-headed windows, probably also of pre-Conquest date, in the wall above the arch leading from the nave to the tower, but these could not be preserved. Early in the thirteenth century the two lower storeys of the tower were erected together with a low, shingled, wooden, pyramidal spire. The chancel was also originally of this period as can be seen from the three blocked lancet windows in the north and south walls dating, like the fine and lofty although mutilated chancel arch, from *c*.1120. In 1751, the present embattled tower replaced the old one, but this was only the prelude to a much larger rebuilding of 1793-95, when much of the earlier work was replaced in what the Victoria County History[58] refers to as 'the plainest sort of meeting-house style'. The whole width of the former south aisle was embraced in a new south side to the nave, thus causing the chancel arch to be off-centre. Though plain, the brickwork is of high quality and was still in good condition two centuries later. At the same time, the south chancel chapel was converted into the Grantley Mortuary Chapel. (The family owned Wonersh Park for over a century.) Externally, the stonework of the tower and the nave, chancel and chapel (Bargate, rubble, aggregate and ironstone with clunch dressings) contrasts with the brickwork of the 1793-95 rebuilding. The queen-post, butt-purlin timber roof dates from this rebuilding and exceptionally is visible, since the ceiling was later removed. Above the chancel arch can be seen the line of the former nave roof.

The church was spared Victorian 'improvements', but there was further major restoration and rebuilding in 1901-02, carried out by a local architect, Charles Nicholson (later knighted), involving complete repair, re-arrangement of the interior and the provision of additional accommodation and we see the results of his sensitive approach in the building today. The chancel, whilst retaining its original walls, had its east end rebuilt by Charles Nicholson to its original length and height after he had removed the small, shortened Georgian chancel with its apse. Later in 1929, he converted the mutilated thirteenth-century chancel arch into an interesting focal point by providing a screen; this, however, has now had to be moved in order to cope with the greatly increased size of the congregation in recent years. An unusual feature is the tunnel-like crypt entered from the chancel by a flight of steps; this was halved in size when the north chancel chapel was built in the fifteenth century. The south chancel mortuary chapel is now used as an organ-chamber and vestry.

Furnishings
Internally the furnishings and fittings convey a feeling of warmth ('comely and worshipful' as J.C. Cox[59] describes them), to which the wide span of the open queen-post, timber roof covering the whole nave contributes. The rood screen which has caused so much controversy will be removed to a position behind the altar. On the right is a parclose screen made up from fragments of a former medieval screen. The Norman bowl and part of the stem of the font were excavated from the floor in 1901; the cover, designed by Sir Charles, was a gift in 1915 and forms a canopy over a statuette of the Virgin Mary and the Infant Christ, copied from one in Bruges attributed to Michelangelo. In the north chapel there is an attractive marble figure of the Madonna, as the 'Second Eve' treading upon the serpent, in a niche on the right-hand side. Below in the wall is a squint trained on to the chancel altar. The south-east window of the nave contains a panel of richly coloured, early sixteenth-century Austrian stained glass. The east window, portraying the Te Deum, is the first work of A.K. Nicholson (Sir Charles' brother) dated 1914, with strong blues and reds; most of the other glass in the church is also his work. The walls of the nave have dadoes formed from a west gallery front and pew ends, providing an attractive form of panelling. Various Grantley hatchments adorn the walls and in the south-east corner of the nave there is a painted Royal Arms of George III, which is of especial interest in that they retain the French fleur-de-lys. This is a reminder of the time when England laid claim to the Crown of France, not relinquished until the signing of the Treaty of Amiens in 1802. There are several chandeliers of eighteenth-century design, mostly modern Belgian copies but including a fine original Flemish one in the chancel. The paintings are copies, two in the nave, including the 'Madonna of the Rocks' by Leonardo da Vinci, recently cleaned, and two in the north chapel.

The monuments include a large sixteenth-century table tomb on the ground floor of the tower, long stripped of its brasses, which may once have contained the body of a lord of the manor. Another behind the organ dates from the seventeenth century with finely carved heraldry to a later lord of the manor Richard Gwynn (d.1702), described as a 'filezer' (or keeper of the files) of the City of London. At the west end of the nave there are small fragments of the architectural frame of a Jacobean wall tablet roughly carved but with good Italian Renaissance work; the inscription and side columns are missing. There is an attractive modern tablet on the other side of the door. Brasses on the chancel floor commemorate Thomas Elyot (d.1467) and his wife Alicia, and Henry Elyot (d.1503), his wife Johanna and twenty-three children.

WOODHAM, All Saints

The parish of All Saints, Woodham was created out of the parishes of Addlestone, Horsell and a small part of Christ Church, Woking to meet the growing needs of local residents. Building was in two phases and took some time to complete, the foundation stone being laid in October 1893, the final consecration not taking place until July 1907. The architect was W.F. Unsworth who had erected Christ Church a few years earlier. The exterior is typical Surrey vernacular with red tiled roofs and an abbreviated tower, having louvred belfry windows and short, tiled, overlapping spire. The nave walls are of Bargate stone. The lavishly furnished interior consists of a nave of five bays, which was extended by two bays in the second building phase, chancel, Lady Chapel and aisles. The sanctuary floor is laid with American marble tiles and the steps are of Swedish marble. Round the walls of the Lady Chapel runs a dado of green tiles.

Furnishings
The furnishings have been added as various donors came forward with their gifts, the earliest being the Caen stone font, largely given by children receiving catechism and designed by the architect; it was dedicated in 1895. The font cover, also given by children, which carries a replica in oak of the figure of Christ in the Thorwaldsen Museum in Copenhagen, did not follow until 1909. The altar and rails, the latter made of olive, ebony, cedar and oak, date from 1907, the oak pulpit from 1913, the chancel reredos from 1915 and the oak rood from 1929. The three-manual organ, built by Harrison & Harrison, dates from 1928, and the mural decorations by James Powell & Sons from 1911. Of the windows, the east window, showing Christ in Glory, is by Heaton, Butler & Bayne and dates from 1912. The second window from the east (1902) in the north aisle, known as the Children's Window, is by C.E. Kempe. In the south aisle to the right of the entrance door, a recent window commemorating Wyndham Gillard (1934-1985) depicts Matthew, seated on a scroll, being called by Jesus to follow Him. There are two items of older date – a panel in the Lady Chapel reredos, which is believed by some experts to date from the tenth century and was retrieved from the ruins of a church destroyed by an earthquake in 1883, in the island of Ischia, Italy; the other is a brass Incense Boat of uncertain date dug up when foundations were being prepared for building 'Woodhambury' in Woodham Lane about 1887.

WORPLESDON, St Mary the Virgin

This place of worship is mentioned in Domesday Book and the chantry chapel where the organ stands is of eleventh-century date, but most of the church is Perpendicular work of the fifteenth century, built of durable heathstone. The chancel, however, is of thirteenth-century construction, built of roughly coursed flint and carstone, but was lengthened by ten feet in a poor restoration of 1866. The chapel on the south side was added in the restoration and converted in 1975 into an attractive modern room for worship and fellowship.

The earliest mention of patronage is in 1292 when the living was granted by Ledereyna, wife of William de Valoynes, to Sir John de Cobham, with whose family it remained, except for a short period at the end of the fourteenth century when Sir John de Cobham was sentenced to be hanged, drawn and quartered – commuted to banishment to Jersey – for being a member of the Council of 1386. He was restored to favour, however, with the accession of Henry IV in 1399, and the patronage continued with the family until the attainder of Lord Henry Cobham in 1603. It then passed to the Crown for most of the seventeenth century until 1693 when it was exchanged with Eton College for Petworth, since when it has remained with the College.

Conspicuously sited above the village, unusual in Surrey, St Mary's presents one of the finest towers in the county (*see fig. 1*), heightened – as an inscription on the inner face attests – by 14 feet, at the expense of Richard Exfold towards the end of the fifteenth century. The tower has diagonal buttresses and a stair turret at the north-east corner, which is flush with the east wall, making this side broader than the west. An engaging feature is the little cupola from the stables of the old rectory, the bell in which originally summoned the coachmen from the pub at the end of the service, but now strikes the hour. A sturdy five-light window above a well carved doorway with Tudor roses in the spandrels completes the picture. The south porch dates from 1591, bearing over the entrance the initials E.R. The arcades between the nave aisles consist of round piers and capitals. A Surrey feature, seen at Compton and Wanborough, is the decoration with crimped plaster around the arcade arches, the rectangular windows of the aisle and the south door. The chancel arch was heightened and widened in the 1866 restoration, and the tower arch is impressively large. At the east end there is an authentic Curvilinear window similar to that of Old Woking. The small fifteenth-century clerestory windows are of Wealden stone, with one or two lights under trefoil heads. At the east end of the south aisle is a lancet window.

Furnishings
Chief amongst the furnishings is the fourteenth-century glass in the aisle windows (*Colour Plates XI & XII*). This was originally in the chancel east window, but transferred to make way for a Clayton & Bell window depicting Christ in Glory surrounded by worshipping angel faces. Below is a knightly figure who may be St George or an archangel, with shield and red sword. The predominant hue is silver with touches of blue and red. Clayton & Bell retained the old glass in the tracery. Of the fourteenth-century glass transferred to the aisles, there are delightful figures of St Cecilia and St Etheldreda (sometimes referred to as an Annunciation) with the Virgin in green and the angel in yellow, against a deep red background and under canopies. There is much armorial glass, mainly on the south side, including at the west end of the south aisle the arms of Henry VIII impaling the arms of Anne Boleyn granted to her on her marriage in 1530. Eton College provided the altar rails, adapted to fit, the seventeenth-century font and cut down pulpit. The font is of baluster shape with octagonal fluting at the top and base of stem. The organ came from Dorset and was rebuilt in 1961. There are two empty ogee-headed canopies in the north chapel, dating from the fourteenth century. There is a tablet on the south wall of the chancel to Stephen Sleech, a former Rector and also Provost of Eton, who died in 1765. The lancet window at the west end of the north aisle dates from 1912 and commemorates Sir Donald Tovey, scholar of Balliol College and Rector of Worplesdon. He edited the works and letters of the poet Thomas Gray. Below is a tablet to his son, a noted musicologist, the Reid Professor of Music at Edinburgh from 1914 to 1940, who established the Reid Orchestral Concerts in

1917. At the foot of the tablet is the musical score for the first line of the Benedictus canticle.

In September 1947, the Queen, before her accession, was present with Prince Philip and Princess Margaret at the baptism of her god-daughter, Rosemary Elizabeth Elphinstone, the daughter of the Revd. Andrew Elphinstone and Mrs. Jean Elphinstone, one of her Ladies-in-Waiting, and, among other occasions, in January 1967 when her god-daughter was married.

From 1826 until demolished in 1851, an Admiralty Semaphore Tower stood to the north of the church. Like the remaining one at Chatley Heath, Cobham, it was an octagonal brick structure, 180-feet high, higher than the church itself. Chatley Heath was used for relaying messages on the route from London to Portsmouth, including the one-o-clock time signal each day. Worplesdon was the first tower on the uncompleted line to Plymouth, so it is doubtful if it saw much service.

WOTTON, St John

This interesting church is set in some of Surrey's most beautiful scenery against the backcloth of Ranmore Common and approached by a road winding down from the A25. Its history goes back to pre-Conquest times and, since the beginning of the seventeenth century, has been closely associated with the Evelyn family who retain a share in the patronage. The most famous member, John (called Sylva because of his knowledge and love of trees), was born in Wotton House, the family home, in 1620 and died there in 1706. Apart from his diaries and essays, he was the first great landscape gardener to break away from Tudor formality and was one of the founders of the Royal Society. According to his diary he received his early schooling in the old porch, but this may have been the space under the tower. Recent excavations have revealed traces of a pre-Conquest church west of the tower and the base of the tower and most of the original nave was of the same period. The rest of the church, apart from the Evelyn Mausoleum, the vestry and the south porch, were added between 1190 and 1220, the old eleventh-century chancel being adapted to become the nave and the parts west of the tower demolished. The latter thus became a west instead of a central tower, the western arch being blocked up and a single arched window inserted. In 1579, the north chapel became the Evelyn Chapel and c.1630 the arch from the chancel into the chapel was also blocked up. The Mausoleum was added about 1680 in the north-east corner. Considerable alterations, including a new chancel arch, an east window inserted, replacing three earlier lancets and a vestry were carried out in 1856-58 but much of the earlier work remains.

Lying between the chalk of the North Downs and the greensand to the south, St John's is built of Bargate stone with its warm brown and yellow tints, the county's best stone. The exterior is enhanced by the use of Horsham slates for the roof and by the west tower (*see fig. 12*) which was restored in 1957/58. The top, dating possibly from the seventeenth or eighteenth century, is of the two-tiered pyramidal type making it a conspicuous stranger, for this type is normally found in Shropshire (as at Clun, Hopesay and More, where it is described by Pevsner [60] as 'rather jaunty-looking'), and the Monmouthshire part of Gwent (as at Rockfield and Skenfrith). The Evelyn Mausoleum is of brick in English bond with a large round window at the east end. The brick is separated from the stone of the vestry by the rough-cast of the restored chancel, making a rather indigestible mixture. The 1857 south porch has an attractive barge-board, which is modern, together with the outer oak doors dating from 1954, but the inner arch of the doorway leading into the church dates from the thirteenth century and has fine arch mouldings with jambs which have shaft-rings.

Contemporary with this doorway are eight tiny but well-carved heads only three inches high, the lower two being a restoration; there is much speculation as to who they represent. Some say that they refer to people concerned in a dispute between King John and the Pope at the election of Stephen Langton as Archbishop of Canterbury, but this has been doubted.[61] The church consists of a restored and partially rebuilt chancel, a largely rebuilt nave (although the lofty narrow tower arch is the oldest datable feature other than the base of the tower), the original north chapel, which became the Evelyn Chapel in 1579, the north-east mausoleum of *c.*1680, and the vestry and south porch of the mid-nineteenth century. Three original lancet windows remain at the east end of the Evelyn Chapel, also two on the north side (one blocked). One in the chancel is covered by the vestry but beyond is another, restored in Bath stone with a low side window below similarly restored. The other windows are of the nineteenth century.

Furnishings
The Evelyn Chapel is entered from the north aisle through a balustraded oaken screen with the date 1632 marked on it. There are two fonts, one of the nineteenth century with thirteenth-century themes and the other in the Evelyn Chapel of seventeenth-century date in classical style with a simple ogee cover. Many of the other furnishings are recent gifts. A sedile, however, on the south wall of the chancel is probably of the thirteenth century and there is some old stained glass in the top of the narrow lancet in the west wall. Although not of outstanding sculptural merit, the monuments are the most interesting features of the interior. They are mainly to members of the Evelyn family, starting with the wall monument in the chapel to George Evelyn, who bought the Wotton Estates and died in 1603. He is shown kneeling in an elevated position between his two wives, Rose and Joan, by whom he had twenty-four children, shown in two groups below in a horizontal strip. (Four in swaddling clothes denote that they died in infancy.) To the left and next to it is a memorial to Richard Evelyn (d.1640) and his wife Ellen, also kneeling but with figures at the sides holding back drapes; their more modest family of five children also appear in a strip below – John Evelyn is the second of the boys. A rather better half-length work opposite commemorates Elizabeth Darcy (d.1634), daughter of Richard; it is in the form of a bust with head leaning on hand and a baby in swaddling clothes below. John Evelyn himself (d.1706) and his wife Mary (d.1709) are, in complete contrast, commemorated by two raised, coffin-shaped, stone slabs with entire absence of ornamentation, but with inscriptions (long in the case of John who did not wish to be left in the gloomy mortuary). John's slab is under the south window and Mary's against the south wall. Other family monuments include a tablet to George Evelyn (d.1829) by Westmacott. In the churchyard there are a number of wooden 'bed-boards' or 'bed-heads' mostly of the eighteenth century. Near the outer door of the mausoleum is the Glanville monument, surmounted by a white marble urn. Richard Glanville, nephew of John Evelyn, left money for a competition to encourage poor boys in the parish to be apprenticed to some trade. The competition is at present in abeyance because of the lack of eligible boys, but efforts are made each year to revive it.

REFERENCES

Abbreviations:

B.O.E.	Buildings of England.
S.A.C.	Surrey Archaeological Collections.
V.C.H.	Victoria County History.

1. John Betjeman (ed.), *Collins Guide to English Parish Churches*, Collins (1958), p 359.
2. C.T.Cracklow, *Views of Surrey Churches*, (1828) reprinted by Phillimore (1979).
3. Ruth Dugmore, *A Study of the Church of St John Baptist, Puttenham*, P.C.C. (1969).
4. William Morris, quoted in *A Brief Guide to Dunsfold Parish Church*, n.d. (c. 1975).
5. Eric Parker, *Highways & Byways in Surrey*, Macmillan (1909), p. 181.
6. **B.O.E.** *(Surrey)*, Penguin (1971), p. 245.
7. *Ibid.* p. 220.
8. Anon, *Battersea Parish Church*, P.C.C. (1972), p.7.
9. **B.O.E.** *(Surrey)*, Penguin (1971), p. 114.
10. C.T. Cracklow, *op. cit.* in note 2.
11. P.M. Johnston in **V.C.H.** *(Surrey)*, Vol. 2. (1905), p.245.
12. **B.O.E.** *(Surrey)*, Penguin (1971), p. 121.
13. *Ibid.* p. 433.
14. *Ibid.* p. 424.
15. Richard Faulkner, *The Church and School in Englefield Green*, P.C.C. (1973), p. 6.
16. **B.O.E.** *(Surrey)*, Penguin (1971), p. 421.
17. *Ibid.* p. 109.
18. Alec Clifton-Taylor, *English Parish Churches as Works of Art*, Batsford (1986), pp. 51-52.
19. John Ruskin, *Seven Lamps of Architecture*, George Allen (1849); *Collected Works*, (commenced 1908), Vol. 8, p.242.
20. C. A. Ralegh Radford, 'The Church of St Mary, Stoke D'Abernon', *Archaeological Journal*, Vol. 118 (1963), p.165.
21. **B.O.E.** *(Surrey)*, Penguin (1971), p. 85.
22. *Ibid.* p. 180.
23. *Ibid.* p. 60, 89.
24. *Ibid.* p. 98.
25. *Ibid.* p. 99.
26. *Ibid.* p. 114.
27. Louis Jennings, *Field Paths & Green Lanes* (1877).
28. **B.O.E.** *(Surrey)*, Penguin (1971), p. 121.
29. L.R. Stevens & H. Cook, *The Parish Church of St Mary, Byfleet*, P.C.C. (1977), p. 16.
30. R. Williams, *Chaldon Church, Surrey*, P.C.C. (1933), p. 12.
31. **B.O.E.** *(Surrey)*, Penguin (1971), p. 181.
32. William Morris, *op. cit.* in note 4.
33. **B.O.E.** *(Surrey)*, Penguin (1971), p. 209.
34. *Ibid.* p. 226.
35. *Ibid.* p. 248.
36. *Ibid.* p. 280.
37. Rev. B. F. L. Clarke, in Betjeman, *op. cit.* in note 1., p.362.
38. *Ibid.*
39. **B.O.E.** *(Surrey)*, Penguin (1971), p. 357.
40. Bruce Watkin, *Surrey - a Shell Guide*, Faber (1977), p.134.
41. **B.O.E.** *(Surrey)*, Penguin (1971), p. 374.
42. *Ibid.* p. 407.

43. *Ibid.* p. 408.
44. *Ibid.* p. 422.
45. *Ibid.* p. 426.
46. Bruce Watkin, *op. cit.* in note 38, p. 155.
47. **B.O.E.** *(Surrey)*, Penguin (1971), p. 433.
48. Maxwell Fraser, *Surrey*, Batsford (1975), p. 83.
49. John Waterson, *Windows of Stoke d'Abernon and their background*, Author (1986).
50. John Coales (ed.), *The Earliest English Brasses*, Monumental Brass Society (1987).
51. Alec Clifton-Taylor, quoted in **B.O.E.** *(Surrey)*, Penguin (1971), p. 474.
52. M. Fraser, *op. cit.* in note 46, p. 132.
53. G. Zarnecki, *English Romanesque Lead Sculpture*, Tiranti (1957), p. 5.
54. **B.O.E.** *(Surrey)*, Penguin (1971), p. 512.
55. *Ibid.* p. 515.
56. *Ibid.* p. 528.
57. *Ibid.* p. 533.
58. **V.C.H.** *(Surrey)*, Vol. 3. (1911), p.124.
59. J. C. Cox, *Surrey - The Little Guide*, Methuen (1926) p. 208.
59. **B.O.E.** *(Shropshire)*, Penguin (1958), p.24.
60. P.M. Johnston, 'Remarks upon some Carved Heads on a Doorway in Wotton Church, Surrey, **S.A.C.**, Vol. 24 (1911), p. 70.

Tailpiece - The Pulpit at Nutfield.

INDEX

The references refer to page numbers, those in italics to illustrations. Roman numerals relate to Colour Plates.

230